SPACE DIARY

FACT
FINDER

SPACE
DIARY

K E N N E T H · G A T L A N D

CRESCENT BOOKS
New York

A SALAMANDER BOOK

First published by Salamander Books Ltd, 52 Bedford Row,
London WC1R 4LR, United Kingdom

© Salamander Books Ltd 1989

This 1989 edition published by Crescent Books,
distributed by Crown Publishers, Inc.,
225 Park Avenue South, New York, New York 10003,
United States of America

Printed and bound in Belgium.

ISBN 0-517-66778-9

hgfedcba

Library of Congress Cataloging-in-Publication Data

Gatland, Kenneth William, 1924-
    Space diary/Kenneth Gatland.
    P. cm.
    ISBN 0-517-66778-9
    1. Astronautics – History.   2. Rocketry – History.   I. Title.
    TL788.5.034   1989
    629.4'09 – – dc19
                                                    88-33063
                                                        CIP

CREDITS

Editor:
Philip de Ste. Croix

Editorial assistant:
Roseanne Eckart

Designer:
SallyAnn Jackson

Map artwork:
Richard Natkiel
© Salamander Books Ltd

Filmset:
Modern Text Typesetting Ltd, England

Color reproduction:
Scantrans Pte Ltd, Singapore

Printed in Belgium by
Proost International Book Production

THE AUTHOR

Kenneth W. Gatland has a long association with the aerospace industry and is the author of many books and papers on rockets and space exploration. He began his career with the famous design department under Sydney Camm responsible for the Hurricane, Typhoon and Tempest interceptors of World War II. His first book, *Development of the Guided Missile* (Iliffe), published in 1952, was quickly translated by the Soviets and re-published in Moscow. A past-President of the British Interplanetary Society, he contributed to a study of small satellite launchers between 1948-51 which led to Project Orbiter and the first American Earth satellite, Explorer 1. His other books include *The Inhabited Universe; Astronautics in the Sixties; Spacecraft and Boosters; Manned Spacecraft; Frontiers of Space; Missiles and Rockets,* and *The Illustrated Encyclopedia of Space Technology.* He edited the BIS monthly publication, *Spaceflight,* from 1959-81, and became Fleet Street's first Space Correspondent contributing to the *Sunday Telegraph.* As well as being a Fellow of the BIS, he is a Fellow of the Royal Astronomical Society. He is currently working for British Aerospace at Kingston-upon-Thames.

PICTURE CREDITS

The publishers would like to thank the many private individuals, aerospace manufacturing companies, and public institutions who have supplied the photographs included in this book. We are particularly indebted to Theo Pirard of the Space Information Center and David Shayler of Astro Info Service who supplied many photographs from their private collections.

Anglo-Australian Telescope Board: 1
Arianespace: 44 middle (Bernard Paris), 51 right,
    62 upper and lower right
Astro Info Service: 39 lower left
Boeing Aerospace: 57 upper
British Aerospace: 32 lower, 52 upper right
CAST: 54 right
CGWIC: 43 left
Phillip Clark Collection: 17 right
CNES/Intercosmos: 34, 52 left
Department of Defence, Australia: 37 lower
Deutsches Museum, Munich: 12 upper
DoD, Washington: 40 lower, 44 left, 48
ESA: 28 right, 38 upper, 49 left, 59 right
GEC-Marconi: 22 lower
Glavkosmos: 55
Harris: 39 upper right
Hasselblad: Front cover upper right, 20 lower,
    23 lower right, 25 lower
Hughes: 35 right, 36 upper right
IAI: 60 right
Imperial War Museum, London: 12 lower
ISAS, Tokyo: 21 right
ISRO: 54 middle
JPL/NASA: Front cover lower right, 18 lower,
    25 upper, 27 lower right, 28 left, 29 right,
    30 lower, 49 right, 62 lower left
MBB: 56 right, 58 lower left
NASA: Front cover left, back cover inset, 3, 7 right,
    8 left, 9 right, 13 lower, 14 right, 15 right, 16 left
    and right, 17 left and middle, 18 upper, 19, 20
    upper, 21 left, 22 upper, 23 upper and lower left,
    24 upper and middle, 26, 31, 33 upper,
    35 left, 37 upper, 38 lower, 40 upper, 41 middle,
    42, 44 right, 45, 46, 47 lower, 49 middle, 50,
    61 lower, 63
NASDA: 52 middle, 54 upper left, 56 left
New York Public Library: 7 left
Novosti Press Agency, Moscow: 15 left, 16 middle,
    27 upper, 41 right, 61 upper
OSC: 59 left

Planeta Publishers, Moscow: 29 left and
    middle, 33 lower, 47 upper
Rockwell International: 30 upper
Royal Observatory, Edinburgh: Cover background
    picture
SIC: 39 lower right
David Skinner, World Space Foundation: 6 right,
    9 left
Smithsonian Institution: 7 middle, 10, 11
Tass News Agency: 32 upper, 43 right, 51 left, 53,
    57 lower
TRW: 22 middle
USAF: 36 lower, 41 left, 58 right
US Army: 15 middle
US Navy: 13 upper, 14 left

THE SPACE AGE

When the Soviets launched the first Sputnik on 4 October 1957, people stood in awe of a fantastic achievement. The satellite was little more than a radio transmitter in a metal sphere, but its regular "bleep-bleep" as it passed around the world announced the dawn of a new age. When, three and a half years later, Yuri Gagarin girdled the Earth in his Vostok spacecraft on 12 April 1961 – proving that man could go into space and live to tell the tale – it was clear that mankind had embarked on a thrilling new adventure. Just eight years after that epic flight, on 20 July 1969, two Americans, Neil Armstrong and Edwin Aldrin, landed their *Eagle* Lunar Module on the Moon and walked on its surface. Armstrong called it "one small step for a man, one giant leap for mankind".

By 1972 twelve men, all Americans, had left footprints in the lunar dust. But space research is more than exploration. Satellites have spun a web of communications around our world, linking nations by telephone, telegraph and television. Other kinds of satellite serve as "radio-stars" helping our ships and planes navigate safely in all weathers. Observation satellites keep us informed about weather, ocean conditions, sea ice, destructive storms, pollution and the health of agricultural crops and forests. The pictures they take, in different parts of the electromagnetic spectrum, help us find minerals and fossil fuels.

Still other satellites keep watch on military activities around the world and help to police arms limitation agreements. So effective are their cameras that objects on the Earth's surface smaller than 1.0ft (0.3m) wide can be discriminated.

We have also seen the first space stations – Russia's Salyuts and Mir and America's Skylab – in which men and women have begun to experiment with new ways of making things in the microgravity environment of space. In prospect are space factories manufacturing new high-strength/lightweight alloys, super crystals for the electronics industry and the purest vaccines and serums.

Scientists expect to exploit these techniques flying to and from orbit in re-usable space shuttles. *Buran* (Snowstorm) allied to the new Soviet heavy-lift booster Energiya now takes its place alongside the NASA Space Shuttle, restored to service after the agonising disaster to *Challenger*. The European Spacelab, which remains fixed in the cargo bay of the American Shuttle, allows scientists to commute to and from orbit with their experiments.

In the meantime, the use of telescopes and other instruments above the atmosphere has thrown revealing light upon the Universe. And although mankind has yet to travel beyond the Moon, his robot emissaries are spreading his quest across the Solar System.

In this illustrated *Space Diary* we record some of the ideas and practical advances that have engendered this immense blossoming of human knowledge and experience. The value of a diary format is that it allows events to be compared in a chronological context. We include consideration of military developments because of the importance of their technological spin-off.

Clearly, it is impossible to detail every launching in a book of this size. The Soviets alone put up more than 90 satellites a year and new challengers of the space frontier have emerged in the shape of Europe, China, Japan, India and many others. However, diary entries will be found for every manned space flight to date and most of the unmanned launchings carried out by nations other than the United States and the Soviet Union.

As we look towards the 21st century, a bold new epoch of exploration is dawning. The Soviets have teams routinely commuting to the Mir space station, including foreign nationals. Twelve countries have agreed to a $23 billion US-led plan for a permanently manned space station which, alongside Soviet ambitions, could lead, eventually, to the setting up of scientific bases on the Moon and Mars.

We may hope that further improvements in the East-West political climate will result in these huge endeavours being mounted in concert by the entire human family.

Kenneth W. Gatland
Ewell, Surrey, England
May 1989

LAUNCH CENTRES

UNITED STATES

1	Kennedy Space Center, Florida Cape Canaveral Air Force Station	28.5°N, 81°W
2	Vandenberg Air Force Base, California	34.7°N, 120.6°W
3	Wallops Station, Wallops Island, Virginia	37.9°N, 75.4°W

USSR

4	Baikonur Cosmodrome	45.6°N, 63.4°E
5	Plesetsk	62.8°N, 40.1°E
6	Kapustin Yar	48.4°N, 45.8°E

JAPAN

7	Kagoshima Space Centre	31.2°N, 131.1°E
8	Tanegashima, Osaki	30.4°N, 131°E

CHINA

9	Jiuquan Satellite Launch Centre (Shuang-ch'eng-tzu)	40.6N, 99.8°E
10	Xi Chang Satellite Launch Centre	28.1°N, 102.3°E
11	Taijuan Satellite Launch Centre	37.8°N, 111.5°E

E.S.A.

12	Guiana Space Centre, Kourou, French Guiana	5.2°N, 52.8°W

ITALY

13	San Marco, Formosa Bay	2.9°S, 40.3°E

INDIA

14	Sriharikota Launching Range (SHAR)	13.9°N, 80.4°E

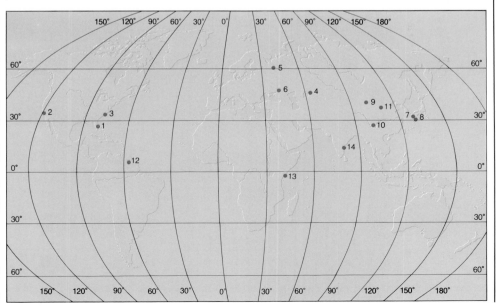

360 BC

Hollow model of a pigeon suspended by a string over a flame is made to move by steam issuing from small exhaust ports (described by Aulus Gellius in *Noctes Atticae*, "Attic Nights").

c. AD 62

Hero (or Heron), a Greek resident of Alexandria, invents the "Aeolipile", a hollow sphere with canted nozzles which spins on pivots by the reaction of steam jets. One of the supports on which the sphere rotates is hollow to admit steam generated in a "boiler" supported over a fire.

c. 850

Chinese use some form of gunpowder in making fireworks to celebrate religious festivals.

1232

Chinese repel Mongols besieging the town of Kai-fung-fu with "arrows of flaming fire". (If these are true rockets, as seems likely, the Chinese must have discovered how to distil organic salt-petre to increase rate of burning.)

Early Chinese solid-fuel fire-arrows.

1242

Roger Bacon, an English Franciscan monk, produces secret formula for "gunpowder": saltpetre 41·2; charcoal 29·4; sulphur 29·4. He also distils salt-petre — the oxygen-producing ingredient — to achieve faster rate of burning. The formula is concealed in an anagram written in Latin which (freely translated) reads: "... but of saltpetre take 7 parts, 5 of young hazel twigs, and 5 of sulphur; and so thou wilt call up thunder and destruction, if thou know the art".

1280

In *The Book of Fighting on Horseback and with War Engines*, the Syrian military historian al-Hasan al-Rammah gives instructions for making gunpowder and rockets which he describes as "Chinese arrows".

1379

Gunpowder rockets used in the siege of Chioggia, near Venice, Italy.

1680

Peter the Great establishes the first Rocket Works in Moscow (later transferred to St. Petersburg) to make signal illuminating rockets for the Russian Army.

1687

Sir Isaac Newton enumerates Laws of Motion; eg, in his third law he states that: "for every action there is an equal and opposite reaction" (principle of the rocket).

1770s

Capt Thomas Desaguliers examines rockets brought from India to Royal Laboratory, Woolwich, England, but fails to reproduce reported range or accuracy. (Some will not even lift from their stands.)

1780s

Indian ruler Hyder Ali, Prince of Mysore, employs iron-cased rockets with 8-10ft (2·4-3·0m) balancing sticks against troops of the East India Company. Weighing 6-12lb (2·7-5·4kg), they travel up to 1·5 miles (2·4km).

1789

Innes Munroe publishes *A Narrative of the Military Operations on the Coromandel Coast*. Describes an incident in 1761, when an Indian rocket corps of 1,200 men led by Hyder Ali of Mysore defeated British in the Battle of Panipat. Rockets volleyed at enemy cavalry 2,000 at a time travelled over half a mile (0·8km).

1792

Troops of Hyder Ali's son, Tippu Sultan (who enlarges rocket corps from 1,200 to 5,000 men and supplies them with larger rockets) use rockets against British in Third Mysore War. Tippu Sultan defeats British several times between 1782 and his death in battle at Seringapatam in 1799.

1804-05

Colonel William Congreve (later knighted) requests large rockets to be made at Woolwich to his specification. Because rockets have no recoil, he believes that they may be launched from ships as well as from land. Within one year he produces a 24lb (10·9kg) rocket with a range of 2,000yds (1,830m). He then produces 32lb (14·5kg) iron-cased rockets: length of casing 42in (107cm) x 4in (10cm) diameter; charge of 7lb (3·17kg); detachable balancing stick 15ft (4·6m) long. He develops a faster-burning powder to increase range.

Congreve tests rockets at Woolwich Arsenal, increasing range and accuracy. By 1805 he has demonstrated that a 6lb (2·7kg) rocket can travel about 6,000ft (1,830m) — approximately

Sir William Congreve (by J. Lonsdale).

twice as far as Indian rockets. (A 6lb rocket refers to the weight of a lead ball loaded into the cylindrical motor case; not the weight of the fuelled rocket.)

1806

October 8 First use of Congreve rockets during the Napoleonic Wars, when 18 rocket boats with sail and oarsmen attack Boulogne harbour. The iron-cased rockets are 32-pounders (14·5kg), 3·5ft (1·06m) long x 4in (10·1cm) diameter, to which are attached 15ft (4·6m) balancing sticks. Range is about 3,000yds (2,743m). Many of the rockets overshoot the French invasion fleet, setting fire to parts of the town.

1807

September 2-7 Congreve rockets are launched against Copenhagen, setting fire to large parts of the town. Blunt warheads discharge carbine balls; pointed heads have holes through which an incendiary mixture squeezes out after impaling wooden ships and buildings.

1813

A Treatise on the Motion of Rockets by William Moore, published by the Royal Military Academy, Woolwich, includes a mathematical description of the trajectories of rockets, including the motion of the rocket both in air and vacuum according to Newton's Third Law of Motion.

1814

September 13-14 British use Congreve rockets in the attack on Fort McHenry, Baltimore, inspiring Francis Scott Key to compose *The Star-Spangled Banner* which includes the phrase "... the rocket's red glare"

1828-29

Solid-fuel rockets designed by Alexander D. Zasyadko (1779-1837) are used in the Russo-Turkish War.

1840s

William Hale, an Englishman, produces spin-stabilised rockets by placing three curved metal vanes in the rocket exhaust. Employed by US forces in the Mexican War (1846-48), in the Crimean War (1853-56), in Hungary, Italy, Prussia, and during the American Civil War (1861-65).

1853-56

Some Russian ships are armed with rockets during the Crimean War.

1857

September 17 Konstantin Eduardovich Tsiolkovsky — who becomes the Father of Cosmonautics in the USSR — is born in the village of Izhevskoye, Spassky Uyezd, Ryazan Gubernia. (Died, Kaluga, 19 September 1935).

1865

Jules Verne, in his novel *De la Terre à la Lune* ("From the Earth to the Moon"), puts his passengers into a huge aluminium bullet fired towards the Moon from a giant cannon buried in Florida soil. Although the "space cannon" is impossible, the choice of Florida as the launch site is oddly prophetic of the actual Apollo Moon shots at Cape Canaveral, 100 years later.

The weightless environment of space as pictured in Jules Verne's novel, "De la Terre à la Lune".

Achille Eyraud (France), in his novel *Voyage à Venus,* makes first serious suggestion of the reaction principle as a means of space travel.

1869-70

A story published in *Atlantic Monthly*, "The Brick Moon" by Edward Everett Hale, contains first known proposal for a habitable Earth satellite of 200ft (60·9m) diameter. Hale considers weather, communication and navigation aspects.

1879

Jules Verne, in his novel *Les ang cents millions de la Begum,* suggests launching Earth satellites by means of rockets fired from a huge cannon.

1881

Nikolai Ivanovich Kibalchich (1853-1881), a Russian revolutionary sentenced to death by the Tsar, sketches a design for a man-carrying rocket platform stabilised by tilting the rocket motor in a gimbal frame. He proposes feeding gunpowder cartridges successively into a blast chamber. (The same steering principle is used in modern rockets.)

1882

October 5 Robert Hutchings Goddard — who becomes the Father of Astronautics in the United States — is born at Worcester, Massachusetts. (Died, Baltimore, 10 August 1945).

1883

Konstantin E. Tsiolkovsky, in *Outer Space,* develops the theory of reaction propulsion, arguing that a rocket will work in the vacuum of space.

Konstantin Tsiolkovsky at work in the study of his home in Kaluga, which is now a national museum.

1890

Hermann Ganswindt (Germany) proposes a reaction-powered spaceship fuelled with steel cartridges charged with dynamite.

1894

June 25 Hermann Julius Oberth, who became the Father of German Rocketry, is born in Sibiu on the northern slopes of the Transylvanian Alps.

1897

Kurt Lasswitz publishes science-fiction novel *Auf Zwei Planeten* ("On Two Planets"). Years later, Willy Ley applies the term "Repulsor", from the space rockets in this book, to the rockets for the VfR (Verein für Raumschiffahrt).

1898

H.G. Wells, in his novel *War of the Worlds,* describes a Martian invasion of Earth in which the invaders are eventually vanquished by terrestrial diseases.

1901

H.G. Wells, in his novel *The First Men in the Moon'* "invents" an anti-gravity

material, Cavorite, to transport his spaceship to the Moon.

1903

Tsiolkovsky, in treatise on space travel, advocates use of liquid propellants and establishes principles of spaceship design. First treatise is entitled: *Exploration of the Universe with Rocket-Propelled Vehicles;* supplements appear in 1911, 1912 and 1914.

Tsiolkovsky describes cylindrical spin-stabilised space habitat with artificial gravity and a "space greenhouse" with a closed ecological system in "The Rocket Into Cosmic Space", *Science Survey,* Moscow, 1903.

1909

Professor Robert H. Goddard (1882-1945) begins study of liquid-propellant rockets, concluding that liquid oxygen and liquid hydrogen would be an excellent combination.

A 1916 picture of Robert H. Goddard holding a circular vacuum tube.

1917

January 5 Goddard receives grant of $5,000 from Smithsonian Institution for work on rockets to probe the upper atmosphere.

1918

Goddard postulates nuclear-propelled "ark" carrying civilisation from a dying

Solar System towards another star. Manuscript ("The Ultimate Migration", dated 14 January 1918) is sealed into an envelope for posterity and is not published (*The Goddard Biblio Log,* Friends of the Goddard Library) until 11 November 1972.

November 7 Goddard demonstrates tube-launched solid-propellant rockets (forerunners of "Bazooka") at Aberdeen, Maryland.

1919

Goddard publishes monograph, *A Method of Attaining Extreme Altitude,* containing basic mathematics of rocketry. One section entitled "Calculation of Minimum Mass Required to Raise One Pound to an 'Infinite Altitude'" is Goddard's carefully-worded reference to space flight, at this time a subject considered to lack the dignity of serious scientific enquiry. He outlines a scheme by which a rocket, with rapid-fire solid-propellant feed, might be made to impact the shadow side of the Moon with a charge of flash powder to announce its arrival. (Smithsonian Miscellaneous Collections, Vol 71, No 2).

1921

Soviets establish state-laboratory for research on solid-propellant rockets. Founder: N. I. Tikhomirov (1860-1930).

Fridrikh A. Tsander suggests a composite "aerospace" vehicle which takes off with propellers like an aeroplane; at altitude, liquid-fuel rocket engines are started and metallic parts of the vehicle no longer useful for flight are fed to a furnace to be used as fuel.

1923

H. Oberth's classic work, *Die Rakete zu den Planetenräumen,* is published.

November 1 Goddard operates small rocket motor burning liquid oxygen and gasoline fed by pumps, on a test stand.

1924

In book *Cosmic Rocket Trains* Tsiolkovsky considers multi-staged rockets in which the lower stage returns to Earth after expending its propellants

Tsiolkovsky, in an article "The Spaceship", proposes use of the atmosphere as a braking medium for vehicles returning from outer space. (Others reaching the same conclusion are Fridrikh A. Tsander in his article "Flight to Other Planets", and Yu V. Kondratyuk, who shows that a properly designed aerofoil could result in large savings of propellant on re-entry.)

1925

Walter Hohmann in his book *Die Erreichbarkeit der Himmelskörper* ("The Attainability of Celestial Bodies") defines principles of rocket motion in space.

1926

March 16 Goddard achieves world's first flight of liquid-propellant rocket at Auburn, Massachusetts.

Goddard's rocket just before launch.

1927

July 5 A group of German rocket enthusiasts, inspired by Oberth, form Verein für Raumschiffahrt. (Society for Space Travel). Meeting takes place in the parlour of an alehouse, the "Goldenen Zepter" (Golden Sceptre), Schmiedebrücke 22, Breslau. Principals: Johannes Winkler, Max Valier, Rudolf Nebel.

Max Valier proposes rocket aircraft developed from Junkers G.23.

1928

Dr Frank von Hoeff proposes 30-tonne rocket-powered lifting-body capable of taking off from water like a hydroplane. Upper stage is assumed to have orbital capability.

Capt Potocnik (pseudonym "Hermann Noordung") postulates three-element space station in Earth orbit: "Wohnrad" (living wheel), "Maschinenhaus" (machine station) and "Observatorium" (observatory). The "Wohnrad" assumes diameter of 98ft (30m).

Professor Hermann Oberth is contracted by UFA film company to build liquid-propellant rocket for launching on the day of the première of Fritz Lang film, *Frau im Mond* ("Woman on the Moon"). Assistants are: A.B. Scherschevsky (author of *Die Rakete für Fahrt und Flug*, or "The Rocket for Transport and Flight"), and Ing Rudolf Nebel (then employed as an advertising engineer with Siemens und Hulske, Berlin). Together they build and test a rocket chamber designed by Scherschevsky, fuelled with gasoline and liquid oxygen, fitted with *Spaltduese* ("slit nozzle") designed by Oberth. Although the chamber is inefficient ("burning like a blowtorch"), with the *Spaltduese* they achieve a thrust of 5·5lb (2·5kg). Oberth aims at a rocket intended to reach an altitude of at least 62 miles (100km), but later this is reduced to 12·4 miles (20km). Propellants are to be either methane or alcohol with LO₂. Proposed launch site is the island of Horst on the Baltic coast. After experiencing difficulties with leaking tanks and pipework — and problems with getting the liquid oxygen into the tank — the rocket is set up in Horst and promptly explodes. The project is abandoned.

February 1 Robert Esnault-Pelterie and André Hirsch, a French banker, establish the REP-Hirsch International Astronautics Prize of 5,000 Fr to be awarded annually for the best original scientific work, either theoretical or experimental, that will advance the state-of-the-art in space travel or related sciences. (First recipient is Hermann Oberth for second edition of his book *Wege zur Raumschiffahrt*, "The Roads to Space Travel", 1929.)

June 11 Sailplane *Ente* (Duck) flies from Wasserkuppe Mountain, Germany, powered by two Sander solid-propellant rockets. After catapult launch, it flies more than three-quarters of a mile (1·2km) in about 60 seconds. Pilot: Fritz Stamer.

1928-32

Nikolai A. Rynin publishes nine-volume encyclopedia *Interplanetary Communications*, covering myths and legends of space travel, science fiction (Verne and Wells), methods for communicating with other worlds, rocket history, mathematics of propulsion, long-range artillery, aircraft, international rocket pioneers (including the work of Tsiolkovsky, Goddard, Esnault-Pelterie), astronavigation, and information on the Moon and planets. Extensive bibliography.

1929

Group for development of electric and liquid-propellant rocket engines is formed within Gas Dynamics Laboratory (GDL) under V.P. Glushko. Location: Admiralty building and St John Ravelin of the Peter and Paul Fortress, Leningrad.

J.D. Bernal (*The World, the Flesh and the Devil*, Methuen & Co, London) and Olaf Stapledon (*Star Maker*, K. Paul, Trench, Trubner & Co, London) describe concepts of artificial planets and self-contained worlds.

Yuri V. Kondratyuk publishes his best-known work, *The Conquest of Interplanetary Space*. Contains first known statement of orbital technique for landing on planetary bodies: "The entire vehicle need not land; its velocity need only be reduced so that it moves uniformly in a circle as near as possible to the body on which the landing is to be made. Then the machine part (*landing module. Ed*) separates from it, carrying the amount of active agent (*propellant*) necessary for landing and subsequently rejoining the remainder of the vehicle".

Kondratyuk proposes a lifting surface to brake the speed of a spacecraft returning to Earth from outer space. The craft, having entered the atmosphere, performs braking ellipses, slowly shedding speed by aerodynamic drag, and finally descends as a glider. Alternatively, the craft makes a direct descent through the atmosphere (like the Space Shuttle).

July 17 Goddard launches a "weather rocket" with a barometer, thermometer and camera. Instruments are recovered by parachute.

September 30 Fritz von Opel flies a rocket glider at Rebstock, near Frankfurt, powered by 16 solid-propellant

Fritz von Opel in the cockpit of his RAK-1 rocket glider; with him are Stamer (left) and Fridrikh Tsander.

---

rockets, each of 50lb (22·7kg) thrust. There is no catapult. The glider reaches 95mph (153km/h), is airborne for about 75 seconds, and travels nearly 5,000ft (1,525m).

November 23 Col Charles A. Lindbergh visits Goddard and subsequently arranges a grant of $50,000 from Guggenheim Fund for the Promotion of Aeronautics to support Goddard's work with rockets.

1930

Glushko designs USSR's first liquid-propellant rocket engine, the ORM-1.

Esnault-Pelterie, French rocket pioneer, publishes his major work *L'Astronautique*, ranging from consideration of sounding rockets to projects for interplanetary travel and including extensive mathematical treatment of rocket performance and trajectories. Work is an expansion of lectures to the French Astronomical Society (1927) and a book *L'Exploration par Fusées de la Très Haute et la Possibilité des Voyages Interplanétaires* (1928).

April 4 American Interplanetary Society is founded by G. Edward Pendray, David Lasser and others at apartment of Mr and Mrs Pendray, 450 West 22nd Street, New York City. Four years later (6 April 1934) name is changed to American Rocket Society (incorporated within Institute of Aeronautics and Astronautics, formed by merger of Institute of the Aerospace Sciences [IAS] and ARS, 1 February 1963).

May 17 Max Valier is killed by exploding steel-cased rocket motor, fuelled by kerosene/water mixture and liquid oxygen, at Heylandt factory in Berlin-Britz. Motor is being static tested for demonstration in rocket car Rak 7.

Max Valier seen making a bench test of a liquid-propellant rocket motor at the Heylandt factory.

July 23 Oberth's *Kegelduese* is static tested at the Chemisch-Technische Reichanstalt.

October 19 Gottlob Espenlaub flies rocket glider at Düsseldorf, powered by Sander solid-propellant rockets, reaching 55·9mph (90km/h).

December 30 Goddard launches 11ft (3·3m) long liquid-propellant rocket at Roswell, New Mexico, which achieves altitude of 2,000ft (609m) and speed of 500mph (805km/h). Propellants liquid oxygen/gasoline, gas-pressure feed.

1931

Esnault-Pelterie starts development of rocket engine employing liquid oxygen/hydrocarbon for static testing.

Dr Eugen Sänger begins series of rocket-motor experiments at University of Vienna. Test motor has a spherical jacketed combustion chamber of approximately 2in (5·08cm) diameter with 10in (25·4cm) long nozzle. Light fuel oil is circulated through jacket before being injected into chamber for combustion with liquid oxygen. High combustion pressure of 30 to 50 atm obtained by

Bosch injector of type used in contemporary Diesel engines. Average thrust 55lb (25kg); burning times up to 15 minutes.

January Klaus Riedel and Rudolf Nebel design a new combustion chamber after an idea of Guido von Pirquet. A cylinder of aluminium is spun into two hemispheres and fitted with an entry section for a conventional nozzle, the parts being welded together. The chamber is provided with a water-jacket for cooling and propellants are fed by upstream injection (as formerly proposed by Winkler). According to Engel, the motor is 10 times lighter than the *Kegelduese* and for the same propellant consumption gives 2·2lb (1kg) more thrust. A series of these motors is built, each having a dry weight of just 8·75oz (250g).

February Austrian engineer Friedrich Schmiedle establishes first officially-recognised rocket mail service. His solid-fuel rockets project mail for a distance of some 2 miles (3·2km) over mountainous country between the Austrian towns of Schöckel and Radegund. A parachute is automatically released after the rocket has ceased firing.

February 21 Johannes Winkler launches his HW-I (Hückel-Winkler) rocket, fuelled with methane and liquid oxygen, at Breslau. It hops 6·56ft (2m) into the air, turns over and falls back to the ground.

March 14 Winkler re-launches HW-I rocket fitted with stabilising fins. It climbs 295ft (90m), turning horizontally, and lands some 656ft (200m) from the point of departure. (This is the first known liquid-propellant rocket to fly in Europe).

April Klaus Riedel enlarges dimensions of aluminium rocket motor to give thrust of 70·5lb (32kg).

April 11 Rocket car of Heylandt/Valier team makes test run under thrust of improved liquid-propellant motor built by chief engineer Alfons Pietsch. New and more efficient propellant injector is designed by Arthur Rudolph. Motor weighing 39·7lb (18kg) is capable of producing up to 350lb (160kg) thrust for a few minutes. Another test run is made on 3 May.

April 15 Near Osnabrück, Reinhold Tiling demonstrates 6ft (1·82m) solid-propellant rocket of aluminium construction, with folding wings which open out for recovery.

May Johannes Winkler begins design of HW-II rocket.

May 10 First (unintentional) flight of liquid fuel rocket by VfR. A water-cooled Mirak III, developed by Riedel, "broke loose from its test stand and went up 60ft (18·3m)".

May 14 Same VfR rocket which made unscheduled flight on May 10, now re-named Repulsor 1, ascends 200ft (61m). It is a so-called "two-stick

Repulsor", named from the fuel/nitrogen tank layout beneath the motor in the head.

June 9 Goddard patents design for rocket-propelled aircraft.

July-August Constantin Generales, an American medical student, and Wernher von Braun conduct in Zürich first known experiment in "space-medicine". They build a primitive centrifuge in which they place a number of mice to determine the effects of high rates of acceleration. Generales then dissects the mice to obtain physiological data.

August VfR launches a Repulsor rocket to an altitude of 3,300ft (1,006m), recovered by parachute.

September 20 *Gesellschaft für Raketenforschung* (Society for Rocket Research) is founded in Hanover by Albert Püllenberg and Albert Löw.

September 29 Goddard launches 9·94ft (3·03m) by 12in (30·5cm) rocket. Flight lasts 9·6 seconds, reaching 180ft (59m).

October 13 Goddard rocket with simplified combustion chamber climbs more than 1,700ft (518m). Length 7·75ft (2·36m) by 12in (30·5cm) diameter.

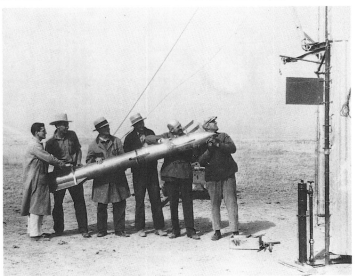

Goddard and assistants placing the October test rocket in the tower.

November 13 *Gruppa Isutcheniya Reaktivnovo Dvisheniya* ("Group for the Study of Reaction Propulsion") is formed in Leningrad under auspices of the Osoaviakhim (LenGird).

November 18 "Group for the Study of Reaction Propulsion" is formed in Moscow under auspices of Central Council of the Osoaviakhim (MosGird). Principal: F.A. Tsander.

1931-32

Glushko makes 100 static firings of series ORM rocket engines.

1932

Tsander publishes his book, *Problems of Flight by Jet Propulsion*.

Rolf Engel (with support from Hugo A. Hückel) forms rocket group within the *Verein Deutscher Ingenieure* (Society of German Engineers) — a voluntary labour service for young engineers during the depression. Group is formed in Dessau, where a large number of engineers from the Junkers company are unemployed. Participants include Heinz Springer, Werner Preuss and (later) Werner Brügel. Activities end with arrest of Engel and Springer by Gestapo on grounds of "negligent high treason" (ie, communicating information about German rocket activities to enthusiasts abroad).

Spring Officials of Ordnance Department of the Reichswehr visit *Raketenflugplatz*, near Berlin: Col Prof Karl Becker, Chief of Ballistics and Ammunition; Major von Horstig, ammunition specialist; and Capt Dr Walter Dornberger, in charge of powder rockets for the German Army.

April 19 Goddard launches gyro-controlled liquid-oxygen/petrol rocket. Nitrogen gas pressure feeds propellants to thrust chamber and operates bellows working coupled air/exhaust control vanes.

July Klaus Riedel, Rudolf Nebel and Wernher von Braun stage rocket demonstration for Ordnance Department at Army Proving Grounds at Kummersdorf, about 60 miles (96·5km) south of Berlin. Mirak II, which reaches altitude of about 200ft (60·9m), crashes before parachute can open.

September Goddard resumes full-time teaching at Clark University, allowing him to make experiments in the laboratory under grant from Smithsonian Institution.

October 6 HW-II rocket built by Johannes Winkler, Rolf Engel, Hans Bermüller and Heinz Springer explodes on launch stand because of a malfunction of the liquid oxygen and liquid methane control valves.

November 1 Wernher von Braun becomes civilian employee of the German Army at Kummersdorf, under Dornberger, charged with the development of liquid-propellant rockets.

November 12 First liquid-fuel rocket built by American Interplanetary Society produces 60lb (27kg) of thrust for 20-30 seconds during static test, Stockton, New Jersey. Damaged and never flown. Basis of design: German "two-stick" Repulsor.

December 21 At Kummersdorf-West a 20in (50·8cm) liquid-oxygen/ ethyl-alcohol rocket motor explodes on static test. Participants: Walter Dornberger, Walter Riedel, Heinrich Grünow and Wernher von Braun.

1933

Goddard receives grant from Daniel and Florence Guggenheim Foundation making possible further improvement of rocket components: welding techniques for light metals, pumps, thrust chambers, insulators, etc.

January At Kummersdorf, von Braun bench-tests a small, water-cooled rocket motor which develops a thrust of 308lb (140kg) for 60 seconds.

Von Braun, at Kummersdorf, makes plans for "A"-series of experimental rockets. A-1 rocket has regeneratively-cooled liquid-oxygen/alcohol motor of 661lb (300kg) thrust. Explodes on test stand within 0·5 second. Development abandoned.

May 14 American Interplanetary Society's Rocket No 2 ascends about 250ft (76m) from Great Kills, Staten Island, New York; then liquid oxygen tank bursts due to a stuck valve.

August 17 USSR launches world's first hybrid (solid/liquid propellant) rocket GIRD 09, from the Nakhabino Polygon, near Moscow. Propellants: liquid oxygen and gasoline and colophony, a dark-coloured resin obtained from turpentine. Rocket attains an altitude of about 1,312ft (400m), although motor burns through. Designed by M.K. Tikhonravov and built by a group which includes S.P. Korolev. Length 7·9ft (2·4m); launch weight

41·9lb (19kg); average thrust 66·1lb (30kg).

October Rocket engines OR-2 and OR-10 designed by Tsander are static tested.

Soviet liquid-propellant rocket engines ORM-50 and ORM-52 designed by Glushko (GDL) are static tested.

October 10 Reinhold Tiling, his laboratory assistant Miss Angelika Buddenböhmer, and Friedrich Kuhr, are fatally injured by an explosion while compressing some 40lb (18kg) of black powder into fuel pellets for rockets.

October 13 British Interplanetary Society is founded in Liverpool by P.E. Cleator. Because Explosives Act of 1875 precludes the development and testing of rockets on unlicensed premises, Society concentrates on theoretical studies in astronautics.

October 31 Soviets establish Reaction Propulsion Institute (RNII) on the basis of GDL and MosGird. Glushko's GDL group for the development of electric and liquid-propellant rocket engines continues as a department of RNII.

November 25 First Soviet fully liquid-propellant rocket, GIRD X, attains altitude of nearly 262ft (80m). Engine OR-2 designed by F.A. Tsander employs liquid oxygen and petrol. Overall length 7·2ft (2·2m); weight less than 66·1lb (30kg); thrust 154lb (70kg).

GIRD X, the first Russian liquid-propellant rocket to fly. It used a Tsander-designed OR-2 motor.

1934

Arthur Rudolph, one of Valier's assistants, joins the Kummersdorf group.

June 5 William G. Swan reaches altitude of 200ft (61m) in his "Steel Pier Rocket Plane" in Atlantic City, New Jersey, USA.

William Swan at the controls of his "Steel Pier Rocket Plane" which was powered by 12 powder rockets.

September 9 Successful flight test of fourth liquid-fuel rocket built by American Rocket Society, from Marine Park, Staten Island, New York, achieves distance of 1,338ft (407m), splashing into New York Bay. Has single-thrust chamber with four canted nozzles. (Originally tested 10 June 1943, but did not fly because fuel ports too small.)

December Two A-2 rockets, "Max" and "Moritz", launched by von Braun group from island of Borkum, North Sea, attain altitudes of about 1·5 miles (2·4km).

1934-35

Goddard begins testing A-series of rockets, employing pressure-feed and stabilised by gyro-controlled exhaust vanes, at Roswell, New Mexico.

1935

Glushko and G.E. Langemak publish their book, *Rockets, Their Design and Applications.*

March 8 Goddard flies liquid oxygen/ gasoline rocket with pendulum stabiliser, reaching speed of more than 700mph (1,126km/h) and landing about 9,000ft (2,743m) from launch tower.

March 28 Goddard launches 14·8ft (4·51m) rocket which reaches 4,800ft (1,463m) altitude, travelling 13,000ft (3,962m) at average speed of 550mph (885km/h). Rocket corrected its path by action of gyro on vanes in the exhaust.

Summer Rocket motor installed in Heinkel He-112 is static-tested by

Kummersdorf group (which now comprises some 80 people). Von Braun's group receives 5 million marks from Luftwaffe and 6 million marks from the Army (before this the annual budget did not exceed 80,000 marks!).

1935-36

Goddard begins new series of experiments in which the aim is to develop a more powerful liquid oxygen/gasoline rocket motor of 10in (25·4cm) diameter.

1936

Soviets launch "Aviavnito" sounding rocket to an altitude of 3·5 miles (5·6km). Length 10ft (3·05m), weight 213lb (96·6kg).

Glushko publishes *Liquid Propellants for Reaction Engines,* based on his course of lectures at Zhukovsky Air Force Academy.

February GALCIT Rocket Research Project is initiated at California Institute of Technology by Dr Frank J. Malina, J.W. Parsons, and E.S. Forman. It pioneers work on hypergolic (self-igniting) propellants. Rocket experiments are made in the Arroyo Seco, north of Pasadena (now the site of the Jet Propulsion Laboratory). First application, in 1940, is JATO (jet-assisted take-off) for aircraft; later the Corporal and Sergeant missiles for the US Army, and the WAC-Corporal (first successful US sounding rocket), launched by a German A-4 in "Bumper Project".

November 7 Goddard launches four-chamber liquid-propellant L-7 rocket, which climbs 200ft (61m), at Roswell, N.M.

1936-37

Rocket motor built by Esnault-Pelterie develops a thrust of 275lb (125kg) for 60 seconds.

1937

Dr Walter Thiel takes over von Braun's rocket facility at Kummersdorf "to study and perfect liquid propellant rocket motors".

February Walter H_2O_2 rocket engine assists take-off of Heinkel He-72 Kadett in experiment sponsored by German Air Ministry.

April Rocket engine of 2,200lb (1,000kg) thrust, fuelled by alcohol and liquid oxygen, installed in Heinkel He 112, is flight tested. (Static trials began in the summer of 1935.)

April Wernher von Braun's group moves into newly-constructed rocket research establishment at Peenemünde on the Baltic coast of Germany. More workers from Raketenflugplatz co-opted: Klaus Riedel, Hans Hueter, Kurt Heinish and Helmuth Zoike.

May 9 H.F. Pierce (American Rocket Society) launches a liquid-fuel rocket to about 250ft (76m) altitude at Old Ferris Point, Bronx, New York.

May 19 Goddard flies rocket with excellent automatic stabilisation.

July 28 Goddard flies 18·5ft (5·64m) by 9in (22·8cm) diameter rocket with movable tailpiece steering, wire-wound tanks, barograph payload. Reaches altitude of 2,055ft (626m), but parachute opens prematurely.

August 27 First Soviet gas-generator GG-1, designed by Glushko, completes bench tests.

An A-3 rocket during static test.

Autumn Three A-3 rockets are launched from Greifswalder Oie. Much improved design has three-axis gyro control system operating exhaust vanes for control at low speeds. Also, liquid nitrogen pressurisation system, vaporiser, alcohol and oxygen valves, and two-stage propellant flow which largely eliminates ignition explosions. On first launch parachute opens prematurely after five seconds and rocket crashes into the sea. On second and third launches parachutes are omitted, but rockets still go out of control.

1937-38

Soviet ORM-65 rocket engine completes 30 ground tests in RP-318-1 glider designed by S.P. Korolev. Propellants: nitric acid/kerosene; thrust: 110 to 386lb (50 to 175kg); multi-start capability. Specific impulse 210-215.

Korolev, a giant of Soviet rocketry.

1938-42

Dr Eugen Sänger and Dr Irene Bredt conduct research into development of "antipodal rocket bomber" at Research Institute for the Technique of Rocket Flight, Trauen, near Hanover, Germany. Overall length 91·8ft (28m); wing span 49·2ft (15m); launch weight 100 tonnes; maximum velocity 13,596mph (21,880km/h); maximum range 14,596 miles (23,490km). Launch method: captive rocket booster riding a monorail track 1·8 miles (2·9km) long; launch velocity Mach 1·5. After climbing at 30° under rocket power aircraft is intended to follow a ballistic trajectory of 100 miles (161km) apogee, followed by a series of aerodynamic "skips" in the upper atmosphere. Project abandoned 1942.

1938

April 20 Goddard rocket with barograph reaches 4,215ft (1,285m) altitude, landing 6,950ft (2,121m) from tower. Motor operated for 25·3 seconds.

Summer Successful launchings of A-5 rockets are made without guidance system at Greifswalder Oie.

December 10 American Rocket Society tests 90lb (41kg) thrust regeneratively-cooled liquid-fuel rocket motor designed by James H. Wyld. (An improved Wyld motor subsequently [1941-42] becomes the basis for a US Navy contract to develop rocket-assisted take-off units for seaplanes).

1938-39

Goddard concentrates on development of small high-speed centrifugal pumps.

1939

British Interplanetary Society concludes two-year engineering study of technique for landing men on the Moon.

Glushko's rocket group separates from RNII to become independent design group of Moscow-based aero-engine factory.

June 20-July 3 Heinkel He-176, first rocket-plane employing liquid propellants, is test-flown at Peenemünde by Erich Warsitz. It is powered by a Walter engine of 1,100lb (500kg) thrust and has a pressurised cockpit which can be separated from the fuselage and recovered by parachute.

Autumn First A-5 with new gyro-control system operating exhaust vanes is launched from Greifswalder Oie —and recovered by parachute. (Approximately 25 of these test rockets —

forerunners of the A-4 —are launched over the next two years, some of them several times. Programme tests three different guidance systems. At first launchings are vertical, reaching altitudes of 8 miles (12·9km); then inclined. Radio guide beams are also tested.)

1940

February 28 Russian rocket glider RP-318-1 designed by S.P. Korolev flies under power from modified ORM-65 rocket engine burning nitric acid/kerosene. Thrust is variable from 110 to 386lb (50 to 175kg); top speed 124mph (200km/h). Pilot: Vladimir P. Fyodorov. Tow aircraft: P-5.

June DFS 194, powered by 600lb (272kg) thrust Walter rocket engine, is test-flown by Heini Dittmar.

August 9 Goddard makes first rocket flight with propellant pumps at Roswell, N.M. Rocket attains 300ft (91·4m) altitude at velocity of only 10 to 15mph (16 to 24km/h).

1941

January 6 Goddard motor on static test develops highest thrust to date: 985lb (447kg).

September Goddard group begins work under contract from US Navy Bureau of Aeronautics and US Army Air Corps.

September 10 First glide test of Russian BI-1 rocket fighter designed by A. Ya Bereznyak and A.M. Isayev, from military airfield near Sverdlovsk. Tow aircraft: twin-engined bomber.

October 2 Me 163 rocket-powered interceptor, based on Lippisch tailless concept, attains 624mph (1,004km/h) during early test flight.

December 18 American pioneer rocket company— Reaction Motors, Incorporated— is formed by leading members of the American Rocket Society; James H. Wyld, Lovell Lawrence, John Shesta and Hugh F. Pierce. Subsequently produces engines for various applications, eg, Bell X-1, X-15 research aircraft, Viking sounding rocket.

1942

March 19 American pioneer rocket company— Aerojet Corporation— is officially incorporated in California. (An outgrowth of the GALCIT Rocket Research Project begun by Dr Frank J. Malina and under the direction of Dr Theodore von Karman, California Institute of Technology).

May 15 Rocket interceptor BI-1 making low-level run under power flies into the ground, killing the pilot G. Ya

Bakhchivandzhi. Aircraft is powered by RNII's D-1-A-1100 liquid-propellant rocket engine.

July Goddard group moves to Naval Engineering Experimental Station, Annapolis, Maryland. (Developments to July 1945 include liquid-propellant take-off unit for flying boats; also, variable-thrust rocket motors).

October 3 First successful A-4 rocket is launched at Peenemünde. It travels a distance of 118 miles (190km), reaching a maximum altitude of 53 miles (85km).

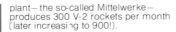

First flight of Soviet RD-1 engine installed in tail of Pe-2R aircraft.

May-June Germans make operational test launchings of V-2 rockets at Blizna, Poland.

August 17-18 Six hundred RAF bombers raid Peenemünde rocket establishment causing some 800 casualties, about half being Soviet prisoners of war. Dr Walter Thiel, currently in charge of the A-4 power plant, is killed.

1944

Two versions of RD-1 engine are put into production by State Defence Committee (GKO). In 1944-45 flight trials are made in Pe-2, La-7, Yak-3 and Su-6 aircraft.

Soviet design bureau (OKB) is established under A.M. Isayev to design cryogenic liquid-propellant rocket engines.

Spring Disused underground oil depôt south of Harz Mountains, Germany, converted into underground assembly

A US soldier inspects a V-2 at the Mittelwerke underground plant.

plant—the so-called Mittelwerke—produces 300 V-2 rockets per month (later increasing to 900!).

June 22 California Institute of Technology receives US Army Ordnance contract for research and development of long-range rockets:

September 7 First V-2 rocket with one-tonne amatol explosive warhead is

A mobile battery of three V-2s ready for launch in September 1944.

launched against London in retaliation for Allied air attacks on Germany. Civil Defence records show that about 4,320 V-2s are launched between 6 September 1944 and 27 March 1945, of which about 1,120 are directed against London and its suburbs, killing 2,511 people and seriously injuring nearly 6,000.

1945

Soviet GDL-OKB under V.P. Glushko begins development of high-thrust liquid-propellant rocket engines.

February Bachem Ba 349, first vertically-launched rocket interceptor, crashes on first and only manned test flight, killing the pilot. At 492ft (150m) cockpit cover carrying pilot's headrest flies off; the plane turns on its back, climbs inverted to 4,921ft (1,500m) at 15 degrees to the horizontal, and then dives into the ground. Powerplant: Ba 349A-HWK 109-509; Ba 349B-HWK 109-509D with cruise chamber.

May Arthur C. Clarke, in memorandum placed before British Interplanetary Society, advocates geostationary (24hr) orbit for global telecommunications by satellite.

May 2 General Dornberger, Dr Wernher von Braun and other Peenemünde personnel, having fled westward in a convoy of vehicles, surrender to US 7th Army.

May 5 German rocket establishment at Peenemünde, on island of Usedom, and the port of Swinemünde, are taken by Second White Russian Army under General Konstantin K. Rokossovsky. Installations have been largely destroyed by retreating Germans.

September 20 Wernher von Braun and other leading German rocket engineers arrive in United States under "Project Paperclip".

October First group of German rocket engineers arrives at White Sands Proving Ground, New Mexico.

1945-46

GDL-OKB makes flight trials of RD-100 rocket engine for long-range ballistic missile (Soviet version of the German V-2) and a geophysical rocket (1RA-E).

1946

Soviet occupation forces reorganise V-2 rocket production in Germany. Ex-Peenemünde engineer Helmut

Gröttrup is put in charge of Germans working at Zentralwerke, Niedersachswerfen. Instead of launching V-2s, they are static-tested at Lehesten under Soviet rocket engineer V.P. Glushko.

Work begins in United States on intercontinental ballistic missile programme (Project MX-774).

April 16-September 19 1952 Sixty-four V-2s—including six two-stage "Bumper" rockets—are launched from White Sands, N.M. Two "Bumper" rockets are launched from the Long Range Proving Ground, Florida (now USAF Eastern Test Range and Kennedy Space Center). One V-2 is launched from an US aircraft carrier.

June 28 V-2 rocket instrumented by Naval Research Laboratory (NRL) for upper air research reaches altitude of 67 miles (108km).

July-August Soviet rocket engineer S.P. Korolev designs "stretched V-2", lengthening propellant tanks by about 9ft (2.74m) and increasing engine thrust from 55,116 to 70,540lb (25,000 to 32,000kg), using two turbopumps in tandem.

August 18 Soviet Air Force flypast at Tushino, Moscow, includes demonstration of RD-1X3 rocket engine in S.A. Lavochkin's 120R aircraft.

September 28 Dr Frank Malina and Prof Summerfield of JPL (Caltec) give results of theoretical study on "The Problem of Escape from Earth by Rocket" at 6th International Congress for Applied Mechanics (Paris) (*J. Inst. Aero Sc.*, Vol 14, No 8) setting out requirements for multi-stage rockets capable of achieving escape velocity. Contains the suggestion that instrument could measure cosmic radiation. (Malina is responsible for developing at JPL the WAC-Corporal sounding rocket which, at Summerfield's suggestion, is launched as second stage from a German A-4 rocket in 1949.)

October 28 German rocket engineers recruited by USSR arrive in Moscow. They are divided into two groups: one (including Helmut Gröttrup) is established in Moscow suburb, near Datschen (Nii-88); the other, on the island of Gorodomlya in Lake Seliger, some 150 miles (241km) northwest of Moscow.

November 29 Academician M.V. Keldysh appointed chief of RNII.

December 23 Study group of British Interplanetary Society (R.A. Smith and H.E. Ross) submits re-design of German V-2 as a man-carrying rocket with a separable pressurised cabin to give a man experience of space flight, including periods of weightlessness (*JBIS*, May 1948). Although proposal submitted to (then) Ministry of Supply is not adopted, the work is fully vindicated in the US Mercury-Redstone project, in which US astronauts (Shepard and Grissom) are exposed to short periods of zero-g, in 1961.

1947

GDL-OKB designs RD-101 engine for V-2-A medium-range missile and geophysical sounding rocket.

May 22 Corporal E surface-to-surface missile, launched at White Sands, New Mexico, is first to employ radar system of ground control.

June 20 "Bumper Project" for development of two-stage launcher based on German V-2 rocket and modified WAC-Corporal is initiated by US Army Ordnance.

Autumn German groups in USSR under Helmut Gröttrup design R.10 rocket of conical configuration: length 46·5ft (14·1m); maximum diameter 5·3ft (1·6m); launch weight 40,490lb (18,366kg); empty weight 4,235lb (1,921kg). Engine: improved A-4 type employing LO₂/ethyl alcohol; thrust 70,400lb (31,993kg). Propellant tanks of very thin steel are to be pressurised, forming integral part of structure. Warhead—with ablative wood covering—designed to separate after propulsion ends. Guidance: beam-riding. Design range 570 miles (917km). Although the R.10 is not produced as such, it undoubtedly plays a part in formulating ideas for Soviet missiles of the 1950s, developed under S.P. Korolev.

October 30 Soviets begin launch tests of V-2 type missiles near the village of Kapustin Yar, some 75 miles (121km), east of Stalingrad (now Volgograd). First missile flies almost due east for nearly 175 miles (281km), landing "not too far from the target". Another V-2, launched the next day, goes out of control and crashes from a height of about 500ft (152m). Present are Sergei Korolev and Helmut Gröttrup.

1948

Winter-Spring German rocket group in Moscow (Nii 88) merges with existing group at Gorodomlya, where Soviets continue to use personnel as consultants on various problems of rocket engineering. Work includes study of an R.12 multi-stage rocket to launch a 2.200lb (998kg) warhead to a distance of approximately 1,500 miles (2,413km).

December 29 US Secretary of Defense James V. Forrestal reveals the existance of an "Earth Satellite Vehicle Programme". Studies undertaken within the framework of the RAND Corporation include such companies as Douglas, North American Aviation and Aerojet-General. The studies look towards military applications which would involve considerable engineering effort and heavy expenditure. RAND, for example, recommend a 500lb (227kg) satellite launched by a three-stage liquid oxygen/alcohol rocket; launch weight 233,669lb (105,992kg). Launch vehicle estimated to cost (1948 prices) $150 million. A later project recommends a liquid oxygen/liquid-hydrogen multistage rocket of 82,000lb (37,195kg) estimated to cost some $82 million. US Navy advocates a single-stage LO₂/LH₂ rocket, launch weight 101,000lb (45,805kg), named HATV (High Altitude Test Vehicle). Responding to this study are North American Aviation, Bureau of Aeronautics, Glenn L. Martin and Aerojet-General. The idea is that the entire vehicle will become the satellite, telemetering back data from instruments contained in the nose. None of these proposals is, in fact, taken up.

This V-2 was the first large rocket to be launched from the deck of a ship.

September 6 V-2 rocket is launched from aircraft carrier USS *Midway*.

October 14 Bell X-1 rocket-powered research aircraft, powered by four-chamber 6,000lb (2,722kg) thrust Reaction Motors RMI engine, makes first manned supersonic flight in history. Pilot: Charles E. Yeager. Launch aircraft: modified B-29.

Chuck Yeager pilots X-1 No.1 during the first manned supersonic flight.

1948-49

Two Britons, Dr L.R. Shepherd, a Harwell physicist, and A.V. Cleaver, a leading British rocket engineer, examine feasibility of applying nuclear energy to rocket propulsion in classic series of papers published by the British Interplanetary Society. (*JBIS*, September, November 1948; January and March 1949).

1948-51

British Interplanetary Society advocates reducing scale and cost of engineering to achieve early experience of orbital flight with instrumented satellite, in series of studies, culminating in paper "Minimum Satellite Vehicles" by K.W. Gatland, A.M. Kunesch and A.E. Dixon, given at 2nd IAF Congress in London (*JBIS*, November 1951). Calculated that a three-stage rocket with "balloon tanks" and liquid oxygen/hydrazine propellants, with launch weight of about 16 tonnes, could orbit radar-reflecting inflatable balloon and single cosmic ray experiment. Conclusions are taken into account in early planning (1952) of Project Orbiter by Office of Naval Research, Washington, D.C., which leads to first US satellite Explorer 1.

1949

Dr Chien Hsueh-Sen, a member of the California Institute of Technology, proposes a boost-glide hypersonic aircraft of 3,107 miles (5,000km) range. (See also entry 1972 November!)

February 24 Two stage V-2/WAC-Corporal rocket launched from White Sands, N.M., attains record altitude of 244 miles (393km). American WAC-Corporal—designed and developed under direction of Dr Frank J. Malina at JPL—is propelled by an RFNA/aniline rocket engine with gas pressure feed producing 1,500lb (680kg) thrust for 45 seconds.

April German group at Gorodomlya prepares design study of R.14 rocket to launch a 6,600lb (2,994kg) warhead a distance of 1,800 miles (2,897km). Characteristics: single stage; balloon tanks of pressurised stainless steel or aluminium alloy; length 77·6ft (23·6m); diameter 9ft (2·74m); launch weight 156,200lb (70,852kg); dry weight 15,400lb (6,985kg); propellants LO₂/ethyl alcohol; thrust 220,000lb (99,792kg). Engine test stand of this thrust value established near Zagorsk, about 36 miles (58km) northeast of Moscow.

1949-52

Systematic research into the effects of space flight on living organisms begins at Kapustin Yar. Dogs are rocketed to altitudes of some 60 miles (96·5km) within recoverable nose-cones of Pobeda rockets.

1950

May 11 Viking 4 sounding rocket is launched to record altitude of 106 miles (170km) from research ship USS *Norton Sound*, a converted sea-plane tender. Maximum velocity 5,160ft/sec (1,573m/sec). Location: near Christmas Island, Pacific Ocean. Object: to determine relationship between Earth's magnetic field and cosmic rays.

Viking 4 rocket lifts off from the USS Norton Sound in the Pacific.

September 30-October 2 First International Astronautical Congress in Paris leads to formation of International Astronautical Federation (IAF) in London one year later. Principals: Gesellschaft für Weltraumforschung (GfW), West Germany; Groupement Astronautique, France; British Interplanetary Society.

November Arthur C. Clarke suggests possibility of mining the Moon and launching lunar material into space by electromagnetic catapult. ("Electromagnetic Launching as a Major Contribution to Space-Flight", *JBIS*, November 1950).

1951

March 21-November 28 1953 German rocket engineers taken to work in Soviet Union are repatriated to Germany in stages, beginning with lower-grade technicians and ending with senior design engineers, including

Helmut Gröttrup and family. Among last to leave are rocket guidance specialists.

August Viking 7 sounding rocket achieves record altitude for single-stage rockets of 135 miles (217km) and speed of 4,100mph (6,597km/h).

1951-55

Dr Walter Dornberger —former commandant at Peenemünde —and Dr Krafft A. Ehricke undertake design at Bell Aircraft Corporation of two-stage winged rocket aircraft under Project Bomi (Bomber Missile). Sub-orbital and orbital versions are envisaged, taking off vertically from a launch pad. Studies by USAF at Wright-Patterson Air Force Base. Project abandoned 1955.

1952

March Dr Wernher von Braun proposes a spinning wheel-shaped space station of 250ft (76·2m) diameter orbiting 1,062 miles (1,730km) above the Earth. ("Crossing the Last Frontier", *Colliers*, 22 March 1952).

May US Air Force announces that mammals —two monkeys ("Pat" and "Mike") and two mice— have been recovered alive and unharmed after being launched in an Aerobee sounding rocket to an altitude of some 200,000ft (60,960m) from Holloman AFB. The animals were subjected to a brief acceleration of about 15g, lasting less than one second, and to a force of 3-4g lasting 45 seconds. Animal compartments were in nosecone of Aerobee which descended by parachute. Total programme includes three Aerobee launchings: 18 April 1951: monkey killed on impact; 20 September 1951: monkey and 11 mice recovered; 21 May 1952: two monkeys and two mice recovered. Conclusion: "Weightlessness does not appear to affect the animals' heart rates, blood pressure or respiration systems."

July Dr L.R. Shepherd considers "Noah's Ark" starship— a nuclear-powered million-tonne colony shaped like an oblate spheroid. ("Interstellar Flight", *JBIS*, July 1952).

1953

August 31 Douglas D-558-II, powered by 6,000lb (2,722kg) thrust engine, attains unofficial world's altitude record of about 15 miles (24·1km). Pilot: Lt-Col Marion E. Carl.

November 20 D-558-II flies at 1,325mph (2,132km/h), nearly twice the speed of sound. Pilot: A. Scott Crossfield.

December 12 Bell X-1A sets new unofficial speed record of more than 1,600mph (2,575km/h).

1954

GDL-OKB begins development of RD-107 and RD-108 rocket engines for central core and strap-on boosters of first Soviet ICBM. Propellants: liquid oxygen/kerosene.

Design bureau under S.A. Kosberg begins work on aircraft rocket engine using monopropellant (isopropyl-nitrate).

1955

United States initiates research into nuclear rocket propulsion under Project Rover, a joint activity of the US Atomic Energy Commission and the US Air Force. Research is centred on graphite reactor design at Los Alamos Scientific Laboratory (LASL), concentrating on materials. Project, which initially examines the possibilities of nuclear rockets for military purposes, is switched in 1957 to a programme of nuclear rockets for space propulsion at LASL alone.

May 26 Soviets launch two dogs in geophysical rocket from Kapustin Yar (Volgograd cosmodrome). Seven similar sub-orbital experiments are flown over next two years.

May 31 Construction of the Baikonur cosmodrome begins on the steppes of Kazakhstan. Massive deployment of construction machinery is made to build launch facilities for the R.7 ICBM, preparation and test buildings, control station, highways and dormitory areas with heat and water supply. First stage of work is completed by April 1957. Nearby is site of Zvezdograd (Star City) — now Leninsk—adjoining the old town of Tyuratam.

July 15 President Eisenhower announces decision to launch a small scientific satellite based on Office of Naval Research (ONR) Project Orbiter and modified Jupiter-C launch vehicle. Later, it is decided to base America's first satellite attempt on a "civilian" launcher under Project Vanguard.

September 9 US Secretary of the Navy gives Naval Research Laboratory (NRL) authority to proceed with Project Vanguard satellite launcher for International Geophysical Year (IGY).

Autumn US Department of Defense assigns development of intermediate range ballistic missile of 1,500-mile (2,414km) range to Redstone group at Huntsville, Alabama.

1956

GDL-OKB begins development of RD-214 rocket engine for first stage of SS-4 Sandal MRBM. Propellants: nitric acid/kerosene. Thrust 74 tonnes; chamber pressure 45 atm (abs); specific impulse 264. Sandal is adapted as first stage of small Cosmos satellite launcher (B-1) introduced in 1962.

February 1 US Army Ballistic Missile Agency (ABMA) activated under Maj-Gen John B. Medaris to develop Jupiter IRBM.

July 23 Bell X-2, powered by Curtiss-Wright rocket engine of 15,000lb (6,804kg) thrust, sets unofficial world's speed record of 1,900mph (3,058km/h).

The Bell X-2: capable of Mach 3 +.

September Darell Romick describes cylindrical Space Colony 0·6 miles (1km) long by 980ft (300m) diameter, with hemispherical ends and with 1,640ft (500m) rotating disc at one end, to be inhabited by 20,000 people. ("Manned Earth— Satellite Terminal Evolving from Earth-to-Orbit Ferry Rockets [METEOR]", IAF Congress, Rome, Italy, September 1956).

September 7 Bell X-2 sets new unofficial world's altitude record for manned aircraft exceeding 126,000ft (38,403m).

September 20 Three-stage Jupiter-C launched from Cape Canaveral on sub-orbital trajectory carries an 86·5lb (39·2kg) payload to an altitude of 680 miles (1,094km) and a downrange distance of more than 2,980 miles (4,800km). (At this stage the United States is approaching the ability to launch a small satellite into Earth orbit, but Project Orbiter has been halted by a political decision in favour of Project Vanguard. This is a decision that the Eisenhower administration lives to regret, since history now records that the world's first artificial satellite was launched by the Soviet Union.)

September 27 Bell X-2 sets new unofficial world's speed record for manned aircraft of 2,100mph (3,380km/h). Flight ends tragically when aircraft goes out of control and crashes, killing pilot Capt Milburn G. Apt.

1957

August First Soviet intercontinental ballistic missile, the R.7 (NATO code-name Sapwood), is launched on test from newly-built launch centre north of Tyuratam in Kazakhstan. (Launch centre is later developed as Baikonur cosmodrome.)

October 4 Soviets launch world's first artificial satellite, Sputnik 1, by R.7 ICBM from Baikonur cosmodrome.

An exploded view of Sputnik 1.

November 3 Soviets launch Sputnik 2, containing the dog Laika, by modified R.7 ICBM.

December 6 First US attempt to launch an artificial satellite, by Vanguard three-stage rocket, fails on launch pad at Cape Canaveral. Rocket develops insufficient thrust, topples over and explodes in flames.

1958

GDL-OKB begins design development of RD-219 rocket engine for second

stage application. Thrust 90 tonnes; chamber pressure 75 atm (abs); specific impulse 293. Propellants: nitric acid/dimethylhydrazine. Flight tests 1961.

January 31 First US artificial satellite, Explorer 1, is launched from Cape Canaveral by Juno I. Instrumented by Dr James A. Van Allen, its major discovery is that the Earth is girdled by radiation belts.

Juno I/Explorer 1 at Pad A, LC 26.

March Richard L. Garwin publishes first technical discussion on possibility of using solar radiation pressure to propel a "solar sail" spaceship (Jet Propulsion, JARS, March 1958). Concept appears to have originated in the early 1920s with Konstantin Tsiolkovsky and F.A. Tsander. First mention in the USA of solar sail idea was made by Carl A. Wiley (pen name Russell Saunders) in Astounding Science Fiction, May 1951.

October 1 National Aeronautics and Space Administration (NASA) is formally inaugurated. Administrator: Dr T. Keith Glennan; Deputy Administrator: Dr Hugh L. Dryden.

October 7 NASA formally approves Project Mercury "to send a man into orbit, investigate his capabilities and reactions in space and return him safely to Earth".

December 12 Nosecone containing squirrel monkey "Old Reliable" is lost at sea following launch of a Jupiter IRBM from Cape Canaveral, Florida.

December 18 US launches into Earth-orbit Project Score (Atlas), which broadcasts human voice from space

for first time: a recorded Christmas message from President Eisenhower.

1959

January 2 Soviets launch Lunik (Luna) 1 which misses Moon by 3,100 miles (5,000km) and goes into orbit around the Sun.

April 2 Seven astronauts are selected for Project Mercury: Captains L. Gordon Cooper, Jr, Virgil I. Grissom and Donald K. Slayton, USAF; Lt M. Scott Carpenter, Lt-Cmdrs Alan B. Shepard, Jr, and Walter M. Schirra, Jr, USN; Lt-Col John H. Glenn, Jr, USMC.

May 28 Monkeys "Able" and "Baker" recovered after flight in Jupiter nosecone launched from Cape Canaveral. "Able" later dies during an operation to remove bio-electrodes; "Baker" survives to take up residence at Alabama Space and Rocket Center, Huntsville, Alabama.

September 12 Soviets launch Lunik (Luna) 2, which becomes first man-made object to impact the Moon.

October 4 Soviets launch Lunik (Luna) 3, which circumnavigates the Moon to photograph the far side, returning images to Earth by television.

December 4 Monkeynaut "Sam" recovered in Mercury capsule abort test after launch on Little Joe LJ-2 from Wallops Island, Virginia. On 31 January 1960, "Miss Sam" makes a similar flight in Little Joe LJ-1B.

1960

April 1 First meteorological satellite, Tiros 1, is launched by United States.

Drum-shaped; 22in x 42in (0.56m x 1.07m) diameter; 283lb (128kg) weight.

April 13 First experimental navigation satellite, Transit IB, is launched by United States. Spherical; 3ft (0.91m) diameter; 267lb (121kg) weight.

May 24 First experimental infra-red surveillance satellite, Midas 2, is launched by United States. Cone-cylinder 23ft (7m) long x 5ft (1.5m) diameter; 5,070lb (2,300kg) weight.

August 12 NASA launches Echo 1, the first experimental passive communications satellite. Satellite has the form of a balloon of aluminized Mylar plastic which inflates to a diameter of 100ft (30.5m) in space. It is successfully used to reflect radio waves from ground-based transmitters to receiving Earth stations separated by thousands of miles; e.g., Holmdel, New Jersey, USA— Jodrell Bank,

The 135ft (41m) diameter Echo 2 satellite during inflation testing.

Cheshire, England. LC Cape Canaveral. LV Delta. D 24 May 1968 A 135ft (41.1m) diameter balloon satellite, Echo 2, is launched 25 January 1964, made of thicker material.

August 18 US Air Force launches Discoverer 14 from Vandenberg Air Force Base into orbit of 115 x 500 miles (186 x 805km) x 79.65°. Releases re-entry capsule, first to be air-snatched by aircraft (C-119). A similar capsule, from Discoverer 13, parachuted into the sea, 11 August 1960.

August 19-20 Sputnik 5 is launched from Baikonur cosmodrome with two dog-passengers, Strelka and Belka. First recovery of living creatures from orbital flight. Vostok prototype. LC Baikonur. LV A-1. FT 1.1 days.

October 4 US Army launches active repeater communications satellite, Courier 1B, which records signals from Earth stations and re-transmits them on command.

October 10-14 Two Soviet space rockets "failed in flight" on 10 and 14 October, according to NASA. Believed to be concerned in attempts to launch unmanned spacecraft to Mars while Premier Nikita Khrushchev is attending UN in New York. One source refers to a major accident at the Baikonur cosmodrome.

October 13 Three mice, "Amy", "Sally" and "Moe", make successful sub-orbital flight into space in RVX-2A nosecone of Atlas D ICBM launched from Cape Canaveral. They endure some 20 minutes of weightlessness.

December 1 Soviets launch two dogs, "Pchelka" and "Mushka", in Sputnik 6 (Vostok prototype). After circling the Earth for nearly 24 hours, ground control sends the command for retrofire, but spacecraft is seemingly misaligned: the re-entry trajectory is too steep and the capsule (and dog passengers) burns up in the Earth's atmosphere. LC Baikonur. LV A-1. FT 1 day.

December 19 First Mercury-Redstone flight vehicle (MR-1A) is launched on sub-orbital flight from Cape Canaveral. Unmanned capsule ascends 130 miles (209km) and splashes 235 miles (378km) downrange.

1961

GDL-OKB begins design development of RD-253 topping cycle rocket engine for first stage of Proton launch vehicle. Flight tests begin 1965. (Engines of upper stages developed by Kosberg-OKB.)

Work begins on the Spaceport at Merritt Island, Cape Canaveral, Florida, subsequently the John F. Kennedy Space Center.

January 31 A 137lb (62kg) chimpanzee, "Ham", is recovered after sub-orbital flight in Mercury capsule

"Ham" in the special couch designed for his 16 minute MR-2 flight.

launched by Redstone MR-2 from Cape Canaveral. Height of achieved trajectory is 155 miles (249km); downrange distance 420 miles (676km). Flight is meant to achieve 115 miles (185km) altitude and 290 miles (467km) range, but thrust of booster is "higher than expected".

March 24 Professor Carl Sagan proposes scheme to make Venus habitable by injecting colonies of algae into atmosphere to reduce CO_2 concentration. ("The Planet Venus", *Science*, Vol 133, 24 March 1961, pp. 849-858).

March 25 Last trial launching of Vostok-type spacecraft, making one Earth revolution, before first manned space flight. Includes a dummy cosmonaut and dog, "Zvesdochka". Similar test (with "dog Chernushka") 9 March 1961 also succeeded. LC Baikonur. LV A-1. FT 0·1 day.

April 12 Soviet Union launches first man into space. Lt Yuri Gagarin in Vostok 1 completes one circuit of the Earth in a flight lasting 108 minutes. Orbit ranges between 113 x 204 miles (181 x 327km) x 65° to equator. Total distance travelled is 25,400 miles (40,868km). LC Baikonur. LV A-1. LT 0907 MT. R near village of Smelovaka, Ternov District, near Saratov.

A suited-up Yuri Gagarin in the bus on the way to the Vostok 1 launch pad at Baikonur cosmodrome.

April 20 Harold Graham, 27-year-old engineer, makes first free-flight with Bell Aerosystems rocket belt. Flight lasts 13 seconds and covers distance of 112ft (34·1m). On a later flight Graham flies up and over a 30ft (9·1m) hill with a slope of about 60°, maintaining a parallel course about 3 to 4ft (0·98 to 1·31m) from the ground.

May President Kennedy recommends development of nuclear rocket propulsion technology; this leads to the NERVA Project and the award of a contract to the industrial team of Aerojet-General and Western Electric for the development for flight testing of

a NERVA engine based on the LASL Kiwi-B reactor. The contract then specifies a NERVA engine of 55,000lb (24,948kg) thrust (1,100 MW) and a specific impulse of 760. (NERVA is the acronym of Nuclear Engine for Rocket Vehicle Application.)

May 5 NASA launches Cdr Alan B. Shepard, Jr, in Mercury 3 spacecraft *Freedom 7* on sub-orbital flight lasting 15min 22sec. Maximum altitude 116 miles (186km); distance travelled 297 miles (478km). Astronaut demonstrates ability to achieve manual

Alan Shepard's Mercury capsule is lifted from the Atlantic Ocean.

control of spacecraft under weightlessness. LC Cape Canaveral. LV Modified Redstone. LT 0934 EST. R Atlantic, USS *Champlain*.

May 25 President Kennedy, at a joint session of Congress, declares national space objective: "I believe that this nation should commit itself to achieving the goal, before this decade is out, of landing a man on the Moon and returning him safely to Earth...."

July 21 NASA launches Lt-Col Virgil I. Grissom in Mercury 4 spacecraft *Liberty Bell 7* on sub-orbital flight lasting 15min 37sec. Maximum altitude 118 miles (190km); distance travelled 303 miles (487km). Mission successful but spacecraft sinks; astronaut recovered. LC Cape Canaveral. LV Modified Redstone. LT 0720 EST. R Atlantic, USS *Randolph*.

August 6-7 Major Gherman Titov in Vostok 2 completes 17 Earth revolutions in flight lasting 25hr 18min. Distance travelled 436,656 miles (703,150km). LC Baikonur. LV A-1. LT 1130 MT. R Saratov region, about 450 miles (724km) SE of Moscow.

October 27 First launch of Saturn 1 (Block 1) vehicle demonstrating validity of clustered engines. Launches dummy upper stages on sub-orbital trajectory, reaching 98 miles (157·5km) apogee, 246 miles (396·3km) downrange.

November 10 Monkey "Goliath" dies when Atlas E launched from Cape Canaveral is destroyed in flight by range safety officer. Experiment is 'Small Primate Unrestrained Test' (Spurt).

November 15 First known poem to be sent into space is inscribed on an instrument panel of the satellite Traac launched from Cape Canaveral. Called "Space Prober", it is by Prof Thomas G. Bergin, Professor of Romance Languages, Yale University:
"From Time's obscure beginning, the Olympians
Have, moved by pity, anger, sometimes mirth,
Poured an abundant store of missiles down
On the resigned, defenceless sons of Earth.
Hailstones and chiding thunderclaps of Jove,
Remote directives from the constellations,

Aye, the celestials have swooped
down themselves,
Grim bent on miracles or incarnations.
Earth and her offspring patiently
endured,
(Having no choice) and as the years
rolled by
In trial and toil prepared their counter-
stroke—
And now 'tis man who dares assault
the sky.
Fear not, Immortals, we forgive your
faults,
And as we come to claim our promised
place
Aim only to repay the good you gave
And warm with human love the chill of
space."
Traac—which achieves an orbit of 585
by 695 miles (941 by 1,119km) has a
lifetime of some 800 years.

November 29 NASA launches Mercury 5 capsule with chimpanzee passenger "Enos". Spacecraft is commanded
down after two orbits because of
development of abnormal roll rate.
Chimp recovered in good condition.
LC Cape Canaveral. LV Atlas D.
FT 3·3hr.

December 20 Rhesus monkey "Skat-
back" is launched in Atlas F ICBM from
Cape Canaveral.

1962

February 20 Lt-Col John H. Glenn
becomes first American to orbit the
Earth in space. His Mercury 6 capsule
Friendship 7 completes three Earth
revolutions in flight lasting 4hr 55min
23sec. Retro-rocket pack retained
during re-entry when false signal
indicates possibility of loose heat
shield. Safe recovery. LC Cape Canaveral. LV Atlas D. LT 0947 EST.
R Atlantic, USS *Noa*, about 210 miles
(338km) NW of San Juan, Puerto Rico.

**John Glenn, the first US astronaut
actually to orbit the Earth.**

May 24 Lt-Cdr M. Scott Carpenter in
Mercury 7 spacecraft *Aurora 7* completes three revolutions of the Earth in
flight lasting 4hr 56min 5sec. LC Cape
Canaveral. LV Atlas D. LT 0845 EDT.
R Atlantic, USS *Pierce*, about 125
miles (201km) NE of Puerto Rico.

June 27 North American X-15,
powered by Reaction Motors engine
of 50,000lb (22,680kg) thrust, flies at
4,105mph (6,605km/h). Pilot: Joseph
A. Walker, NASA. Launch aircraft:
modified B-52.

July 10 NASA launches Telstar 1, first
privately-financed communications
satellite (by American Telephone &
Telegraph Company) into elliptical
orbit; this enables Earth stations
tracking the satellite to transmit live
television between North America and

Telstar 1 is readied for launch.

Europe. Periods of communication
limited to about 20 minutes when Telstar is above the horizon of communicating terminals. Serviceable until
February 1963. Weight 170lb (77kg);
diameter 34·5 in (87·6cm). Orbit 592 x
3,500 miles (952 x 5,632km) x
44·79°. Telstar 2 is launched 7 May
1963 into higher orbit to reduce
exposure to damaging radiation in the
Van Allen belt.

August 11-15 Major Andrian G.
Nikolayev in Vostok 3 completes 64
revolutions of the Earth in flight lasting
94hr 22min. First television from a
manned spacecraft. Distance travelled
1,639,190 miles (2,639,600km).
LC Baikonur. LV A-1. LT 1130 MT.
R S of Karaganda (48°02'N, 75°45'E).

August 12-15 Lt-Col Pavel R. Popovich
in Vostok 4 completes 48 Earth revolutions in flight lasting 70hr 57min.
First dual flight with another manned
spacecraft, passing within some
4 miles (6·5km) of Vostok 3. Distance
travelled 1,230,230 miles (1,981,050km).
LC Baikonur. LV A-1. LT 1102 MT.
R S of Karaganda (48°10'N, 71°51'E).

August 27 NASA launches Mariner 2
spacecraft to achieve flyby of Venus on

14 December 1962. Finds heavy
atmosphere, mostly carbon dioxide,
100 times the pressure of Earth's;
surface temperature exceeding 800°F
(426·7°C); no magnetic field.

October 3 Cdr Walter M. Schirra, Jr, in
Mercury 8 spacecraft *Sigma 7* completes six Earth revolutions in flight
lasting 9hr 13min 11sec. Distance
travelled 153,900 miles (247,625km).
Lands 4·5 miles (7·2km) from recovery
ship. LC Cape Canaveral. LV Atlas D.
LT 0815 EDT. R Pacific, USS *Kearsarge*,
about 295 miles (475km) NE of
Midway Island.

November 1 Soviets launch Mars 1
spacecraft from Baikonur. Expected to
pass within 620-6,700 miles
(998-10,780km) of Mars on 19 June,
1963, but communications lost
21 March 1963. Carries photo-TV
system for photographing surface of
Mars; instruments for discovering
organic compounds on planet's
surface, and spectrometer; magnetometer for cosmic rays and radiation
belt investigations, etc. LC Baikonur.
LV A-2-e. Weight spacecraft: 1,970lb
(893·5kg).

December 13 Relay 1, NASA prototype
for an operational communications
satellite, is launched into an orbit of
821 x 4,622 miles (1,322 x 7,439km)
inclined at 47·49° to the equator to
test transmission of television, telephone, facsimile and digital data. Size
2·66ft (0·81m) long x 2·43ft (0·74m)
diameter. Weight 172lb (78kg).

1963

Dandridge Cole suggests Space
Colony habitat made from hollowed-
out asteroid of ellipsoidal form, some

18·6 miles (30km) long, with
landscaped interior, rotating about its
major axis to create artificial gravity.
Mirrors reflect sunlight inside to give
impression of daylight. Similar
concept proposed to achieve
migration to the stars.

May 15-16 Major L. Gordon Cooper,
Jr, in Mercury capsule *Faith 7*,
completes 22 Earth revolutions in
flight lasting 34hr 19min 49secs.
Distance travelled 583,469 miles
(938,801km). LC KSC (Cape Canaveral). LV Atlas D. LT 0904 EDT.
R Pacific, USS *Kearsarge*, about 80
miles (129km) SE of Midway Island.

June 14-19 Lt-Col Valery F. Bykovsky
in Vostok 5 completes 81 Earth revo-
lutions in flight lasting 119hr 6min.
Passes within 3·1 miles (5km) of
Vostok 6. Travels more than
2,050,620 miles (3,300,000km).
LC Baikonur. LV A-1. LT 1459 MT.
R about 337 miles (540km) NW of
Karaganda on latitude 53°.

June 16-19 Junior Lieutenant Valentina
V. Tereshkova, first woman in space,
completes 48 Earth revolutions in
Vostok 6 in flight lasting 70hr 50min.
Travels about 1,242,800 miles
(2,000,000km). LC Baikonur. LV A-1.
LT 1230 MT. R 390 miles (627km) NE
of Karaganda on latitude 53°.

Tereshkova about to enter Vostok 6.

August 22 North American X-15
reaches altitude of 67 miles (108km).
Pilot: Joseph A. Walker, NASA. Under
NASA ruling pilot qualifies as an
astronaut, having exceeded altitude of
50 miles (80·5km).

September 25 Col Yuri Gagarin,
speaking at Paris Congress of the
International Astronautical Federation
(IAF), states: "Techniques being
developed in my country involve the
assembly of components of spacecraft in Earth-orbit and the
introduction of propellant." The
technique is being adopted "because
it was not possible to launch vehicles
of several scores of tons directly to the
Moon".

October Nikita Krushchev talks of
watching the Americans reach the

Moon: "We will see how they fly there, and how they land there ... and, most important, how they will take off and return"

October 4 On sixth anniversary of Sputnik 1, Col Yuri Gagarin writes: "It may, of course, be too bold of me to conclude that interplanetary travel will be a fact within a few years. Preparations for these flights will call for a still greater effort including many more flights into Earth-orbit...." When these experiments are completed, "we shall be able to assemble spacecraft of any size in flight and the refuelling problem, which is so important for protracted space travel, will also be solved".

December 10 US Air Force's X-20 Dyna-Soar project is abandoned. Project began in late 1950s with Boeing as prime contractor; aimed at developing a one-man space-glider capable of orbiting Earth and returning to land on a runway. Booster: Titan III.

December 13 Soviets launch first experimental meteorological satellite, Cosmos 23. Orbit 149 x 381 miles (240 x 613km) x 49°.

1964

July 28 NASA launches Ranger 7 on mission to obtain close-up pictures of lunar surface down to impact. Hits Moon 31 July after 65·6hr flight, Sea of Clouds 8·5°S, 19·5°W. Returns 4,306 photographs.

An Atlas-Agena lifts Ranger 7 towards its encounter with the Moon.

August 19 NASA launches Syncom 3 communications satellite into geostationary orbit above International Date Line. Broadcasts opening ceremonies Tokyo Olympics. Preliminary experiments: Syncom 1 (14 February 1963, radio failed); Syncom 2 (26 July

1963). LC Cape Canaveral. LV Thrust Augmented Delta.

October 12-13 Col Vladimir M. Komarov, Dr (of Sc) Konstantin P. Feoktistov and Dr (of Medicine) Boris G. Yegorov in Voskhod 1 complete 16 Earth revolutions in flight lasting 24hr 17min 3sec. First three-man crew in space; Feoktistov, spacecraft designer, and Yegorov, medical doctor, specialists gaining first-hand experience of space flight. Distance travelled 415,936 miles (669,241km). LC Baikonur. LV A-2. LT 0730.1 MT. R about 194 miles (312km) NE of Kustanai.

November 28 NASA launches Mariner 4 spacecraft to achieve flyby of Mars on 14 July 1965. Twenty-one close-up pictures reveal cratered surface from distance of about 6,000 miles (9,656km). No evidence of "artificial canals" or flowing water. Atmospheric density about one-hundredth that of Earth, mostly carbon dioxide.

1965

February 16 NASA launches Pegasus 1, first Saturn launch vehicle with operational payload (meteoroid detector); first TV from orbiting satellite. Separation of "boilerplate" Apollo CSM from S-4 stage.

March 18-19 Col Pavel I. Belyayev and Lt-Col Alexei A. Leonov in Voskhod 2 complete 17 Earth revolutions in flight lasting 26hr 2min 17sec. Leonov performs world's first spacewalk lasting 10 minutes; total time outside pressurised cabin (including time in extensible airlock) 23min 41sec. Distance travelled 445,420 miles (716,680km). Faulty sensor in attitude control system enforces extra Earth orbit, with manual control of re-entry by Belyayev. LC Baikonur. LV A-2. LT 1000 MT. R near Perm, Urals, some 746 miles (1,200km) NE of Moscow.

March 23 Lt-Col Virgil I. Grissom and Lt-Cdr John W. Young in Gemini 3 complete three Earth revolutions in flight lasting 4hr 53min. First US two-man space mission; first spacecraft to manoeuvre from one orbit to another. LC Cape Canaveral. LV Titan II. LT 0924 EST. R USS Intrepid, Atlantic, off Grand Turk Island.

April 6 First geostationary commercial communications satellite, Early Bird (Intelsat 1), is launched from Cape Canaveral.

April 23 Soviets launch Molniya 1A communications satellite into 12-hr elliptical orbit inclined at 65° to equator for relay of telephone and TV services within USSR.

June 3-7 Capt James A. McDivitt and Capt Edward H. White, II, in Gemini 4 complete 62 Earth revolutions in flight lasting 97hr 56min 31sec. White spacewalks for 21 minutes; manoeuvres in space with gas-gun. First EVA by US astronaut; first extensive manoeuvre of spacecraft by pilot. Distance travelled

Gemini 4: Ed White's spacewalk.

1,609,700 miles (2,590,000km). LC Cape Canaveral. LV Titan II. LT 1015.59 EST. R USS Wasp, Atlantic, 390 miles (628km) E of Cape Canaveral.

July 16 Soviets launch 12·2 tonne Proton 1 automatic space laboratory to study the primary particles of high-and-low energy cosmic rays. Heaviest Soviet payload to date. First use of new heavy launch vehicle. Proton 2 (2 November 1965) and Proton 3 (6 July 1966) similar. LC Baikonur. LV D-1. FT 86·86 days.

August 21-29 Major L. Gordon Cooper, Jr, and Lt Charles Conrad, Jr, in Gemini 5, complete 120 Earth revolutions in flight lasting 190hr 55min 14sec. Demonstrate man's ability to function in space environment for long period. Use fuel cells for electrical power supply; evaluate guidance and navigation system for future rendezvous missions. LC KSC (Cape Canaveral). LV Titan II. LT 0900 EST. R USS Champlain, Atlantic, 335 miles (539km) SW of Bermuda.

December 4-18 Major Frank Borman and Lt-Cdr James A. Lovell, Jr, in Gemini 7, complete 206 Earth revolutions in flight lasting 330hr 35min 17sec. World's longest manned space flight to date. Provide rendezvous target for Gemini 6. Distance travelled 5,716,900 miles (9,198,492km). LC KSC (Cape Canaveral). LV Titan II. LT 1230.03 EST. R USS Wasp, Atlantic, about 700 miles (1,727km) SW of Bermuda; splashdown is 6·4 miles (10·3km) from target.

December 15-16 Cdr Walter M. Schirra, Jr, and Capt Thomas P. Stafford, in Gemini 6, complete 16 Earth revolutions in flight lasting 25hr 51min 43sec. Mission includes rendezvous and station-keeping with Gemini 7, closing to within about one foot (30cm) of that vehicle. LC Cape Canaveral. LV Titan II. LT 0837.26 EST. R USS Wasp, Atlantic, 630 miles (1,014km) SW of Bermuda.

1966

January 31 Soviets launch Luna 9 to the Moon; lands 3 February, Ocean of Storms, west of craters Reiner and Marius. First mechanical object to land in working condition; sends panoramic pictures by television.

March 16 Neil A. Armstrong (C) and Capt David R. Scott in Gemini 8 complete 6½ Earth revolutions in flight lasting 10hr 41min 26sec. Achieve first docking between a manned spacecraft and an unmanned space vehicle — Gemini Agena Target Vehicle (GATV) — but experiment ends prematurely when a thruster in Gemini malfunctions, causing the combined spacecraft to spin. After separating the spacecraft the astronauts make a safe return to Earth. (In subsequent Apollo programme, Armstrong becomes commander of Apollo 11 and "the first man to walk on the Moon" (see 1969 July 16-24). LC KSC (Cape Canaveral). LV Titan II. LT 1141.02 EST. R USS Mason, Pacific, 690 miles (1,110km) SE of Okinawa; splashdown is 1·1 miles (1·8km) from planned target in secondary recovery area.

March 31 Soviets launch Luna 10, which becomes first artificial satellite of the Moon on 3 April.

May 30 NASA launches Surveyor 1, which soft-lands 1 June, after 63hr 36min flight, just north of crater Flamsteed, Ocean of Storms, 2°27'S, 43°13'W. Sends 11,237 pictures by television.

Gemini 9's view of the ATDA; the nose shroud failed to jettison.

June 3-6 Capt Thomas P. Stafford and Lt Eugene A. Cernan in Gemini 9 complete 45 Earth revolutions in flight lasting 72hr 20min 50sec. Achieve rendezvous with Augmented Target Docking Adapter (ATDA), but docking frustrated because nose shroud of ATDA has failed to jettison. Cernan carries out 2hr 8min of EVA, unrelated to ATDA. Distance travelled 1,255,630 miles (2,020,308km). LC KSC (Cape Canaveral). LV Titan II. LT 0839.33 EST. R USS *Wasp*, Atlantic, some 345 miles (555km) E of Bermuda; splashdown 0·38 miles (0·61km) from target.

July 18-21 Lt-Cdr John W. Young and Capt Michael Collins in Gemini 10 complete 43 Earth revolutions in flight lasting 70hr 46min 39sec. First use of target vehicle—Agena—as source of propulsion after docking, setting new altitude record for manned spacecraft of 474 miles (763km). Also rendezvous with Gemini 8 target vehicle. Collins' stand-up EVA 49 minutes; EVA to retrieve experiment from Agena 8min 39sec. LC KSC (Cape Canaveral). LV Titan II. LT 1720.26 EST. R USS *Guadalcanal*, Atlantic, some 529 miles (851km) due E of Cape Canaveral.

August 10 NASA launches Lunar Orbiter 1 which swings into orbit round the Moon on 14 August after 92hr 1min flight. Photographs about 2 million sq miles (5·18 million sq km), including 16,000 sq miles (41,440 sq km) over primary Apollo landing sites.

September 12-15 Lt Charles Conrad, Jr, and Lt-Cdr Richard F. Gordon, Jr, in Gemini 11, complete 44 Earth revolutions in flight lasting 71hr 17min 08sec. Achieve first-revolution rendezvous and docking with Agena target; use Agena propulsion to achieve record altitude of 850 miles (1,368km).

During EVA, Gordon fastens Agena-anchored tether to Gemini docking bar, and spacecraft later make two Earth revolutions in tethered configuration. Gordon EVA time 2hr 43min. LC KSC (Cape Canaveral). LV Titan II. LT 0942.26 EST. R Atlantic, 701 miles (1,128km) E of Miami.

November 11-15 Lt-Cdr James A. Lovell, Jr, and Major Edwin E. Aldrin, Jr, in Gemini 12, complete 59 Earth revolutions in flight lasting 94hr 34min 31sec. Docks with Agena target on third revolution. Aldrin works outside spacecraft, including standup EVAs, for record 5hr 30min. First solar eclipse photo from space. Distance travelled 1,628,510 miles (2,620,272km). LC KSC (Cape Canaveral). LV Titan II. LT 1546.33 EST. R USS *Wasp*, Atlantic.

December 21 Soviets launch Luna 13 to Moon; lands Ocean of Storms (18°52'N, 62°3'W) on 24 December. 360° panoramic camera reveals surface objects down to 0·38 to 0·50in (1·5 to 2·0mm) across. Also carries soil density meter and gamma ray density meter on extensible "flop out" arms.

1967

James E. Webb, NASA Administrator, tells House Space Committee in Washington that Soviet Union is developing a launch vehicle which may have a thrust exceeding 10 million lb (4·5 million kg); it could appear "during 1968 or shortly thereafter".

January 27 Crew of first manned Apollo mission, Lt-Col Virgil I. Grissom, Lt-Col Edward H. White, II, and Lt-Cdr Roger Chaffee, die when fire breaks out in their command module during a launch pad rehearsal at KSC. Capsule had been installed on unfuelled Saturn 1B.

April 23-24 Col Vladimir M. Komarov, making first manned test flight in new spacecraft Soyuz 1, is killed when parachute lines of re-entry module become entangled after returning from orbit. Believed that one of solar panels on spacecraft did not deploy, de-stabilising spacecraft and impeding attitude control. Flight time 26hr 45min; number of Earth revolu-

tions 18. LC Baikonur. LV A-2. LT 0335 MT. R crashed outskirts of Orenburg.

June 14 NASA launches Mariner 5 to achieve flyby of Venus 19 October 1967. Confirms and refines Mariner 2 findings. Finds that exosphere of Venus is made up of hydrogen, as is that of Earth. Detects Venerian ionosphere.

October 30 Cosmos 186 and 188 achieve first automatic rendezvous and docking during 49th Earth revolution of Cosmos 186. TV camera shows act of docking. Spacecraft fly together, linked mechanically and electrically, for 3·5hr. Both craft separate Soyuz-type capsules for recovery 31 October and 2 November 1967 respectively.

November 9 First Saturn V flight, unmanned, from Kennedy Space Center, sending Apollo 4 into Earth-orbit for test of spacecraft re-entry module.

1968

Dr Peter E. Glaser originates concept of Satellite Solar Power Station beaming energy to Earth by microwave. ("Power from the Sun, Its Future", *Science*, Vol 162, 1968).

March 27 Col Yuri Gagarin, first man in space, and flying instructor Col Vladimir Seryogin die in aircraft acci-

dent during routine flight in two-seat MiG-15 from airfield adjoining Star Town cosmonauts' training centre. The MiG takes off at 1019 MT; it is said to have crashed some 30 miles (48·3km) E of Moscow at 1031.

April 4 Second Saturn V flight, unmanned, sending Apollo 6 into Earth orbit. Despite propulsion difficulties in second and third stages, Apollo spacecraft are tested satisfactorily.

June 28 Early Bird (Intelsat 1) in geostationary (Clarke) orbit achieves third anniversary in commercial service, more than doubling original life expectancy, including 220hr of received and transmitted television.

September 14 Soviets launch Zond 5 on first circumlunar flight, returning to the Indian Ocean (32°38'S, 65°33'E). Flies within 1,212 miles (1,950km) of lunar surface. Carries tortoises, wine flies, mealworms, bacteria, plants and seeds; broadcasts tape-recorded voice giving simulated instrument values. Objective: "to perfect systems and units for trajectory manoeuvring and return to Earth".

October 11-22 Capt Walter M. Schirra, Jr, Major Donn F. Eisele and R. Walter Cunningham (C), in Apollo 7 command and service modules, complete 163 Earth revolutions in flight lasting 260hr 9min 03sec. First manned mission of Apollo programme, demonstrating ability of spacecraft, crew and manned space flight network to conduct Earth orbital mission: live TV broadcast from space. LC Cape Canaveral. LV Saturn IB. LT 0711 EDT. R USS *Essex*, Atlantic.

Apollo 7's S-IVB docking target.

October 26-30 Col Georgi Beregovoi in Soyuz 3 completes 61 Earth revolutions in flight lasting 94hr 51min. Beregovoi, at 47, is oldest man in space to date. Manoeuvres near unmanned Soyuz 2 in test of spacecraft modified after Soyuz 1 accident. Automatic systems are used in radar search phase, bringing the two craft within 656ft (200m) of each other. Final approach to Soyuz 2 "target" is under manual control, but (apparently) there is no attempt to dock. A second rendezvous man-oeuvre is made after the ships have drawn apart 351 miles (565km). LC Baikonur. LV A-2. LT 1134 MT. R "in pre-set area of Karaganda".

November 10 Soviets launch Zond 6 on circumlunar flight, returning to Soviet Union by aerodynamic "skip" in Earth's atmosphere. Flies within 1,503 miles (2,418km) of lunar surface. Carries automatic camera, biological specimens, nuclear emulsions, micro-meteoroid detectors. LC Baikonur LV D-1-e.

November 16 Soviets launch 17-tonne Proton 4 automatic space laboratory, with 12·5 tonnes of scientific apparatus. Object: to study "the nature of cosmic rays of high and ultra-high energies and their interaction with atomic nuclei". LC Baikonur. LV D-1.

November 30 First attempt by European Launcher Development Organisation (ELDO) fails to orbit a test satellite by Europa I (F7) from Woomera, Australia. Electrical inter-ference in German (Astris II) third stage operates the self-destruct system on separation.

December 21-27 NASA launches Apollo 8 (CSM only) on world's first manned flight to vicinity of the Moon. Col Frank Borman (Cdr), Capt James A. Lovell, Jr (CMP) and Lt Col William Anders (LMP) orbit the Moon 10 times in 20hr 6min, coming within 70 miles (112·6km) of lunar surface, televising scenes to Earth. Total flight time of two-way mission—launch to splash-down—is 147hr 0min 42sec. LC Cape Canaveral. LV Saturn V. LT 0751 EST R USS *Yorktown*, Pacific.

1969

Professor Gerard K. O'Neill begins study of Space Colonies at Princeton University.

January 14-17 Col Vladimir A. Shata-lov in Soyuz 4 completes 48 Earth revolutions in flight lasting 71hr 14min. Achieves first docking between two manned spacecraft. After joining up with Soyuz 5, two cosmonauts, Yeliseyev and Khrunov, spacewalk to Soyuz 4 to join Shatalov for the return flight. Spacecraft separate after 4hr 35min. LC Baikonur. LV A-2. LT 1039 MT. R about 25 miles (40km) NW of Karaganda.

January 15-18 Col Boris Volynov, Aleksei S. Yeliseyev (C) and Col Yevgeny Khrunov in Soyuz 5 partici-pate in major docking experiment with Soyuz 4. Volynov returns alone after his two companions transfer to other craft by EVA lasting about 1 hour. Flight time 72hr 46min; number of

Earth revolutions, 49. LC Baikonur. LV A-2. LT 1014 MT. R about 124 miles (200km) SW of Kustanai.

February 24 NASA launches Mariner 6 to achieve flyby of Mars 31 July 1969. Together with Mariner 7 (launched 27 March 1969; fly-by 5 August 1969) takes some 200 close-up pic-tures that show smooth, cratered and chaotic surfaces. Confirms and refines atmospheric data. Flies within 2,000 miles (3,218km) of planet.

David Scott, in the open hatch of the Apollo 9 CSM, as photographed by Russell Schweickart in the LM.

March 3-13 NASA launches Apollo 9 into Earth orbit in first flight of com-plete spacecraft (CSM/LM). Col James A. McDivitt (cdr); Col David R. Scott (CMP) and Russell L. Schweickart (LMP) (C) complete 151 Earth revolutions in flight lasting 241hr 00min 54sec. Crew evaluate Lunar Module for first time in space, qualify-ing total system for lunar flight. Achieve first docking of CSM with LM. First crew transfer from CSM/LM through interior docking tunnel. EVA from LM, by Schweickart, lasts 37min. LC KSC, LV Saturn V. LT 1100 EST. R USS *Guadalcanal*, about 1,000 miles (1,609km) E of Cape Canaveral.

March 20 Test firings of NASA/AEC NERVA-XE experimental nuclear rocket engine in a vertical stand begin at Nuclear Rocket Development Station, Jackass Flats, Nevada. This is non-flying prototype of 75,000lb (39,019kg) thrust engine intended for flight-testing in late 1970s.

May 18-26 NASA launches Apollo 10 in full dress rehearsal of Moon land-ing. Col Thomas P. Stafford (cdr), Cdr John W. Young (CMP) and Cdr Eugene A. Cernan (LMP) demon-

strate Lunar Module *Snoopy* rendez-vous and docking with CSM *Charlie Brown* in lunar orbit, confirming all aspects of lunar landing procedures except actual descent. Stafford and Cernan fly separated LM to within 9·4 miles (15km) of lunar surface. Number of Moon revolutions by CSM, 31, taking 61hr 34min; 4 revolutions by undocked LM. Total flight time of mission 192hr 03min 23secs. LC KSC. LV Saturn V. LT 1249 EST. R USS *Princeton*, Pacific.

June NERVA experimental rocket engine is run under close to full power 50,000lb (22,680kg) for the first time under simulated altitude conditions. In all, 15 rocket reactors are tested, the last of which, the XE, is started up 28 times. In the course of three tests, a

specific impulse of 825 is demon-strated for extended durations in a flight-size reactor. A range of thrust levels, including the NERVA thrust of 75,000lb (34,019kg), is demonstrated The ability to stop and restart at will is also demonstrated. Despite its success, the project is terminated in the early 1970s.

July 4 Prototype of Soviet super-booster (Type G-1) catches fire and explodes seconds after it had been launched from Baikonur cosmodrome.

July 13 Soviets launch Luna 15 auto-matic Moon probe into lunar orbit, as US attempts first landing by manned spacecraft on Sea of Tranquillity. After manoeuvring in lunar orbit, probe crashes in Sea of Crises (about 17°N, 60°E) some two hours before Apollo 11 astronauts lift-off on return flight.

July 16-24 NASA launches Apollo 11 on first manned lunar landing mission. Astronauts Neil A. Armstrong (C) (cdr); Lt-Col Michael Collins (CMP) and Col Edwin E. Aldrin, Jr (LMP) fulfil the goal set by President Kennedy on 25 May 1961 of landing a man on the Moon within the decade. After separating from CSM *Columbia* in lunar orbit, Armstrong and Aldrin in LM *Eagle* land on Sea of Tranquillity at 1617.43 EDT, 20 July. Armstrong puts his left foot on the Moon at 2056 EDT. Aldrin follows him down some 15 minutes later. Together they deploy US flag and scientific instruments, collect 48·5lb (22kg) of rock and soil samples. Total EVA time, hatch open to hatch close, is 2hr 31min 40sec. Total stay time on Moon is 21hr 36min 21sec. Number of CSM Moon revolutions 30 in 59·5hr. Total flight time of mission 195hr 18min 35sec. LC KSC. LV Saturn V. LT 0932 EDT. R USS *Hornet*, Pacific, SW of Hawaii.

Aldrin about to step onto the Moon from the ladder of LM Eagle.

August 7-14 Soviets launch Zond 7 from Earth-parking orbit on free-return circumlunar trajectory. Equipment includes "a high precision astro-orientation system"; on-board computer controls all phases of flight. Craft has "special protection against radiation". Closest approach to Moon 1,243 miles (2,000km). Re-entry module makes aerodynamic skip in Earth's atmosphere to land in Soviet Union. LC Baikonur. LV D-1-e. R "in predetermined area S of Kustanai.

September 18 President Nixon's space task force advocates manned expedition to Mars "before end of century". One option, recommended by Vice-President Spiro Agnew, chairman of task force, calls for Mars expedition in 1986, with peak expenditure in early 1980s of some $8,000 million a year. More immediately, report calls for "…. very heavy emphasis on proceeding with scientific applications …. Earth satellites for geology, the atmosphere, oceans …. Earth resources …. applying space technology directly to people on Earth".

October 11-16 Col Georgi Shonin and Valery Kubasov (C) in Soyuz 6 complete 75 Earth revolutions in flight lasting 118hr 42min. Participate in non-docking group flight with Soyuz 7 and Soyuz 8. During the mission Kubasov conducts the first welding and smelting experiments in space using automatic "Vulkan" unit, located in orbital module, designed by Academician Boris Paton. LC Baikonur. LV A-2. LT 1410 MT. R about 112 miles (180km) NW of Karaganda.

October 12-17 Col Anatoly Filipchenko, Vladislav Volkov (C) and Col Viktor Gorbatko in Soyuz 7 complete 75 orbits in flight lasting 118hr 41min. Participate in group flight with Soyuz 6 and Soyuz 8. LC Baikonur. LV A-2. LT 1345 MT. R about 96 miles (155km) NW of Karaganda.

October 13-18 Col Vladimir A. Shatalov and Aleksei S. Yeliseyev (C) in Soyuz 8 complete 75 Earth revolutions in flight lasting 118hr 41min. Participate as "flagship" in non-docking group flight with Soyuz 6 and Soyuz 7. Craft change orbits several times in 31 distinct manoeuvres, approaching each other and separating. Target vehicle is Soyuz 7, which other craft approach within "several hundred metres, using manual controls and on-board automatic navigation devices". LC Baikonur. LV A-2. LT 1329 MT. R about 90 miles (145km) N of Karaganda.

November 14-24 NASA launches Apollo 12 on second manned lunar landing mission. Astronauts Cdr Charles Conrad, Jr (cdr): Cdr Richard F. Gordon, Jr (CMP): Cdr Alan L. Bean (LMP). After separating from CSM *Yankee Clipper* in lunar orbit, Conrad and Bean in LM *Intrepid* make "pin-point" landing in Ocean of Storms within walking distance of

ALSEP EVA on the Ocean of Storms.

Surveyor 3 space probe (which landed April 1967). In two EVAs of 3hr 56min and 3hr 49min respectively, astronauts set out ALSEP, collect 74·7lb (33·9kg) lunar samples, and remove TV camera and other parts from Surveyor for examination on Earth. Total stay time on Moon 31hr 31min. Number of CSM Moon orbits, 45 in 88hr 56min. Total flight time of mission 244hr 36min 25sec. LC KSC. LV Saturn V. LT 1122 EST R USS *Hornet*, Pacific.

1970

February 4 NASA launches Space Electric Rocket Test (SERT) 2 from WTR by Thrust Augmented Thor Agena D. Agena carries two electron ion bombardment engines to test ion

engine operation in Earth orbit. Each engine derives thrust by ionising vaporised mercury propellant; the resultant electrically-accelerated and neutralised ion flow produces thrusts of about 0·07oz (2gm). By 17 May 1970 its continuous thrust has raised the spacecraft nearly 29 miles (46km), from an original near-circular orbit of 620 miles (998km).

Ohsumi: Japan's first satellite.

February 11 Japan becomes fourth nation, after USSR, USA and France, to launch an artificial satellite: *Ohsumi* by Lambda 4S-5 from Kagoshima Space Centre.

April 11-17 NASA launches Apollo 13 in attempt to land astronauts on Fra Mauro. Astronauts Lt-Cdr James A. Lovell, Jr (cdr); John W. Swigert, Jr (C) (CMP) and Fred W. Haise, Jr (C) (LMP). Mission is aborted after explosion of fuel cells' oxygen tank in Service Module of *Odyssey* CSM some 205,000 miles (329,845km) from Earth, approaching the Moon. Astronauts are successfully recovered after enforced circumnavigation of Moon, using LM *Aquarius* oxygen and power until just before re-entry into Earth's atmosphere. Flight lasts 142hr 54min 41sec. LC KSC. LV Saturn V. LT 1413 EST. R USS *Iwo Jima*, Pacific.

April 24 People's Republic of China becomes fifth nation—after USSR, USA, France and Japan—to launch an artificial satellite by independent effort. Launched from Shuang-ch'eng-tzu, Inner Mongolia, the 382.5lb (173kg) satellite broadcasts the music of "Tungfanghung" (The East is Red). Believed first attempt failed 1 November 1969. LC Shuang-ch'eng-tzu. LV Long March 1 (based on CSS-2 IRBM).

June 1-19 Col Andrian G. Nikolayev and Vitali Sevastyanov (C) in Soyuz 9 complete 268 Earth revolutions in flight lasting 424hr 59min. They set new duration record for manned

space flight, exceeding time spent in space by US Gemini 7 astronauts in 1965. LC Baikonur. LV A-2. LT 2200 MT. R about 47 miles (75km) W of Karaganda.

June 12 Third attempt by ELDO to orbit a test-satellite from Woomera fails when Italian-built satellite shroud of Europa I (F9) fails to jettison (because an electrical plug is forced out of contact by trapped air pressure behind it, in *vacuo*); also because of imperfect thrust programming of German third stage. Payload impacts in the Caribbean after traversing North Pole.

August 17 Soviets launch Venera 7 spacecraft from Baikonur. Achieves first confirmed landing on Venus, 15 December 1970, following parachute descent; faint signals received indicate atmospheric pressure 90±15 atm, surface temperature 475±20°C.

September 12 Soviets launch Luna 16, first successful unmanned Moon-craft capable of returning soil samples to Earth. Lands Sea of Fertility (0°41'S, 56°18'E) 20 September. Drilling device obtains ·22lb (100g) of soil and rock fragments to depth of 13·8in (35cm) and places sample into return capsule. Injected into trans-Earth trajectory 21 September, capsule soft-lands by parachute 3 days later at 0826 MT, about 50 miles (80km) SE of Dzhezkazgan, Kazakhstan.

October 20-27 Soviets launch Zond 8 from Earth parking orbit on free-return circumlunar trajectory passing within 695 miles (1,118km) of Moon. Vehicle tested "a possible variant of the return of a spacecraft into the atmosphere from the direction of the Northern Hemisphere". LC Baikonur. LV D-1-e. R "in preset area of the Indian Ocean 453 miles (730km) SE of Chagos archipelago".

November Dr George Low, acting NASA Administrator, tells Congress that programme to develop a large Soviet launch vehicle is still moving forward, despite setbacks.

November 10 Soviets launch Luna 17 with first remote-controlled Moon rover, Lunokhod 1. Lands Sea of Rains (38°18'N, 35°W) 17 November. Steered via a TV/radio link from control station in USSR, vehicle travels total distance of 34,588ft (10,542m). Sends more than 200 panoramic pictures; more than 20,000 others. Physical and mechanical properties of lunar soil studied at more than 500 points; chemical composition analysed at 25 points. Laser retroreflector experiments from Earth. Active research programme ends 4 October 1971. LC Baikonur. LV D-1-e. LT 1744 MT.

December 12 Explorer 42 is launched into equatorial orbit from San Marco platform off the coast of Kenya by an Italian crew. First American satellite to be sent aloft by people of another country.

1971

January 31-February 9 NASA launches Apollo 14 on fourth lunar landing mission. Astronauts Alan B. Shepard, Jr (cdr); Major Stuart A. Roosa (CMP); Lt-Cdr Edgar D. Mitchell (LMP). After separating from CSM *Kitty Hawk* in lunar orbit, Shepard and Mitchell in LM *Antares* land in hilly upland region north of Fra Mauro crater. During two EVAs lasting 4hr 48min and 4hr 35min respectively, they set out second ALSEP and collect 98lb (44·5kg) of lunar samples, using small handcart for first time to transport them. Total stay time on Moon 33hr 31min. Number of CSM Moon revolutions, 34 in 66hr 39min. Total mission flight time 216hr 01min 57sec. LC KSC. LV Saturn V. LT 1603 EST. R USS *New Orleans*, Pacific, some 780 miles (1,255km), S of Samoa.

April 23-25 Col Vladimir A. Shatalov, Alexei S. Yeliseyev and Nikolai Rukavishnikov (C) in Soyuz 10 complete 32 Earth orbits in flight lasting 47hr 46min. Spacecraft docks for 5½hr with Salyut 1 (launched 19 April) but cosmonauts do not board. LC Baikonur. LV A-2. LT 0254 MT. R about 74 miles (120km) NW of Karaganda.

May 19 Soviets launch Mars 2 – first new-generation 5-tonne spacecraft. Ejects landing capsule on final approach to Mars, 27 November 1971, which crash-lands. Mothercraft swings into 857 x 15,535 miles (1,380 x 25,000km) orbit; sends TV pictures and data. Orbiter has photo-TV system, IR radiometer, UV spectrometer, etc. Weight spacecraft: 10,253lb (4,650kg). LC Baikonur. LV D-1-e.

May 28 Soviets launch Mars 3 spacecraft. Ejects capsule on final approach to Mars, which lands (45°S, 158°W) 2 December 1971 at height of a dust storm. Transmissions cease as it begins to send TV picture. Mothercraft sends data from orbit. Objectives as Mars 2. Weight spacecraft: 10,253lb (4,650kg). LC Baikonur. LV D-1-e.

June 6-29 Lt-Col Georgi Dobrovolsky, Vladislav Volkov (C) and Viktor Patsayev (C) in Soyuz 11 dock with Salyut 1 for about 22 days to conduct engineering proving trials and experiments in biology and space-medicine. Described as "first manned orbiting scientific laboratory". Crew die while returning to Earth when a pressure equalisation valve opens at the time of separating the orbital module, releasing air from the command module. The CM lands automatically after a flight lasting 570hr 22min. Cosmonauts are the second, third and fourth Russians to die during a space flight. LC Baikonur. LVA-2. LT 0725 MT.

June 24 Second prototype of Soviet super-booster (Type G-1) explodes at 7·4 miles (12km) altitude.

Apollo 15 commander David Scott with LM Falcon in the background.

July 26-August 7 NASA launches Apollo 15 on fifth lunar landing mission. Astronauts Col David R. Scott (cdr), Lt-Col James B. Irwin (LMP) and Major Alfred M. Worden (CMP). After separating from CSM *Endeavour* in lunar orbit, Scott and Irwin in LM *Falcon* land in Hadley-Apennine region near Apennine Mountains. Three EVAs lasting 6hr 34min, 7hr 12min and 4hr 50min respectively. astronauts deploy third ALSEP and collect 173lb (78·6kg) of rock and soil samples. Mission is first of "J" series, doubling stay time on Moon using Lunar Roving Vehicle (LRV) and improved spacesuits which give greater mobility and stay time. LRV travels total of 17·3 miles (27·9km). Lunar surface stay time 66hr 55min. First live TV coverage of LM ascent stage lift-off from Moon. Number of CSM Moon revolutions, 74. Small sub-satellite left in lunar orbit for first time. Worden trans-Earth EVA 38min. Total mission flight time 295hr 11min 53sec. LC KSC. LV Saturn V. LT 0934 EDT. R USS *Okinawa*, Pacific, N of Honolulu.

October 28 Britain becomes sixth nation, after USSR, USA, France,

Technicians check out the Prospero technology satellite before launch.

Japan and China, to launch a satellite by independent effort, placing 145lb (66kg) Prospero (X-3) technology satellite into orbit of 334 x 990 miles (537 x 1,593km) x 82°. LC Woomera, Australia. LV Black Arrow (R.3). LT 0409 GMT.

November 5 First (and only) attempt by ELDO to orbit a test satellite from French Equatorial range at Kourou, Guiana, South America, by Europa II (F11), fails because of stoppage of guidance computer (subsequently traced to electrical interference in German third stage). Violent manoeuvres just before first stage separation cause vehicle to break up. Main debris fall into Atlantic about 253 miles (407km) downrange.

1972

January 5 President Nixon announces approval to develop NASA Space Shuttle: "an entirely new type of space transportation system designed to help transform the space frontier of the 1970s into familiar territory easily accessible for human endeavour in the 1980s and 1990s". Shuttle will ferry four people and freight to and from orbiting space stations. Development over six years, followed by test flights estimated to cost \$5,500 million. Choice of booster to be made known later

(see March 15).

February 14-25 After manoeuvring in lunar orbit, Luna 20 softlands on NE edge of Sea of Fertility (3°32'N, 56°33'E). Automatic drilling device obtains core sample of lunar material, transferring this to return capsule. Injected into trans-Earth trajectory by rocket stage, capsule soft-lands by parachute in blizzard some 25 miles (40km) NW of Dzhezkazgan, Kazakhstan. LC Baikonur. LV D-1-e.

March 3 NASA launches Pioneer 10 on 21-month fly-by mission to Jupiter. Will become first man-made object to escape from Solar System. LC KSC. LV Atlas-Centaur-TE-M-364-4.

Adjustments are made to Pioneer 10's magnetometer boom at TRW's plant.

March 15 NASA announces that Space Shuttle orbiter will have solid-propellant boosters in parallel-stage configuration. Overall development cost reduced from estimated \$5,500 million to \$5,150 million, with some increase in estimated cost per mission. Horizontal test flights to begin 1976; manned orbital flight tests 1978. Payload 65,000lb (29,500kg) into 100 n. mile (185km) due east orbit.

March 29 United States, Soviet Union and United Kingdom sign in Washington convention on international liability for damage caused by space objects. (The three nations are depository states for the treaty, to which many other nations later add signatures.) The convention complements two earlier treaties governing Man's space activities: the Outer Space Treaty of 1967 and the Astronaut Rescue Agreement of 1968.

April 16-27 NASA launches Apollo 16 on sixth lunar landing mission. Astronauts Capt John W. Young (cdr), Cdr Thomas K. Mattingly, II (CMP) and Col Charles M. Duke, Jr (LMP). After separating from CSM *Casper* in lunar orbit, Young and Duke in LM *Orion* land in Descartes highlands region, 18,000ft (5,486m) higher than Apollo 15 site. In three EVAs lasting

7hr 11min, 7hr 23min and 5hr 40min respectively, they deploy fourth ALSEP, set up first lunar astronomical observatory, and collect 210-213lb (95·2-96·6kg) of rock and soil samples. This is second "J" series mission, including LRV, which travels total of 16·8 miles (27km). Total stay time on Moon 71hr 2min. Number of CSM Moon revolutions, 64. Releases sub-satellite in lunar orbit. Mattingly trans-Earth EVA 84min. Total mission flight time 265hr 51min 05sec. LC KSC. LV Saturn V. LT 1254 EST. R USS *Ticonderoga*, Pacific.

May 24 President Nixon and Premier Kosygin in Moscow sign agreement providing for cooperation in the exploration of outer space for peaceful purposes, and the docking in space in 1975 of a US and a Soviet spacecraft.

May 26 NASA announces retirement of Dr Wernher von Braun, Deputy Associate Administrator for Planning, effective 1 July 1972.

July 23 NASA launches first Earth Resources Technology Satellite (ERTS-1) — later re-named Landsat 1 — from Western Test Range, California.

A mosaic of Italy generated from 46 Landsat 1 infra-red images.

November Dr Chien Hsueh-Sen, a pioneer member of the American rocket team at the California Institute of Technology, who returned to China in 1955 during the Un-American activities campaign of the late Senator Joseph McCarthy, returns on a visit to United States as Director of the Dynamics Research Institute, Academy of Sciences, People's Republic of China. He has played a leading role in establishing China's missile and space programmes.

November 10 NASA launches Anik 1 (Telesat A), first of a series of geostationary communications satellites to provide transmission of TV, telephone and data services throughout Canada.

November 24 Third prototype of Soviet super-booster (Type G-1) explodes at 24·8 miles (40km) altitude.

Harrison Schmitt collecting samples of lunar rock near Apollo 17's Taurus-Littrow landing site.

December 7-19 NASA launches Apollo 17 on seventh and last lunar landing mission of series. Astronauts Capt Eugene A. Cernan (cdr), Lt-Cdr Ronald E. Evans (CMP) and Dr Harrison H. Schmitt (C) (LMP). After separating from CSM *America* in lunar orbit, Cernan and Schmitt (a geologist) in LM *Challenger* land in Taurus-Littrow region. In three EVAs lasting 7hr 12min, 7hr 37min and 7hr 16min respectively, they deploy fifth ALSEP and collect 243lb (110kg) of rock and soil samples. This is third "J" series mission, including astronauts' LRV which travels total of 21·7 miles (35km). Total stay time on Moon 74hr 59min 38sec. Number of CSM Moon revolutions, 75. Released sub-satellite in lunar orbit. Evans trans-Earth EVA 66min. Total mission flight time 301hr 51min 59sec. LC KSC. LV Saturn V. LT 0033 EST. R USS *Ticonderoga*, Pacific.

1973

January 16 After manoeuvring in lunar orbit, Luna 21 softlands inside Le Monnier crater near eastern rim of Sea of Serenity at 0135 MT. Discharges remote-controlled Lunokhod 2 from ramp at 0414 MT.

April 3 Soviets launch Salyut 2 orbital laboratory which develops fault, spins and breaks up. Orbit: 128 x 154 miles (207 x 248km) x 51·56°. Telemetry 19·944 MHz. Lifetime 55 days. May carry some military research equipment.

April 6 NASA launches Pioneer 11 on fly-by mission to Jupiter (December 1974) and Saturn (September 1979).

May 11 Soviets launch structure resembling Salyut space laboratory (called Cosmos 557) which fails upon orbital insertion. Orbit 133 x 151 miles

(214 x 243km) x 51·59°. Lifetime 11 days.

May 14 NASA launches Skylab 1 space station into Earth orbit from KSC by two-stage Saturn V. Station is damaged by air pressure during ascent, which rips away meteoroid shield of orbital workshop and one solar "wing", leaving other solar "wing" in closed position, trapped by piece of torn metal. Astronaut teams (Skylabs 2, 3 and 4) carry out repairs and conduct full range of experiments. Station decays from orbit 11 July 1979.

Skylab in orbit; note missing solar panel and meteoroid shield.

May 25-June 22 NASA launches Skylab 2 ferry with astronauts Capt Charles Conrad, Jr, Dr Joseph Kerwin (C) and Capt Paul J. Weitz. Their spacecraft is modified Apollo CSM. After some difficulty they dock with, and board, Skylab 1, erect sun shield and release stuck solar "wing" during EVA. Astronauts obtain data on 46 of 55 planned experiments; perform three spacewalks totalling 5hr 41min. Number of Earth revolutions 404. Total flight time 672hr 49min 49sec. LC KSC. LV Saturn IB. LT 1400 BST. R USS *Ticonderoga*.

July 21 Soviets launch Mars 4 spacecraft. Passes Mars at a distance of 1,367 miles (2,200km), 10 February 1974, when braking engine fails to place it into orbit; takes pictures. LC Baikonur. LV D-1-e.

July 25 Soviets launch Mars 5 spacecraft. On 12 February 1974 it swings into orbit around Mars ranging between 1,093 and 20,195 miles (1,760 and 32,500km), inclined at 35° to equator. LC Baikonur. LV D-1-e.

July 28-September 25 NASA launches Skylab 3 ferry with astronauts Capt Alan L. Bean, Major Jack R. Lousma and Dr Owen K. Garriott. En route to dock with Skylab 1 space station an attitude control thruster on their Apollo CSM ferry begins leaking; on 2 August (while docked with station) a second thruster develops leaks. At KSC an Apollo rescue ship is prepared, but the problem proves less serious than feared and the men are allowed to complete the mission and use their own Apollo CSM for return. Number

Owen Garriott during a Skylab 3 EVA at the Apollo Telescope Mount. He has just deployed an experiment.

of Earth revolutions 858. Three EVAs totalling 13hr 44min; new sunshield deployed, rate gyros replaced. Total flight time 1427hr 09min 04sec. LC KSC. LV Saturn IB. LT 1208 BST R USS New Orleans.

August 1 X-24B lifting body with NASA pilot John Manke makes first flight, unpowered, from B-52 "mother" at 40,000ft (12,192m), landing after 4min 11·5sec at Edwards Air Force Base, California.

August 5 Soviets launch Mars 6 spacecraft. On 12 March 1974, it ejects a capsule which parachutes through atmosphere of Mars, obtaining scientific data, but stops transmitting just before it lands (24°S, 25°W). Mothercraft continues in heliocentric orbit. LC Baikonur. LV D-1-e.

August 9 Soviets launch Mars 7 spacecraft. On 9 March 1974 it ejects a capsule which misses Mars by 808 miles (1,300km). Mothercraft continues in heliocentric orbit. LC Baikonur. LV D-1-e.

September 27-29 Lt-Col Vasily Lazarev and Oleg Makarov (C) in Soyuz 12, test modification of basic spacecraft for ferry missions to Salyut orbital laboratories. In this configuration extensible solar panels are replaced entirely by chemical batteries. Flight lasts 47hr 16min. First manned test flight following Soyuz 11 disaster, in which third crewman is replaced by a life-support system allowing a two-man crew to wear spacesuits for added protection during launch, docking and undocking, and the separation of spacecraft modules before re-entry. The suits are removed during orbital operations. LC Baikonur. LV A-2. LT 1518 MT. R some 248 miles (400km) SW of Karaganda.

November 3 NASA launches Mariner 10 by Atlas-Centaur from KSC on double-planet mission to Venus (5 February 1974) and Mercury (29 March 1974). Spacecraft makes two further working encounters with Mercury from heliocentric orbit. Obtains first pictures of Mercury's heavily cratered surface; detects magnetic field.

A photomosaic of Mercury's surface derived from Mariner 10 images.

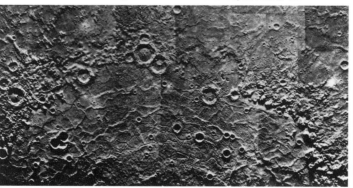

November 16-February 8 1974 NASA launches Skylab 4 ferry with astronauts Lt-Col Gerald P. Carr, Dr Edward G. Gibson (C) and Lt-Col William R. Pogue. Final Skylab 1 visit. Replenishes coolant supplies, repairs antenna, observes Comet Kohoutek. Four EVAs totalling 22hr 21min. Sets record for EVA duration of 7hr 1min. Number of Earth revolutions 1214. Total flight time, 2017hr 15min 32sec. LC Cape Canaveral. LV Saturn IB.

LT 0901 EST. R USS New Orleans, Pacific, about 175 miles (281km) SW of San Diego.

December 18-26 Major Pyotr Klimuk and Valentin Lebedev (C) in Soyuz 13 complete 128 Earth revolutions in flight lasting 188hr 55min. Conduct experiments in biology, Earth resources observation and astrophysics. Spacecraft has extensible solar panels for electrical power supply. LC Baikonur. LV A-2. LT 1455 MT. R about 124 miles (200km) SW of Karaganda.

1974

May 30 NASA launches Applications Technology Satellite ATS-6 to pioneer educational satellite transmission by satellite from geostationary orbit. After a year of operation above a position near the Galapagos Islands, serving the United States, the satellite is moved to a position above East Africa, providing educational programmes to some 5,000 Indian villages. The satellite is returned to its original location in 1976, for continuing experiments in the USA. It is subsequently moved out of geostationary orbit by firing onboard rocket motors to avoid interference with other satellites in this congested orbit. LV Cape Canaveral. LV Titan IIIC. Lifetime indefinite.

June 25 Soviets launch Salyut 3 into orbit of 133 x 157 miles (213 x 253km) x 51·58°. Telemetry frequencies 19·944 MHz; 143·625 MHz. Capsule ejected and recovered 23 September 1974. Orbit after manoeuvres 159 x 181 miles (256 x 292km). Lifetime in orbit 214 days. Some military experiments. Related missions: Soyuz 14 and 15.

July 3-19 Col Pavel Popovich and Lt-Col Yuri Artyukhin in Soyuz 14 dock with Salyut 3 orbital laboratory for 353hr 33min. Flight lasts more than 370hr. LC Baikonur. LV A-2. LT N.A. (orbital insertion 2151 MT).

August 26-28 Lt-Col Gennady Sarafanov and Col Lev Demin in Soyuz 15 fail to dock with Salyut 3 orbital laboratory on 27 August because of fault in automatic control

system. Flight lasts 48hr 12min. LC Baikonur. LV A-2. LT 2258 MT. R about 30 miles (48km) SW of Tselinograd.

September 23 A recoverable module containing "materials of research and experiments" is separated from unmanned Salyut 3. "The engines were started at a set time and the module began its descent to Earth landing in the predetermined area of the USSR."

December 2-8 Col Anatoly Filipchenko and Nikolai Rukavishnikov (C) in Soyuz 16 conduct flight tests of spacecraft modified for forthcoming ASTP mission. Craft has extensible solar panels for electrical power supply. Cosmonauts test docking system and reduction of cabin pressurisation (see page 192). Flight lasts 5days 22hr 24min. LC Baikonur. LV A-2. LT 1240 MT. R 1104 MT.

December 26 Soviets launch Salyut 4 into orbit of 131 x 156 miles (212 x 251km) x 51·57°. Telemetry frequencies 15·008 MHz; 922·75 MHz. Orbit after manoeuvres 208 x 216 miles (336 x 349km). Lifetime 770 days. Related missions: Soyuz 17, Soyuz anomaly, Soyuz 18B, Soyuz 20.

1975

January 11-February 9 Lt-Col Alexei Gubarev and Georgi Grechko (C) in Soyuz 17 dock with Salyut 4 orbital laboratory for extensive series of experiments. Total flight time is 29days 13hr 20min. LC Baikonur. LV A-2. LT 0043 MT. R 68 miles (110km) NE of Tselinograd, Kazakhstan, 1403 MT.

April 5 Lt-Col Vasily Lazarev and Oleg Makarov (C) in Soyuz 18A fail to reach orbit because of launch vehicle upper stage malfunction. They are recovered safely in Western Siberia near Gorno-Altaisk inside their command module. The craft had been intended to dock with the Salyut 4 orbital laboratory. LC Baikonur. LV A-2. LT N.A.

May 24-July 26 Lt-Col Pyotr Klimuk and Vitaly Sevastyanov (C) in Soyuz 18B dock with Salyut 4 orbital

The Soyuz 18B cosmonauts in training.

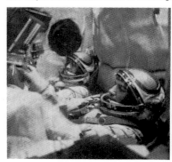

laboratory for extensive series of experiments. Total flight time is 1511hr 20min. LC Baikonur. LV A-2. LT 1758 MT. R about 35 miles (56km) NE of Arkalyk.

June 8 Soviets launch Venera 9 spacecraft from Baikonur. Releases landing capsule being going into orbit around Venus 22 October 1975. Capsule, which transmits from surface for 53 minutes, sends first TV picture of surface conditions: confirms pressure 90 atm, temperature 485°C. Position 30°N, 293° long.

June 14 Soviets launch Venera 10 spacecraft from Baikonur. Releases landing capsule before going into orbit around Venus 25 October 1975. Capsule, which transmits from surface for 65 minutes, sends second TV picture of surface conditions: surface pressure 92 atm, temperature 465°C. Position 15°N, 295° long.

July 15-21 Col Alexei Leonov and Valery Kubasov (C) in Soyuz 19 participate with US Apollo 18 CSM/DM in Apollo-Soyuz Test Project Number of Earth revolutions 96. Total flight time 142hr 30 min. LC Baikonur. LV A-2. LT 1520 MT. 0820 EDT. R54 miles (87km) NE of Arkalyk, Kazakhstan.

July 15-24 Brig-Gen Thomas P. Stafford, Vance D. Brand (C) and Donald K. Slayton (C) in Apollo 18 participate with Soviet cosmonauts in Apollo-Soyuz Test Project (ASTP). (Slayton, at 51, oldest man in space). They dock with Soyuz 19 flown by Col. Alexei Leonov and Valery Kubasov at 1209 EDT on 17 July, remaining together (including undocking and redocking exercise 19 July) for about two days. Number of Earth revolutions 138. Total flight time (Apollo 18) 217hr 28 min. LC KSC. LV Saturn IB. LT 1550 EDT. R USS *New Orleans*, Pacific, about 270 miles (434km) W of Hawaii.

The view from Apollo 18 as Soyuz 19 gently manoeuvres towards docking.

July 26 People's Republic of China launches China 3 heavy (two-tonne) military satellite into low Earth orbit. Similar launchings on 26 November 1975 (China 4; returns capsule to earth); 16 December 1975 (China 5); 7 December 1976 (China 7; returns capsule to earth); 26 January 1978 (China 8; returns capsule to earth). LC Shuang-ch'eng-tzu. LV FB-1, also known as CSL-2.

August 20 NASA launches Viking 1 spacecraft to Mars; inserted into orbit 19 June 1976, releases Lander which

Viking's view of the Martian desert.

soft-lands *Chryse Planitia* (22·46°N, 48·01°W), 20 July 1976. Transmits pictures from Martian surface, examines soil in automatic laboratory, obtains "met" data. Mothercraft observes from orbit.

September 9 NASA launches Viking 2 spacecraft to Mars; inserted into orbit 7 August 1976, soft-lands *Utopia Planitia* (47·97°N, 25·67°W) 3 September 1976. Transmits pictures from Martian surface, examines soil in automatic laboratory. Mothercraft observes from orbit.

November 17-February 16 1976 Soviets launch unmanned Soyuz 20 which docks with Salyut 4 automatically in space station re-supply rehearsal. After separating from station 16 February 1976, re-entry module is recovered "in pre-set area of USSR".

1976

February 10 Pioneer 10 crosses the orbit of Saturn on its way out of the Solar System.

March 17 NASA announces four crews for early flights of the Space Shuttle from Kennedy Space Center: Capt John W. Young; Cdr Robert L. Crippen; Col Joe H. Engle; Cdr Richard H. Truly; Fred W. Haise, Jr (C); Lt-Col Jack Lousma; Vance D. Brand (C); Lt-Col Charles G. Fullerton.

June 22 Soviets launch Salyut 5 into orbit of 129 x 144 miles (208 x 233km) x 51·6°. Telemetry frequency 19·944 MHz. Orbit after manoeuvures 133 x 159 miles (214 x 257km). Some military experiments. Returns two re-entry capsules to USSR. Lifetime 412 days. Related missions Soyuz 21, Soyuz 23, Soyuz 24.

July 6-August 24 Col Boris Volynov and Lt-Col Vitaly Zholobov in Soyuz 21 dock with Salyut 5 on 7 July. Cosmonauts perform extensive series of experiments (page 185). Total flight time 49days 6hr 24min. LC Baikonur. LV A-2. LT 1509 MT. R about 124 miles (200km) SW of Kokchetav, Kazakhstan.

August 17 Indonesia—celebrating 31st year of independence—becomes first nation in Southeast Asia to operate its own telecommunications system, via Hughes-Palapa satellite located 83°E longitude over Indian Ocean. Launched by NASA on 8 July, geostationary satellite provides telephone, television, radio, telegraph and data services to populated areas on some 5,000 of the nation's 13,000 islands, which extend more than 3,100 miles (5,000km).

August 18 Luna 24, after manoeuvring in lunar orbit, soft-lands in south-eastern region of Sea of Crises (12°45'N, 62°12'E). Returns core sample from depth of some 6·5ft (2m); landing 22 August, 124 miles (200km) SE of Surgat, Kazakhstan.

September 15-23 Col Valery F. Bykovsky and Vladimir Aksyonov (C) in Soyuz 22 complete 127 Earth revolutions in independent flight lasting 7days 21hr 54mins. Spacecraft, which embodies extensible solar "wings" for electrical power supply, carries MKF-6 multi-spectral camera made by Carl Zeiss Jena, GDR. LC Baikonur. LV A-2. LT 1248 MT. R about 93 miles (150km) NW of Tselinograd.

October 14-16 Lt-Col Vyacheslav Zudov and Lt-Col Valery Rozhdestvensky in Soyuz 23 fail to dock with Salyut 5 because of a fault in spacecraft's automatic control system. Flight lasts 48hr 6min. Re-entry capsule, blown off course by a snow storm, in darkness and at sub-zero temperature splashes into Lake Tengiz some 121 miles (195km) SW of Tselinograd, Kazakhstan. Cosmonauts rescued by helicopter and boats. First occasion that a Soviet space crew has come down on water. LC Baikonur. LV A-2. LT 2040 MT.

November 24 Reported in Washington that China has begun trials of CSS-X-4 full-range ICBM; estimated range 6,835 miles (11,000km).

December 15 Soviets launch double re-entry test payload Cosmos 881/882, both returning same day to Soviet recovery area. Orbits: C.881— 124 x 150 miles (201 x 242km) x 51·6°; C.882— 118 x 132 miles (191 x 231km) x 51·6°. Similar test missions: Cosmos 997/998 and Cosmos 1100/1101. Probably related to future manned space programme.

1977

February 7-25 Col Viktor Gorbatko and Lt-Col Yuri Glazkov in Soyuz 24 dock with Salyut 5 orbital laboratory. Test and replace units aboard station, including some parts of onboard computer. Continue research programme: photograph Earth; study crystal growth; soldering experiments and casting of metal spheres; also biological and bio-medical experiments. Flight lasts 17days 16hr 08min. LC Baikonur. LV A-2. LT 1912 MT. R about 23 miles (37km) NE of Arkalyk, Kazakhstan.

July 17-2 February 1978 Soviets launch Cosmos 929—a large unmanned space vehicle—into 51·6° inclination orbit; it performs several power manoeuvres over a period of months. Possible test of a new propulsion system for space station or space tug.

August 12 Space Shuttle Orbiter *Enterprise* with astronauts Fred W.

Haise, Jr (C) and Lt-Col Charles G. Fullerton makes first free flight from Boeing 747 "mother" after release at 22,800ft (6,950m) above NASA's Dryden Flight Research Center, Edwards, California. Flight test includes practice flare about 20 seconds after separation at 19,700ft (6,004m) before making two left turns to line up with dry lake runway. Final approach from 8 miles (13km) range at 9° glide angle, landing gear being deployed at 180ft (55m), about 20 seconds before touchdown at just under 200kt (407km/h). Flight lasts 5min 23sec.

August 20 NASA launches Voyager 2 spacecraft on multiplanet, gravity-assist, fly-by mission to: Jupiter (July 1979), Saturn (August 1981), and possibly Uranus (January 1986) and Neptune (1989).

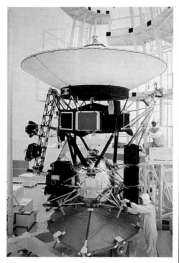

A Voyager test model is checked out in the SAEF-1 facility at KSC.

September 5 NASA launches Voyager 1 on fly-by mission to Jupiter (March 1979) and Saturn (November 1980).

September 13 Space Shuttle Orbiter *Enterprise*, flown by Col Joe H. Engle and Cdr Richard H. Truly, makes second free flight from back of Boeing 747. After separating at 24,000ft (7,315m), craft completes series of manoeuvres before landing on dry lake runway at 185kt (342km/h). Flight lasted 5min 28sec.

September 23 Space Shuttle Orbiter *Enterprise*, flown by Fred W. Haise Jr (C) and Lt-Col Charles G. Fullerton, makes third free flight from back of Boeing 747. After separating at 23,800ft (7,254m), lands on dry lake runway some 5min 34sec later. Glide test includes a "hands off" manoeuvre with the Orbiter on autopilot — also test from 8,000 to 3,000ft (2,438 to 914m) of ground-based microwave device which controls glide path automatically.

September 29 Soviets launch Salyut 6 into orbit of 133 x 159 miles (214 x 256km) x 51·59°. Telemetry frequencies: 15·008 MHz/ 922·75 MHz. Lifetime: de-orbited 29 July 1982. Related missions: Soyuz 25, 26, 27, 28, 29, 30, 31, 32, 33, 34, Soyuz-T, 35, 36, T-2, 37, 38, T-3, T-4, 39, 40; Progress 1, 2, 3, 4, 5, 6, 7, 8, 9, 10, 11, 12; Cosmos 1, 267; LC Baikonur. LV D-1.

October 1 Lt-Gen Vladimir A. Shatalov, commenting on future Salyut missions, says Soviet scientists "contemplate future stations much larger than present Salyuts with crews of 12 to 20 people". However, the potential of present stations will have to be exhausted first. Shatalov envisages orbital stations being increasingly used for producing "super pure metals, monocrystals, vaccines and other useful products".

October 9-11 Lt-Col Vladimir V. Kovalenok and Valery Ryumin (C) in Soyuz 25 fail to dock with Salyut 6 space station. Flight lasts 2days 46min. LC Baikonur. LV A-2. LT 0540 MT. R about 115 miles (185km) NW of Tselinograd.

October 12 Space Shuttle Orbiter *Enterprise* with astronauts Col Joe H.

Enterprise separates from the 747 during the fourth free flight test.

Engle and Cdr Richard H. Truly, makes fourth free flight from Boeing 747; first in which streamlined tail fairing is removed and three dummy SSME rocket engines are exposed in "high-drag" configuration. Flight lasts 2min 34sec.

October 26 Space Shuttle Orbiter *Enterprise*, with astronauts Fred W. Haise, Jr (C) and Lt-Col Charles G. Fullerton, makes fifth and last flight from Boeing 747. After separating at 17,000ft (5,181m) directly in line with Runway 22, glide lasts 1min 59sec.

December 10-March 16 1978 Lt-Col Yuri Romanenko and Georgi Grechko (C) in Soyuz 26 dock with Salyut 6 on 11 December. Soviet authorities reveal that orbital laboratory has two

docking ports, one fore and one aft. Soyuz 25 attempted to dock at the front; Soyuz 26 docks at the rear in case the other port is faulty or has sustained damage. On 20 December, the cosmonauts perform an EVA lasting 1hr 28min, Grechko emerging from the actual docking hatch while Romanenko assists his activities from the depressurised transfer compartment. They find the docking unit undamaged. On-board experiments include use of MKF-6 multi-spectral camera, medical examinations, processing of materials, biological experiments, astronomical studies using sub-millimetre telescope. Flight lasts 96days 10hr, breaking US space endurance record of 84days 1hr 15min set by last Skylab crew between November 1973 and February 1974. Soyuz 26 returns Soyuz 27 crew; Romanenko and Grechko return in Soyuz 27. LC Baikonur. LV A-2. LT 0419 MT. R about 165 miles (265km) W of Tselinograd at 1419MT (Soyuz 27).

1978

January 10-16 Lt-Col Vladimir Dzhanibekov and Oleg Makarov (C) in Soyuz 27 dock at forward airlock of Salyut 6, achieving first three-spacecraft complex, on 11 January. On 16 January the cosmonauts

separate from the station in Soyuz 26, leaving the aft airlock free for another ferry mission. Their total flight time is 6days 4min. LC Baikonur. LV A-2. LT 1526 MT. R 1530 MT, about 192 miles (310km) W of Tselinograd (Soyuz 26).

January 20-February 9 Soviets launch unmanned, expendable, transport spacecraft Progress 1, containing 2,205lb (1,000kg) of propellants and 2,866lb (1,300kg) of compressed air, food, water, films and other cargo. After docking with Salyut 6 at 1312 MT on 22 January, the resident cosmonauts transfer supplies. Craft separates from station with waste material on 7 February and is made to re-enter the atmosphere and burn up over the Pacific Ocean. LC Baikonur. LV A-2.

March 2-10 Col Alexei Gubarev and Capt Vladimir Remek (first Czechoslovakian cosmonaut) in Soyuz 28 dock with Salyut 6/Soyuz 27 complex on 3 March. In conjunction with resident cosmonauts Romanenko and Grechko, they carry out medical examinations, conduct experiments in materials processing and make Earth resources observations. Flight lasts 188hr 16min. LC Baikonur. LV A-2. LT 1828 MT. R about 192 miles (310km) W of Tselinograd.

April 10 Fang Wi, deputy prime minister for science and technology, People's Republic of China, says plans over the next eight years include a major research centre, scientific and applications satellites, manned space flight and an orbital laboratory. National communications satellite project is planned for launch 1981-82.

May 18 British Interplanetary Society publishes *Project Daedalus*, a 192-page report on the world's first engineering study of an unmanned spaceship for exploring the nearer stars.

May 20 NASA launches Pioneer Venus 1 which swings into orbit round Venus on 4 December 1978. Conducts detailed survey of planet in conjunction with entry probes of Pioneer Venus 2.

June 8 Talks open in Helsinki between Soviet Union and United States on possible agreement to ban the use of anti-satellite weapons.

June 15-November 2 Col Vladimir V. Kovalenok and Alexander Ivanchenkov (C) in Soyuz 29 dock with Salyut 6 on 17 June for extensive series of experiments. On 29 July they perform an EVA, from the hatch in the side of the forward transfer compartment, lasting 2hr 5min. Ivanchenkov replaces externally-mounted equipment and retrieves certain specimens which have been exposed to the space environment for nearly 10 months. Returning in Soyuz 31, their mission lasts a record 139days 14hr 48min. LC Baikonur. LV A-2. LT 2317 MT. R about 111 miles (180km) SE of Dzhezkazgan.

June 27-July 5 Col Pyotr Klimuk and Major Miroslaw Hermaszewski (first Polish cosmonaut) in Soyuz 30 dock with Salyut 6/Soyuz 29 complex on second airlock. Objectives: biomedical experiments using equipment made in Poland; Earth resources photography; materials processing. Total flight time 7days 22hr 04min. LC Baikonur. LV A-2. LT 1827 MT. R about 186 miles (300km) W of Tselinograd.

July 7-August 4 Soviets launch unmanned Progress 2 with 1,322lb (600kg) of propellant for Salyut 6 re-supply, plus scientific equipment, air, water, food and film. Docks 9 July; undocks 2 August and subsequently is made to re-enter over Pacific Ocean. LC Baikonur. LV A-2. LT 1426 MT.

August 8-23 Soviets launch unmanned Progress 3 for Salyut 6 re-supply. Docks with Salyut 6/Soyuz 29 complex on second airlock 10 August; undocks 21 August and subsequently de-orbited over Pacific Ocean. LC Baikonur. LV A-2. LT 0131 MT.

August 8 NASA launches Pioneer Venus 2. On 9 December 1978, craft separates into five entry probes that measure Venus' atmosphere as they descend to the surface. Although not designed to survive after landing, one probe transmits data for 67 minutes after impact. LC Cape Canaveral. LV Atlas-Centaur.

August 26-September 3 Col Valery F. Bykovsky and Lt-Col Sigmund Jaehn (first East German cosmonaut) in Soyuz 31 dock with Salyut 6/Soyuz 29 complex on 27 August, on second airlock. After carrying out joint experiments with resident cosmonauts (Kovalenok and Ivanchenkov), Bykovsky and Jaehn return in Soyuz 29. Total flight time 7days 20hr 49min. LC Baikonur. LV A-2. LT 1751 MT. R about 87 miles (140km) SE of Dzhezkazgan.

October 1 President Carter, during a visit to the Kennedy Space Center, Florida, states that US reconnaissance satellites have contributed immensely to international security and are an "important factor" in monitoring arms control agreements.

October 4-26 Soviets launch unmanned Progress 4 for Salyut 6 re-supply. Docks with Salyut 6/Soyuz 31 complex on second airlock, 6 October; undocks 24 October and subsequently de-orbited over Pacific Ocean. Before undocking, it is used to boost space station complex into higher orbit of about 230 miles (370km). LC Baikonur. LV A-2. LT 0209 MT.

December 27 Capsules released by Venera 11 and 12 reach the surface of

Exhibition model of Venera 11/12.

Venus some 497 miles (800km) apart. On-board instruments detect presence of key argon isotopes during descent phase: argon 40 and Argon 56, in 200 times the proportions found on Earth. Surface pressures about 88 atm, temperatures 466°C. Mother-craft continue in heliocentric orbit, Venera 12 parent also conducting Franco-German programme of research into solar and galactic gamma rays.

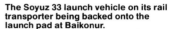

February 25-August 19 Lt-Col Vladimir A. Lyakhov and Valery V. Ryumin (C) in Soyuz 32 dock with Salyut 6 on forward airlock, 26 February. During their protracted mission the cosmonauts perform a wide range of experiments and erect and deploy KPT-10 radio telescope delivered to them in kit form by Progress 7 supply craft. When 32ft (10m) antenna becomes hooked up on the end of the space station, they perform EVA to release it. Ryumin spends 1hr 23min in open space. Cosmonauts are eventually recovered in Soyuz 34 after spending record total of 175 days 36min in space. LC Baikonur. LV A-2. LT 1454 MT. R *Tass* reports re-entry module of Soyuz 32 "has been returned to Earth unmanned".

March 5 Voyager 1 flies within 177,720 miles (286,000km) of Jupiter's cloud tops providing startling new information about the Jovian system. Jupiter's atmosphere is complex, with layers of colourful clouds above a deep atmosphere of hydrogen and helium. The atmosphere, more turbulent than had been expected, appears to be controlled by forces far below the visible cloud tops. The Great Red Spot, large enough to swallow several Earths, is an immense atmospheric storm that rotates counter-clockwise, once every

Jupiter and the satellites Io (left) and Europa as seen by Voyager 1 from about 20 million km distance.

six days. A thin ring is discovered around Jupiter 18-20 miles (29-32km) thick. Biggest surprise: the moon Io has at least nine active volcanos, some with plumes extending 175 miles (280km). Other moons examined include Ganymede, Europa and Callisto.

March 12-April 5 Soviets launch unmanned Progress 5 for Salyut 6 re-supply. Docks with Salyut 6/Soyuz 32 complex on second airlock, 14 March. Raises orbit of Soyuz 32/Salyut 6/Progress 5 complex, 30 March to 176 x 222 miles (284 x 357km); adjusts 2 April. Undocks next day and subsequently made to re-enter over Pacific Ocean. LC Baikonur. LV A-2. LT 0847 MT.

April 10-12 Nikolai Rukavishnikov, first Soyuz civilian commander, and Major Georgi Ivanov (Bulgaria) in Soyuz 33 fail to dock with Salyut 6/Soyuz 32 complex when a propulsion unit used to align the craft with the space station "was found to be deviating from the normal". Cosmonauts are recalled, landing in darkness. Flight time 1day 23hr 01min. LC Baikonur. LV A-2. LT 2034 MT.

The Soyuz 33 launch vehicle on its rail transporter being backed onto the launch pad at Baikonur.

R about 199 miles (320km) SE of Dzhezkazgan. Failure to dock with Salyut 6 leads to Soyuz 34 being launched unmanned on 6 June 1979 to retrieve long-stay cosmonauts, whose original space ferry Soyuz 32 has exceeded safe period in orbit.

April 30 British Interplanetary Society moves into new Headquarters Building in London (27-29 South Lambeth Road, SW8) as part of a Development Programme to promote international astronautics. HQ incorporates Golovine Conference Room and Arthur C. Clarke Space Library.

May 1 Space Shuttle *Enterprise* is rolled out of the Vehicle Assembly Building at the Kennedy Space Center, Florida, on the Mobile Launch Platform and the crawler-transporter and placed on Launch Complex-39A for compatibility checks with pad and service tower. It is returned to the VAB on 23 July 1979.

May 13-June 9 Soviets launch unmanned Progress 6 for Salyut 6 re-supply; 2·5 tonne payload includes propellant, food, water, scientific equipment and mail. Docks Salyut 6/Soyuz 32 complex second airlock 15 May; undocks 8 June and subsequently de-orbited over the Pacific Ocean. LC Baikonur. LV A-2. LT 0717 MT.

May 17 Soviets launch first of new series of Earth resources satellites, Cosmos 1099, from Northern Cosmodrome into orbit of 134 x 153 miles (215 x 247km) inclined at 81·35° to the equator. Spacecraft apparently is based on Cosmos reconnaissance satellites, returning a capsule to Earth after 12 days.

June 6-August 19 Soviets launch unmanned Soyuz 34 which docks with Salyut 6/Soyuz 32 complex on second airlock, 8 June. Undocks 14 June; then re-docks to first airlock after space station "turn-around" manoeuvre. Undocks again 19 August, returning to Earth Soyuz 32 cosmonauts who have set new duration record for manned space flight of 175days 36min. LC Baikonur. LV A-2. LT 0913 MT. R about 105 miles (170km) SE of Dzhezkazgan.

June 28-July 20 Soviets launch unmanned Progress 7 for Salyut 6 re-supply. Docks with Salyut 6/ Soyuz 34 complex on second airlock, 30 June; undocks 18 July and subsequently de-orbited over Pacific Ocean. LC Baikonur. LV A-2. LT 1225 MT.

July 9 Voyager 2 flies within 399,560 miles (643,000km) of Jupiter's cloud tops. Examination is made of Jupiter's banded clouds, Red Spot, "white ovals", thin ring system (discovered by Voyager 1), and the moons Io, Europa, Callisto, Ganymede and Amalthea. Additional discoveries of joint mission included three new satellites, and auroras and cloud-top lightning bolts, like super-bolts on Earth.

Computer-enhanced Voyager 2 image of Jupiter's turbulent atmosphere.

July 11 Skylab space station decays from orbit over the Indian Ocean and some debris falls on south-western Australia. However, there is no damage to life or property.

September 1 Pioneer 11 flies within 13,000 miles (20,880km) of Saturn's cloud tops, some 1,000 million miles (1,600 million km) from Earth, after a six-year journey. The probe spends 10 days photographing and measuring the ringed planet. Discovers two new outer rings ("F" and "G") and a new—11th—Saturnian moon (1979S1), estimated diameter 250 miles (400km), near outer edge of Saturn's rings. Also confirms that Saturn has a magnetic

field, magnetosphere and radiation belts. At the time of encounter, Saturn's gravity swings the probe almost 90° on a change of course toward the edge of the Solar System.

September 25-October 13 Soviets launch Vostok-type biosatellite Cosmos 1129 in first international experiment to breed mammals in space. Payload includes 38 white rats prepared by Soviet and Bulgarian scientists; also 60 Japanese quail eggs. Material from USA includes carrot seeds and carrot slices inoculated with bacteria which form tumours in plants. Capsule lands in Kazakhstan, 13 October 1979.

December 16-March 25 1980 Soyuz T-1 is launched unmanned and docks with Salyut 6 space station under computer control at 1405, 19 December, on forward airlock. Mission includes complete test of basic systems in conjunction with ground control. Previous spacecraft of this type were Cosmos 1001 and Cosmos 1074. Orbital module—a 2,778lb (1,260kg) spheroid, 7·5ft (2·3m) in diameter—separated from spacecraft before retro-fire; decayed from orbit about 28 May 1980. Flight time 100days 9hr 20min. LC Baikonur. LV A-2. LT 1230 GMT.

December 18 United Nations "Moon Treaty"—more properly the "Agreement governing the activities of States on the Moon and other Celestial Bodies"—is opened for signature.

December 24 European Space Agency (ESA) launches Ariane heavy satellite vehicle on maiden flight from Guiana Space Centre, Korou, at 1714·38 GMT. L01 mission is a total success, placing a CAT (Capsule Ariane Technologique) into an orbit of

The 3-stage, liquid-fuelled Ariane L01 lifting off from the Kourou launch pad in French Guiana at 1714 GMT.

125 x 22,217 miles (202 x 35,753km) inclined at 17·55° to the equator.

1980

March 27-April 26 Soviets launch Progress 8 unmanned cargo craft which docks with Salyut 6 on aft airlock at 2001 GMT, 29 March. Engine burn trims orbit of Salyut/Progress complex, 30 March, in readiness for launch of Soyuz 35. Orbit is 216 x 224 miles (348 x 360km) x 51·6°; period 91·4min. On 24 April, Progress engine fires again for 81sec to raise station's orbit to 211 x 228 miles (340 x 368km). Undocks at 0654 GMT, 25 April, and next day at 1654 GMT is made to re-enter the atmosphere and

burns up over Pacific Ocean. LC Baikonur. LV A-2. LT 2153 MT; 1853 GMT.

April 9-11 October Lt-Col Leonid Popov and Valery V. Ryumin (C) in Soyuz 35 dock with Salyut 6 on forward airlock at 1516 GMT, 10 April, to carry out servicing and maintenance tasks before starting long series of experiments. They transfer fuel and other supplies from Progress 8, which has docked automatically 29 March 1980. Ryumin (who only returned from record 175-day space mission the previous August) replaces Valentin Lebedev, who injured his knee in a trampoline accident during training in early March. Research programme includes more smelting experiments in Splav and Krystall furnaces and a new experiment, Lotos, to improve methods of obtaining structural materials from polyurethane foam under weightless conditions. Popov and Ryumin returned in the Soyuz 37 capsule on 11 October 1980, landing some 112 miles (180km) SE of Dzhezkazgan at 1250 MT and setting a new space endurance record of 184days 20hr 12min. LC Baikonur. LV A-2. LT 1638 MT.

April 27-May 22 Soviets launch Progress 9 unmanned cargo craft which docks automatically with Salyut 6/Soyuz 35 complex on aft airlock, 29 April. Supplies include food, water, clothing, dust collectors, regeneration equipment, spare parts, tools, scientific instruments, films and mail. Engine burn trims orbit of Salyut 6/Progress 9 to 216 x 229 miles (349 x 369km) x 51·6°, 16 May. After on-board cosmonauts have transferred cargo, craft is undocked at 2115 MT on 20 May, "with rubbish and used-up equipment", for disposal over the Central Pacific, 22 May. LC Baikonur. LV A-2. LT 0924 MT.

May US scientists prove by experiment that giant planet Jupiter could be a future source of huge quantities of hydrocarbon products to serve Earth's industries. A mixture of gases identified in Jupiter's atmosphere has been irradiated with UV rays, obtaining some 50 polymers and hydrocarbon components, including butane, ethane, propane, benzine and toluene from which fuel oil, plastics, fibres, lubricants, rubbers, solvents and explosives can be produced. Researchers: Professors Carl Sagan and B.N. Khare (Cornell University, N.Y.) and Eric Bandurski and Bartholomew Nagy (University of Arizona).

May 18 People's Republic of China launches ICBM test vehicle CSS-X4 between space centre near Shuangch'eng-tzu and target area of 70 miles (112km) radius centred at 7°S, 171° 33'E in the South Pacific. Splashdown of inert warhead observed by Royal Australian Navy at approximately 0230 GMT, about 750 miles (1,207km) NNW of Fiji. A second test is made on 21 May, ending the test series. Distances travelled respectively are about 5,000 miles (8,046km) and 4,200 miles (6,759km).

May 23 Ariane space rocket (L02) launched from Kourou, French Guiana, crashes into the Atlantic after successful lift-off. One of four first-stage engines loses pressure, leading to pressure drop in other three and activation of "destruct" system. Lost with the rocket are two West German satellites, Firewheel and Amsat (Oscar 9).

May 26-June 3 Valery Kubasov (C) and Capt Bertalan Farkas (Hungarian) in Soyuz 36 dock with Salyut 6/Soyuz 35 complex on aft airlock at 2256 MT on 27 May for series of experiments in conjunction with resident crew (Popov and Ryumin). Flight time 7days 20hr 46min. Land in Soyuz 35 3 June at 1807 MT, 87 miles (140km) SE of Dzhezkazgan. LC Baikonur. LV A-2. LT 2121 MT.

Kubasov (left) and Farkas during survival training in preparation for their Soyuz 36 mission.

June 5-9 Lt-Col Yuri V. Malyshev and Vladimir V. Aksyonov (C) in Soyuz T-2 spacecraft dock with Salyut 6/Soyuz 36 complex on aft airlock at 1858 MT 6 June. Intended docking was automatic under computer control but a suspected fault (spurious as it happened) made the cosmonauts control the docking manually from a distance of about 700ft (213m). Soyuz 36 had been re-docked 4 June on forward airlock by resident cosmonauts Popov and Ryumin who pulled away about 600ft (183m) while Salyut was turned through 180 deg. Soyuz T-2 re-entry module landed with cosmonauts Malyshev and Aksyonov about 124 miles (200km) SE of Dzhezkazgan at 1541 MT. Total flight time 3days 22hr 22min. Soyuz T-2 orbital module (separated before retro-fire) decayed from orbit about 5 September 1980. LC Baikonur. LV A-2. LT 1719 MT.

June 29-July 19 Soviets launch Progress 10 unmanned cargo craft which docks automatically with Salyut 6/Soyuz 36 complex on aft airlock 1 July. The ship "brought expendable materials and various cargoes" to the resident cosmonauts Popov and Ryumin and raised the orbit in preparation for next cosmonaut visit. Undocked 17 July and subsequently re-entered over Pacific Ocean. LC Baikonur. LV A-2. LT 0741 MT.

July 18 India becomes seventh nation after Soviet Union, USA, France, Japan, China and United Kingdom to launch an artificial satellite by independent effort. The 78lb (35·4kg) test-satellite is launched by the SLV-3-2 Rohini four-stage solid-propellant rocket from Sriharikota island, some 62 miles (100km) N of Madras.

July 23-31 Col Viktor Gorbatko and Lt-Col Pham Tuan (Vietnamese) in Soyuz 37 spacecraft on 24 July at 2302 MT dock with Salyut 6/Soyuz 36 complex on aft airlock. Experiments with resident crew (Popov and Ryumin) included "applied problems of space medicine and biology, space technology, mapping of the surface of land and water". Gorbatko and Tuan returned in Soyuz 36. Total flight time 7days 20hr 42min. LC Baikonur. LV A-2. LT 2133 MT. R about 112 miles (180km) SE of Dzhezkazgan at 1815 MT.

Vietnam's first cosmonaut: Pham Tuan aboard the Salyut 6 station.

September 18-26 Lt-Col Yuri Romanenko and Lt-Col Arnaldo Tamayo Mendez (Cuban) in Soyuz 38 spacecraft dock with Salyut 6/Soyuz 37 complex on aft airlock on 19 September. Experiments with resident crew (Popov and Ryumin) included observation of Cuba's natural resources, the crystallisation of

sucrose and bio-medical tests. They returned in their own spacecraft at 1854 MT. Total flight time 7days 20hr 43min. LC Baikonur. LV A-2. LT 2211 MT. R about 108 miles (175km) SE of Dzhezkazgan.

September 28 Progress 11 is launched on 28 September and docks with Salyut 6 on 30 September under automatic control. After the resident cosmonauts had left the station, the cargo ship refuelled Salyut 6 automatically on 9 December at 1323 MT after the Soyuz T-3 crew had boarded the Salyut 6/Progress complex. It re-entered the atmosphere over the Pacific Ocean on 11 December.

November 12 Voyager 1 flies within 77,000 miles (124,200km) of Saturn's cloud tops making detailed studies of the planet, its spectacular ring system and various moons. Ring system is more complex than previously believed, eg faint rings within Cassini division; dark radial "spokes" or "fingers" extend across B-ring. Some rings have eccentric paths, outer ring "braided like rope". Sizes of particles making up the rings cover a wide range, from microns to metres. Rings probably formed at different times, from different sources. Titan, Saturn's largest moon — "no more than 3,175 miles (5,120km) across" — has an atmosphere composed largely of nitrogen, not methane as previously believed. Atmospheric pressure near surface is 50 per cent greater than that of Earth; surface hidden by dense haze at least 175 miles (280km) thick. Titan believed to have roughly equal amount of rock and ice. Close-up observations of Saturn's smaller moons suggest that they consist of "dirty ice". Some are pockmarked by meteoritic craters collected over eons; others are smoother and therefore younger.

A magnificent view of Saturn taken by Voyager 1 just three weeks before its close encounter with the planet.

Voyager 1 photographed six new Saturnian moons, some that had never been seen before, and some that had been reported as moons but not confirmed.

November 25 Space Shuttle Orbiter *Columbia* is moved from the Orbiter Processing Facility at the Kennedy Space Center, Florida, to the Vehicle Assembly Building for mating with the External Tank (ET) and Solid Rocket Boosters (SRBs). First flight is scheduled "no earlier than 17 March 1981".

November 27 Lt-Col Leonid Kizim Oleg Makarov and Gennady Strekalov in Soyuz T-3 dock with Salyut6/Progress 11 complex on forward airlock, 28 November at 1854 MT. Described as a "new stage in the testing of space hardware and a logical continuation of the testing of the new generation of spaceships". Soyuz T-3 undocked from Salyut 6 at 0910 MT on 10 December and then separated the re-entry module before initiating retro-fire. The craft travelled some 6,090 miles (9,800km) to the landing area to touch down some 81 miles (130km) east of Dzhezkazgan. Parts fitted included a new four-pump hydraulic module for temperature control, telemetry, programming and timing modules. Research tasks include the growth of higher plants, the manufacture of semi-conductor materials and the use of a portable helium-neon laser to obtain a hologram of a crystal being dissolved. A new converter was also fitted to Salyut's fuel system. LC Baikonur. LV A-2. LT 1718MT. R 81 miles (130km) E of Dzhezkazgan at 1226 MT.

December 6 First of a series of Intelsat 5 satellites is launched by Atlas-Centaur from Cape Canaveral for stationing in Clarke orbit. The biggest communications satellite to date, it will relay 12,000 telephone calls and two colour TV programmes. This and others of the planned series of nine satellites will link 105 member countries of the Intelsat consortium.

December 29 Space Shuttle Orbiter *Columbia* and its launch system (STS-1) rolled out of Vehicle Assembly Building at Kennedy Space Center and positioned "hard down" on the pad at Launch Complex-39A in readiness for first flight by John W. Young (C) and Capt Robert L. Crippen. The journey along the crawlerway took 10½ hours.

1981

January 24-March 21 Soviets launch Progress 12 unmanned cargo craft at 1718 MT which docks automatically with Salyut 6 on aft airlock at 1856 MT 26 January. Fuel and oxidant for station's main engine are replenished automatically on command from Earth. (Cosmonauts Kovalenok and Savinykh subsequently unloaded Progress 12 and placed used equipment in cargo compartment for disposal.) Undocked 19 March, re-entered atmosphere over Pacific Ocean 21 March. LC Baikonur. LV A-2.

March 12-May 26 Col Vladimir Kovalenok and Victor Savinykh in Soyuz T-4 dock with Salyut 6/Progress 12 complex on forward airlock at 2333 MT 13 March. Savinykh is world's 100th space traveller. Mission continues programme of occupation of Salyut 6 during which necessary repairs and maintenance are carried out and scientific experiments performed. By end of mission Salyut 6 has operated for total of 676 days with men on board. LC Baikonur. LV A-2 T 2200 MT. R 1638 MT some 77 miles (125 km) E of Dzhezkazgan

March 22-30 Col Vladimir Dzhanibekov and Jugderdemidyin Gurragcha (Mongolia) in Soyuz 39 dock with Salyut 6/Soyuz T-4 complex at 1928 MT 23 March. Work with resident crew Kovalenok and Savinykh includes study of the adaptation of human organism to weightlessness and changes in the acuity and depth of cosmonauts' eyesight; also physical and technological experiments including use of holography for study of materials and seeds under micro-g conditions. For first time holographic images are transmitted by TV to and from the Earth. Mission also includes observation and photography of NW and Central Mongolia to locate possible mineral and water resources and assess condition of pasture land. LC Baikonur. LV A-2. LT 1759 MT. R 1442 MT about 106 miles (170km) SE of Dzhezkazgan.

April 12-14 First orbital test flight of Space Shuttle *Columbia* with John W. Young (commander) and Capt Robert L. Crippen (pilot) includes opening and closing of cargo bay doors in space, emergency donning of pressure suits

Space Shuttle Columbia clears the tower for the first time just seconds into its maiden flight.

and test of basic systems. Discovery that one complete thermal protection system tile and portions of others on the rear OMS pods are missing after launch—fortunately they are not in critical areas that might endanger Orbiter during re-entry heating. Spacecraft flies planned 36 Earth orbits in mission lasting 54hr 21 min 57 sec, returning to Dryden Space Flight Center, Edwards AFB, California. Flight initially scheduled for 10 April was delayed two days by computer fault. LC KSC. LV Space Transportation System (STS)-1. LT 0700.03.98 EST. R Runway 23, Edwards AFB, California.

April 25 Soviets launch 33,069lb (15,000kg) Cosmos 1,267 which executes power manoeuvres before docking automatically with unmanned Salyut 6 space station on 19 June at 1052 MT. Tass News Agency reports that Cosmos 1,267 is testing new spacecraft systems and means of assembling large orbiting stations from modular units. Orbit of docked combination is 208 x 234 miles (335 x 377km) x 51·6°. LC Baikonur. LV D-1. LT 0201 GMT.

May 14-22 Leonid Popov (C) and Dumitry Prunariu (Romania) in Soyuz 40 dock with Salyut 6/Soyuz T-4 complex at 2250 MT on 15 May. Work with resident crew Kovalenok and Savinykh includes

bio-medical experiments, study of effects of outer space on construction materials, Earth resource observation and "methods of obtaining monocrystals of a set profile". (Before arrival of Soyuz 40, engine of T-4 was used to adjust space station's orbit.) LC Baikonur. LV A-2. LT 2117 MT. R 1437 MT 140 miles (225km) SE of Dzhezkazgan.

June 19 European Space Agency Ariane L03 launches Meteosat 2 and APPLE, an Indian experimental communications satellite, into geostationary orbit from Kourou Launch Site, French Guiana. Ariane data capsule is also carried to monitor vehicle performance. It is the third launch of the Ariane test series, and the second success.

Early July Soviet officials reveal that they will abstain from further manned flights for the rest of 1981 while work on a new space station is completed. The assembly will be conducted in orbit by attaching modular elements to a central core with multiple docking points. Cosmos 1,267 docked to Salyut 6 is performing interface tests directly related to this project. The manning levels will vary according to mission requirements, but the station may carry up to 12 cosmonauts at one time.

August 25 Voyager 2 passes within 63,000 miles (101,300km) of the cloud tops of Saturn, some 14,000 miles (22,500km) closer than Voyager 1. Spacecraft surveys the planet's ring system and many of its moons during several days of close encounter. A camera platform fault—subsequently rectified—results in the loss of some pictures. Highlights of the encounter include more detailed examination of the complex ring system and the mysterious spoke-like features; discovery of a narrow ring in the Encke division; improved imagery of the satellite Hyperion; better pictures of Saturn's atmosphere; discovery of a

The complex nature of Saturn's ring system is vividly illustrated in this image returned by Voyager 2.

250 mile (400km) wide crater on Tethys, the largest yet observed in the Saturnian system. Spacecraft now on course for Uranus (1986) and Neptune (1989).

September Report on Soviet military power authorised by Caspar W. Weinberger, US Secretary of Defense, includes reference to Soviet Saturn V-class booster having close orbit capability of 390,000-455,000lb

(176,870-206,350kg). It could launch heavy Soviet space station, large laser weapons. "The Soviet goal of having continuously manned space stations may support both defensive and offensive weapons in space with man in the space station for target selection, repairs and adjustments and positive command and control."

September 19 People's Republic of China launches three satellites – China 9, 10 and 11 – from a single carrier rocket. Largest satellite is an octagonal prism, maximum diameter 3·9ft (1·2m) x 3·28ft (1·0m); carries four rectangular solar panels. Second satellite is cone shaped. Third is a balloon linked to metal sphere by a wire tether. Satellites one and two designed to study Earth's magnetic field, IR and UV radiation, charged particles, X-rays etc. Third satellite, which decayed from orbit in six days, for research into atmospheric density. Orbits: 242 x 994 miles (390 x 1,600km) x 59·4°. LC Shuang-ch'eng-tzu. LV FB-1 (CSL-2). LT 2132 GMT.

September 29 Salyut 6 space station (now unmanned) completes four years in space having made 23,029 revolutions of the Earth. Manned flights to the station have included five long-stay crews and 11 visiting missions. Since the docking of Cosmos 1,267 on 19 June, the orbit of the complex has been raised twice using engines onboard the attached module. It is now 292 x 324 miles (470 x 521km).

October 30 Soviets launch Venera 13 unmanned spacecraft with intention of landing a robot laboratory on Venus in March 1982. The craft is designed to be able to excavate a Venusian soil sample and bring it inside the lander for analysis. LC Baikonur. LV. D-1-e. LT 0602 GMT.

November 4 Soviets launch Venera 14 unmanned spacecraft, the sister ship of Venera 13. The two craft are expected to land in an area southeast of the Beta Shield volcano region. The choice of this site was determined by studying US Pioneer-Venus radar images of the planet supplied through US/Soviet co-operative scientific exchanges. LC Baikonur. LV D-1-e. LT 0530 GMT.

November 12-14 Second orbital test flight of Space Shuttle *Columbia* (STS-2) begins at LC-39A at Cape Canaveral at 1010 EST. Crew are Col Joe H. Engle (commander) and Capt Richard H. Truly (pilot). Mission includes five Office of Space and Terrestrial Application (OSTA)-1 experiments mounted in cargo bay on British Aerospace pallet to explore Earth's natural resources; also test of 50ft (15m) long manipulator arm remotely operated by the crew, built by SPAR of Canada. The flight – intended to last more than five days – is cut short because of a fault in one of the three fuel cells that supply electricity. *Columbia* lands at Edwards AFB, California, on 14 November, having completed some 90 per cent of its tasks. Mission elapsed time is 54hr 13min 11sec. LC KSC. LV STS-2. LT 1010 EST. R Edwards AFB, California. Note: A previous attempt to launch STS-2 on 4 November was frustrated when overheating of *Columbia*'s auxiliary power units (APUs) caused by contaminated lubricating oil made the automatic ground launch sequencer stop the count-down at T-31 seconds. This was the second launch delay as a nitrogen tetroxide spill on 22 September, as the forward reaction control system was being loaded with oxidant, had necessitated the rebonding of some 370 silica tiles and the replacement of

The first test of the SPAR robot arm aboard the Shuttle Columbia.

26 thermal blankets in the nose RCS bay. This work delayed the launch from the scheduled date of 9 October.

November 20 Soviets launch Indian Earth Resources satellite Bhaskara 2. Embodies two TV cameras operating in 0·54-0·66 and 0·75-0·85 micrometres bands and three microwave radiometers operating at 19·35, 22·235 and 31·4 GHz. Orbit 324 x 337 miles (521 x 543km) x 50·64°. LC Kapustin Yar. LV C-1. LT 0825 GMT.

Spacelab 1 being prepared at KSC.

December 11 First flight unit of ESA Spacelab arrives at Kennedy Space Center, Florida, aboard Lockheed C-5A transport which lands on Shuttle runway. Some 80 Space Shuttle sorties with the laboratory are planned between 1983-1995, at first with the now-delivered unit and from 1984 with the second Spacelab.

December 20 European Space Agency's Ariane L04 launches Marecs 1 maritime communications satellite for positioning in geostationary orbit at 26°W to provide fast, high-quality radio links between ships and shore stations. Payload also includes data capsule CAT to monitor vehicle performance. LC Kourou, French Guiana. LV Ariane L04. LT 0129 GMT.

1982

January NASA announces that data supplied by Voyager 2, during close encounter with Saturn August 1981, has led to discovery of four more moons and evidence suggesting possibly two more, making a total of 23. All estimated to be 6·2-12·4 miles (10-20km) across circulating within the orbits of larger moons, Mimas distance 115,580 miles (186,000km), Tethys 183,310 miles (295,000km), Tethys/Dione 217,490 miles (350,000km) and Dione 234,880 miles (378,000km).

January Anatoliy Skripko, Science and Technology attaché, Soviet Embassy, Washington DC, informs American Astronautical Society that USSR may begin development of space shuttle-type vehicle in about five years to support long-duration space station operations. The USSR had not urgently pressed for development of a shuttle because "it is no problem for us now to deliver fuel, food or other supplies" to space stations by using large boosters and Progress supply craft. Major

interest surrounds concept of horizontal launching with full recovery of flight vehicles. Aim to reduce payload cost to a level one-tenth that of US Space Shuttle, ie 20-25 roubles per kg (about $30-37·5). Project will be openly discussed in two to three years; first flight expected 1987. Perhaps Vladimir Shatalov best expresses the philosophy. "The horizontal or aircraft start," he said, "is definitely preferred for a re-usable spacecraft, and we are taking this standpoint. However, the Americans chose a useful and less costly alternative, namely a vertical rocket start which has the advantage that it can carry along a greater load each time. The design has undeniable advantages as well as disadvantages ... We prefer the more advanced second shuttle which proceeds from a horizontal launching device. This gives the further advantage that the device can start from any airfield in the Soviet Union equipped for this purpose; this makes the system more flexible in mission operations."

January NASA announces study of an unmanned heavy launcher SRB-X utilising re-usable Space Shuttle components such as Solid Rocket Boosters and Main Engines. Will place 65,000lb (29,484kg) into low Earth orbit or 12,000lb (5,443kg) into geostationary orbit.

January 2 Subsidiary of US investment banking firm, William Sword Co., Space Transportation Co., reported to be

considering the private procurement of a Space Shuttle Orbiter. Company states: "Our concept is to supply the fifth Orbiter and contribute it to the fleet, and then in effect to become ticket agency for the entire fleet."

January 5 British Aerospace announces that ESA has awarded Space and Communications Division a contract to lead industrial team from seven European countries and Canada in construction of L-Sat, one of world's largest communications satellites, which will beam television programmes into homes, or business communications into offices and factories, via small, roof-mounted, dish antennas. The 5,070lb (2,300kg) L-Sat 1, to be launched by Ariane 3 from Kourou, French Guiana, in 1989, will have solar arrays developing over

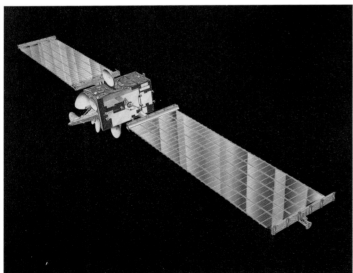

L-Sat as it will appear in orbit.

3,500 watts. It will stand 18·4ft (5·6m) tall and span 88·6ft (27m) over the fully-extended solar arrays. L-Sat (later named Olympus) is expected to develop up to 7,000 watts in subsequent commercial versions.

January 26 European Space Agency approves development of Ariane 4 in

family of six launchers of differing capability. All versions to embody common, lengthened first stage having propellant capacity of 210 tonnes, powered by four uprated Viking engines operating at chamber pressure of 58·5 bar. Second stage, third stage and equipment bay same as Ariane 3. A new, large diameter fairing to be available in three sizes: normal, lengthened and 'dual-launch'. Versions of the launcher differ according to the number of strap-on boosters: either two or four solid-propellant boosters as those of Ariane 3, or two or four liquid propellant boosters using the Viking engine with 40 tonnes of propellant. There are also plans for a hybrid version having two solid-propellant and two liquid propellant boosters, and finally one having no strap-ons. Ariane 4 family will place 2,425 to 9,480lb (1,100 to 4,300kg) into geostationary transfer orbit. Cost per kilogram in orbit should fall to 55 per cent of using Ariane I.

March European Space Agency initiates development of Giotto spacecraft to investigate Halley's comet. Optimum launch date, by Ariane from Kourou, French Guiana, 10 July 1985; Halley encounter 13 March 1986 with comet 0·89 AU from

Sun and 1 AU from Earth; fly-by velocity 42·3 miles/sec (68km/sec). Giotto: spin stabilised, overall height 116in (296cm), diameter over solar cell drum 71in (181cm), launch weight 2,094lb (950kg) reducing to 1,130lb (512kg) when "kick" motor has burnt out and hydrazine propellant used for mid-course attitude and trajectory correction manoeuvres. Cylindrical solar cell arrays (plus four silver cadmium batteries) provide 190W during encounter. High-gain dish antenna diameter 4·8ft (1·47m). Double bumper shield at nozzle end comprises 0·04in (1mm) aluminium front sheet and 0·47in (12mm) Kevlar rear sheet with 9·8in (25cm) gap. Instruments: camera, neutral mass spectrometer, dust impact detector, plasma analysers, energetic particles detector, magnetometer, optical probe. The other two Halley comet spacecraft are:
USSR: Two Venera-Halley spacecraft to be launched 22-28 December 1984 to drop landing modules on Venus 14-22 June 1985; first comet intercept 8 March 1986, second a week later. Fly-by velocity 48·3 miles/sec (77·7km/sec).
Instruments: Wide and narrow angle cameras; three-channel spectrometer; dust counter, plasma analyser.
Japan: ISAS Planet-A intended to penetrate Halley's coma. Launch date: 14 August 1985, Halley encounter 8 March 1986. Depending on trajectory achieved, miss distance will be between 6,214 and 62,140 miles (10,000 and 100,000km). Spacecraft is spin-stabilised, cylindrical, height 27·5in (70cm), diameter 55·1in (140cm), launch weight 298lb (135kg) including 22lb (10kg) scientific instruments, 11lb (5kg) hydrazine for attitude and velocity control. Instruments: UV (Lyman alpha) camera, solar wind analyser. Launch centre: Kagoshima. Launch vehicle: three-stage Mu-3C plus 4th stage "kick" motor.

March 1 Descent craft of Venera 13 soft-lands on Venus, transmitting from surface for 127 minutes, four times longer than planned. Obtains first colour photographs of landscape; first remote analysis of soil samples. Mission sequence: encapsuled lander separates from Venera 13 mothercraft 27 February, some 48 hours before anticipated time of entry into atmosphere of Venus, the latter passing the planet at a distance of some 22,370 miles (36,000km). Lander enters

dense layers of Venusian atmosphere at 0555 MT and 62 minutes later lands in a mountainous area east of Phoebe region at 7°30'S, 303°E. Entry speed about 7 miles/sec (11·3km/sec); after a period of aerodynamic braking and parachute descent to altitude of 29·2 miles (47km) capsule completes descent with help of aerodynamic braking disc. After landing two small television cameras obtain eight panoramic views of surrounding landscape from distance of 4·9ft (1·5m) revealing objects as small as 0·16-0·196in (4-5mm) across; some pictures taken sequentially through red, blue and green filters to obtain colour. Pictures reveal sheets of ancient volcanic lava with traces of chemical erosion; scattering of sharp rocks partly covered with fine dust and sand. Landscape has a brownish hue. Soil sampling device drills the surface rock at the ambient temperature of 457°C (855°F) and pressure of 89 atmospheres. Soil samples are conveyed by suction to an hermetically-sealed chamber in the lander for X-ray and fluorescent analysis. To achieve this, pressure in the chamber is reduced to about one two-thousandth of that outside and a temperature of 30°C (86°F) is maintained by a cooling system. Discovers that soil contains highly alkaline potassium basalts, similar to those of lunar samples obtained by Luna probes, but which do not occur on Earth's surface. Planet's seismic activity and physical and mechanical properties of the ground are investigated by detachable device. The mechanical strength of rocks is determined by a rod powered by springs which impresses a metal stamp into the ground. The same rod is used to measure the electrical conductivity of the ground. During descent and after landing, studies are made of chemical composition of atmosphere and clouds, structure of the cloud cover, and diffused solar radiation. Electric discharges in the atmosphere are also registered. Lander instrument data are relayed to Earth via Venera 13 mothercraft during its close passage of Venus. En route to Venus, and subsequently, studies made of X-rays, inter-planetary plasma and characteristics of cosmic rays and solar wind. Franco-Soviet experiment also investigates location and characteristics of galactic sources of gamma rays. Interplanetary magnetic field studied using a magnetometer of Austrian manufacture.

March 4 UK Government gives approval for direct broadcasting by satellites from 1986, providing BBC with two additional TV channels and three extra high-quality stereo radio channels. Geostationary satellite will broadcast directly to homes with TV sets equipped with signal converters using 35·4in (90cm) dish antenna pointed at the satellite. Alternatively, service will be received by community cable system using a single dish antenna. Three satellites to be built initially based on ECS technology, two operational, one spare, for launch by Ariane rockets from Kourou, French Guiana. Partners in £150 million project to supply satellites — British Telecom, British Aerospace and Marconi — will set up joint company, United Satellites: also discussing with Rothschild Bank possibility of establishing leasing arrangements for the satellites, the three equally to share the equity and the risks.

March 5 Descent craft of Venera 14 soft-lands on Venus, transmitting from surface for 57 minutes. Obtains colour photographs of landscape; soil samples for on-the-spot analysis. Encapsuled lander entered dense layers of Venusian atmosphere at 0553 MT, landing 63 minutes later east of the Phoebe region at 13°15'S, 310°9'E. Surface temperature is 465°C (869°F), pressure 94 atmospheres. Probe lands on a hill about 1,640ft (500m) high. The surroundings, as observed by onboard TV cameras, show large boulders of dark grey rock covered with brownish-black fine-grained material; also small potholes covered by hillside debris. Sky colour is orange or reddish-brown, reflecting appearance of surface. For research objectives, see 1 March, Venera 13.

March 22-30 Third orbital test flight of Space Shuttle *Columbia* (STS-3) begins at LC-39A at Cape Canaveral at 1100 EST, one hour behind schedule because a heater that keeps nitrogen gaseous in the fuel lines failed to start automatically; it was subsequently switched on manually. Crew are Col Jack R. Lousma (commander) and Col C. Gordon Fullerton (pilot). Orbit achieved is 130 x 130nm (240·8 x 240·8km). Mission includes Office of Space Sciences (OSS-1) instruments devoted to astronomy and space physics mounted on British Aerospace pallet in cargo bay; also further test of Spar-built manipulator arm remotely operated by crew including first removal and replacement of a payload in the cargo bay, and test of Orbiter's reaction to thermal extremes at different attitudes with respect to the Sun. Flight preparations, following previous mission of November 1981, included replacement of 499 thermal insulation tiles with densified tiles; replacement of fuel cell No 1 (which failed on STS-2 flight). Lift-off weight 4,478,787lb (2,031,578kg), about 17,000lb (7,710kg) heavier than STS-1 and

STS-3 lifts off. The External Tank is unpainted to save weight.

4,518lb (2,049kg) heavier than STS-2 Problems associated with mission include loss of or damage to some 38 thermal protection tiles from the nose area and aft section of *Columbia,* above the "sear line"; failure of certain radio communications channels; failure of part of close-circuit TV system used to monitor work with manipulator arm; minor drop in cabin pressure; overheated auxiliary power unit (APU 3) and a clogged toilet. Originally intended to land 29 March 1982 (at 1336 local time) at Army Missile Range White Sands, New Mexico, mission extended by one day because of sandstorm conditions in the area. Mission elapsed time is 192hr 4min 49sec instead of pre-planned 171hr 36min. Landing site was changed from Edwards Air Force Base, California, before mission began because of rainstorm damage to landing strip. Number of orbits: 128, re-entry on 129th orbit. LC KSC. LV STS-3. LT 1100 EST. R 0904·49 MST, Northrup Strip, Army Missile Range, White Sands, New Mexico.

March 24 Hughes Aircraft Company wins contract to build five Intelsat 6 communications satellites. Each will carry 33,000 telephone calls and four TV programmes. The spin-stabilised satellite has two nesting concentric cylindrical solar arrays 39ft (11·9m) long when fully deployed; diameter 12ft (3·65m). Launch weight 7,700lb (3,493kg); power 2·2kW; frequencies 4-6GHz and 11·14GHz. Intelsat has options for 11 additional satellites that could eventually raise programme value to $1.6000 million. Hughes' team includes British Aerospace (value of initial participation $100 million); MBB; Nippon Electric; Spar Aerospace; Selenia and Thomson-CSF.

April 10 Insat 1A, world's first combined communications and weather satellite, built for India by Ford Aerospace, is launched from Kennedy Space Center. LV Delta 3910/PAM.

April 19 Soviets launch Salyut 7 space station into orbit of 136 x 173 miles (219 x 278km) x 51·6°: period 89·2 min At present unmanned, "it will be used, like Salyut 6, both in automatic mode and with a human crew". It can accommodate up to five people. Objective is to test modernized systems and equipment and conduct further technical experiments. Communications with the station are being maintained via tracking stations in the USSR and the research ship *Academician Korolev* in the Atlantic. Compared to Salyut 6 there are no fundamental design changes, main consideration being to lighten work load of crew and making long-term living conditions more tolerable. New water supply system, "Rodnik" (Spring) operates as reliably as a domestic tap; hot water constantly available. Station embodies brightly coloured, washable, wall panels, more comfortable crew accommodation, better artificial lighting, "Stroka" teleprinter link Earth-to-space, Delta automatic navigator using on-board computers.

Salyut 7 space station in Earth orbit.

Research programme includes studies of Earth's surface and atmosphere for various departments of the national economy; astrophysical and biomedical studies; technological and technical experiments; tests and adjustments of improved on-board systems and apparatus. "Aelite" multi-purpose unit checks and evaluates cosmonauts' cardio-vascular systems, cerebral activity, blood pressure and circulation. Fresh foodstuffs brought from Earth in Progress cargo ships are stored in a refrigerator. Station has improved docking unit which will allow ships to link up in orbit. LC Baikonur. LV D-1.

May Member countries of European Space Agency (ESA) approve three new projects. 1. Unmanned Spacelab free-flight pallet, Eureca, to carry up to 3,307lb (1,500kg) experiments. Derived from British Aerospace standard pallet mounted in Space Shuttle Orbiter cargo bay, will have solar arrays for power, provision for remote operation, and attitude and thermal control. Flight duration up to six months before Space Shuttle retrieval. First launch 1986, material and life support experiments. 2. Improvements to existing Spacelab module. 3. Studies of manned and unmanned space stations benefitting from Spacelab technology. Participants: Belgium, Denmark, France, Italy, Spain, Switzerland, West Germany and UK. Estimated cost: $160 million (155·9 million accounting units) at mid-1980 prices.

May 13-December 10 Lt-Col Anatoly Berezovoi and flight engineer Valentin Lebedev in Soyuz T-5 dock with Salyut 7 space station on forward airlock at 1536 MT May 14. Orbit of combined vehicles 213 x 224 miles (343 x 360km) inclined at 51·6° to equator. Significant events: 17 May: Cosmonauts release 62lb (28kg) Iskra 2 amateur radio satellite from airlock compartment. 25 June-2 July: They receive Franco-Soviet cosmonauts (who arrive in Soyuz T-6). 30 June: After being in space for 78 days, Berezovoi and Lebedev spacewalk for 153 minutes to replace and fix new instruments on the exterior of Salyut 7; they also assess the use of "different mechanical joints which can be used in assembly work in space". 21-27 August: They receive three more cosmonauts, including the woman Svetlana Savitskaya (who arrive in Soyuz T-7). 18 September: Cosmonauts release amateur radio satellite Iskra 3 from airlock. During their long stay aboard the space station, four automatic Progress cargo ships kept them supplied with air, food, propellant, water, mail and equipment. Progress 16, still attached to the station when the cosmonauts left, was later released by remote control to burn up in the atmosphere. Berezovoi and Lebedev returned in the Soyuz T-7 spacecraft having travelled more than 80 million miles (129 million km) and setting a new duration record of 211 days 8 hours 5 minutes. Of 300 major experiments, the crew made observations and surveys of Earth

Roll-out of a Soyuz T launcher.

including potential areas of oil and mineral deposits and also mapped the distribution of glaciers. More than 60 sessions of photography logged by December included more than 2,000 pictures with the MKF-6M multispectral camera, more than 3,000 with KT-140 topographical camera. The cosmonauts also completed many astrophysical, medical and biological experiments. Astronomical studies included use of Soviet designed X-ray camera and Elena gamma-ray telescope for which fittings were supplied by Bulgaria and Czechoslovakia. Two French-made cameras, Piramig and PSN, obtained more than 1,100 photographs. Pilot production of semi-conductor monocrystals (cadmium selenide and indium antimonide) processed in 300lb (136kg) Korund electric furnace, described as the first manufacture in space for the electronics industry. Products were "highly uniform mono-crystals with properties immensely better than those produced in gravity". Furnace operated at temperatures of 20 to 1,270°C to an accuracy of half a degree. First sample products stated to weigh up to 3·3lb (1·5kg). Cosmonauts landed in a snowstorm, their capsule rolling down a hillside before coming to rest. LC Baikonur. LV A-2. LT 1358 MT. R 2203 MT, 118 miles (190 km) east of Dzhezkazgan.

May 17 Cosmonauts aboard Salyut 7 release 62lb (28kg) artificial satellite Iskra 2 from airlock compartment. Satellite embodies transponder for experiments in amateur radio communications, a memory device, a command radio channel and a telemetry system for relaying scientific and housekeeping information to ground stations. Designed by student design office, Sergo Ordzhonikidze Aviation Institute, Moscow. Orbit 212·5 x 222 miles (342 x 357km) x 51·6° inclination. A similar Iskra 3 was released from airlock on 18 September; orbit 224 x 229 miles (360 x 365km) x 51·6° inclination.

May 23-June 6 Soviets launch unmanned Progress 13 cargo ship which docks with Salyut 7-Soyuz T-5 complex on aft airlock at 1157 MT on 25 May, final link-up being controlled by on-board cosmonauts Berezovoi and Lebedev. Two tonnes of supplies transferred to space station include 1,455lb (660kg) propellants, 290 litres water, life support equipment, research and technical equipment and materials, some 551lb (250kg) being of French supply. Other items include Krystall furnace, electro-photometer EFO-7 (to obtain data from stars), improved Oasis plant growth unit (peas and onions). Modifications to Progress include a "more efficient system for delivering water to the station". Whereas water tanks of earlier craft were internal, water is now contained in spherical bottles on the outside of both Progress and Salyut leaving space for other cargo. After manoeuvring space station complex into lower orbit by two stage engine burn, in readiness for arrival of Soyuz T-6, Progress 13 is separated on 4 June and two days later is de-orbited over Pacific Ocean. LC Baikonur. LV A-2. LT 0957 MT.

June Australia places contracts worth almost $175 million with Hughes Aircraft Company for three Aussat communications satellites, one a ground spare, plus controlling ground stations to be located in Sydney and Perth. Will provide direct-broadcast TV and radio to the outback, relay TV between Australian cities (also services to Papua New Guinea and offshore islands) and supply domestic and data links; also improve air traffic control services and maritime radio coverage. First launch anticipated June 1985; planned geostationary longitudes 156°E, 160°E and 164°E.

June Aérospatiale study looks beyond Ariane 4 to a new family of ESA launchers, some partly re-usable, which could put up to 33,069lb (15,000kg) into low Earth orbit. Three main versions: Ariane 5B: for low Earth orbits. Ariane 5G, with H9 LO$_2$/LH$_2$

third stage, 19,840lb (9,000kg) thrust. Ariane 5H: two-stage variant for use with "Hermes" mini-shuttle studied by CNES.

June 3 Soviets launch test model of winged spacecraft—Cosmos 1374—into 140 miles (225km) circular orbit inclined at 50·7° to equator; makes wing-borne re-entry over Indian Ocean after 1¼ orbits. Royal Australian Air Force reports seven Soviet ships in recovery area some 350 miles (563km) south of Cocos Islands. Test model probably in 2,200lb (1,000kg) class launched by C-1 two-stage rocket from Kapustin Yar about 2130 GMT (est); flight lasts approximately 109 minutes. Project possibly related to planned 40,000lb (18,144kg) class Kosmolyot (spaceplane), designed to resolve thermal heating and control problems. Reminiscent of US Air Force Prime glide-vehicles flown on sub-orbital trajectories by Atlas boosters beginning 1966-70.

June 6 Radio Luxembourg reported to be planning to launch a £200 million satellite system by mid-1980s which could provide new TV channel for Europe, including the UK.

June 18 Soviets conduct successful test of a killer satellite by passing Cosmos 1379 close to target satellite Cosmos 1375. Target, launched from Northern Cosmodrome June 6, entered orbit of 615 x 634 miles (990 x 1,021km) x 65·9°. Interceptor, launched from Baikonur at about 1110 GMT executes plane change of 0·7° 76 minutes later, then manoeuvres into 607 x 628 miles (977 x 1,010km) orbit at 1226 GMT. Re-enters atmosphere 1450 GMT. LC Baikonur. LV F-1. LT 1110 GMT.

June 24-July 2 Soviets launch Soyuz T-6 with first Franco-Soviet crew comprising commander Vladimir Dzhanibekov (USSR), flight engineer

The T-6 crew at work in Salyut 7.

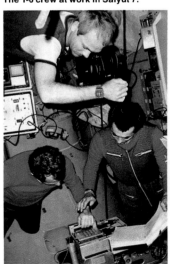

Alexander Ivanchenkov (USSR) and Lt Col Jean-Loup Chrétien (France). Orbit before docking with Salyut 7/ Soyuz T-5 on aft airlock at 2146 MT 25 June, 154 x 172 miles (248 x 277km) x 51·6°. Research programme, in conjunction with resident crew Berezovoi and Lebedev, includes medical experiments—cardio-vascular functions and sensory physiology—biological experiments, studies of Earth's atmosphere, the interplanetary medium and galactic and extra-galactic radiation sources. Also, work with Krystall Magma F electric furnace installed by resident crew including examination of processes of diffusion and crystallisation of metal alloys and improved "space production techniques". French attachment to the furnace measured temperatures at different points in and around the melting zone. Total participation cost to France about £5·5 million including instruments, training and personnel. Dzhanibekov replaced original crew member Yuri Malyshev on medical grounds. Back-up crew: Leonid Kizim (USSR), Vladimir Solovyov (USSR), Patrick Baudry (France). LC Baikonur. LV A-2. LT 1629 GMT. R 1821 MT, about 40 miles (65km) NE of Arkalyk.

Contamination Monitor (IECM) was deployed away from spaceplane and returned. An 8,000lb (3,629kg) military payload, DoD 82-1, fixed in cargo bay, tested IR and UV sensors and space sextant for future surveillance (unofficially reported to include cryogenically cooled IR radiation detection telescope capable of identifying heat from enemy aircraft and missiles). Other experiments include tests of flight instrumentation, thermal effects on external tiles and tile gap heating. In *Columbia's* crew compartment were two materials processing experiments: Continuous Flow Electrophoresis System (CFES) to isolate and purify biological materials, in this case a blend of rat and egg albumins. Mission problems: SRBs failed to develop rated thrust and spaceplane entered orbit some 5 miles (8km) lower than planned; difficulty in closing cargo bay doors which had "warped" under extremes of temperature; failure to salvage the two SRBs which broke up and sank in 3,100ft (945m) of water after main parachutes failed. Fault was traced to a "g" switch designed to close on water impact and release the main parachutes; instead parachutes were

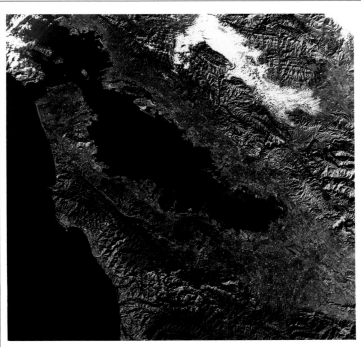

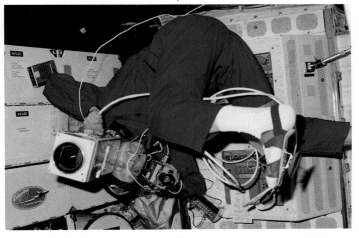

Mattingly in Columbia's mid-deck; note suction-cup-fitted footwear.

June 27-July 4 Fourth and final test flight of Space Shuttle *Columbia* (STS-4) with astronauts Capt Thomas K. Mattingly (commander) and Henry Hartsfield (pilot). First shuttle to fly due east into an eventual 201 x 184 mile (323 x 296km) x 28·5° orbit. Lift-off weight 4,484,585lb (2,034,207kg). Modifications to Orbiter included densification of about 800 thermal tiles and replacement of 10 attitude control thrusters which were contaminated by gypsum during previous landing at White Sands, New Mexico. Objectives include investigation of spacecraft capability under extreme in-orbit conditions of solar heating, and recording of environmental conditions in and around spaceplane; also further testing of Remote Manipulator System arm with which Induced Environment

released from boosters at altitude, some 365 secs after lift-off, when the boosters' frustrums were due to separate. Orbiter's landing is made for first time on concrete runway of minimum length-15,000ft (4,572m). Mission elapsed time is 169hr 14min. LC KSC. LV STS-4. LT 1100 EDT. R 0914 PDT, Runway 22, Edwards Air Force Base, California.

June 30 Space Shuttle *Challenger* is rolled out at Rockwell's factory in Palmdale, California.

June 30 General Georgi Beregovoy, commander of Gagarin Cosmonauts' Training Centre, says two women are training for a space flight which most probably will be to the Salyut 7 space station. Both are married, about 30 years old and already experienced respectively as pilot and flight engineer of aircraft.

July Reagan Administration revives Widebody-Centaur as upper stage for Space Shuttle by approving FY 1982 supplemental of $80 million for conversion work to start. Will replace two-stage Inertial Upper Stage (IUS) in projects Galileo and International Solar Polar Mission (ISPM). Galileo-Jupiter mission will slip to May 1986 but transit time will be reduced to about two years. Estimated development cost: $250 million. Estimated cost of modifications to KSC launch pad and *Challenger* and *Discovery* Orbiters: $125 million. Each payload bay door of Orbiter will include orifice for LO_2 and LH_2 to allow fuelling on the pad; vents through rear of spacecraft will allow dumping of propellants for emergency landing.

July 10-August 13 Soviets launch unmanned Progress 14 cargo ship which docks with Salyut 7-Soyuz T-5 complex on aft airlock at 1141 GMT, 12 July. After replenishing the space station, Progress 14 is de-orbited over the Pacific Ocean on 13 August. LC Baikonur. LV A-2. LT 0958 GMT.

July 16 NASA launches 4,273lb (1,938kg) Earth resources satellite Landsat 4 on its way into Sun-synchronous orbit of 422 x 435 miles (680 x 700km) inclined at 98·3° to equator. Objective to provide continuous remote sensing information and to encourage continued national and international participation in land remote sensing programmes; assess capability of new thematic mapper and exploit new areas of IR and visible light spectra at higher resolution. On-board thematic mapper

A Landsat 4 Thematic Mapper image of the San Francisco, Oakland, San Jose area of California.

provides 98·4ft (30m) resolution in six visible-light spectral bands; an additional IR band gives 394ft (120m). Scanning images processed at Goddard Space Flight Center, Green-belt, Maryland. After six months satellite turned over to National Oceanic and Atmospheric Administration, Department of Commerce. LC Vandenberg AFB. LV Delta 3920 (first use). LT 1059 PDT.

July 22 NASA announces that two mercury ion thrusters will be embodied in USAF research satellites Ion Auxiliary Propulsion System (IAPS). Built for Lewis Research Center by Hughes Aircraft, the small electric rocket engines will be used for attitude control and orbit manoeuvring.

July 29 Life of Salyut 6 space station is ended after four years ten months by attached "Star" module (Cosmos 1267) which uses its rocket engine to brake the station and direct it into the atmosphere over the Pacific Ocean. Five main expeditions of cosmonauts and 11 short-stay expeditions visited the station; nine included people of other socialist countries. Manned occupation lasted total of 676 days, and 35 dockings with manned and automatic spacecraft were made.

August Official China News Agency announces new multi-stage liquid propellant rocket CZ-3 designed to place large satellites into geo-stationary orbit.

August 19-27 Soviets launch Soyuz T-7 with cosmonauts Col Leonid Popov, flight engineer Alexander Serebrov and researcher-cosmonaut Svetlana Savitskaya (second woman in space). Docks with Salyut 7 space station on 20 August. Objectives: scientific, technological and bio-medical experiments jointly with resident cosmonauts Berezovoi and Lebedev. Serebrov is qualified engineer concerned in design and testing of spacecraft. Savitskaya, 34, has flown more than 20 types of aircraft, has 1,500 flying hours to her credit and is a qualified test pilot, second class. She holds 18 world records in aviation and was world aerobatic champion in 1970. Crew returned in the spacecraft Soyuz T-5 originally used by Berezovoi and Lebedev. Brought to Earth results of experiments performed on Salyut 7 by resident crew during previous three months, and by crew of five cosmonauts in the course of their joint work. Cosmonauts photographed selected regions of land and oceans, carried out astrophysical and geophysical

Svetlana Savitskaya, cosmonaut.

experiments using Soviet, Czech and French equipment. One experiment obtained "ultrapure biologically active materials" under conditions of weightlessness. Biomedical studies showed "no substantial differences in the reactions of the female and male organisms to space flight". LC Baikonur. LV A-2. LT 2112 MT. R 1904 MT, 43 miles (70km) north east of Arkalyk.

September 1 United States establishes Space Command within US Air Force

USAF Space Command F-15 carries an ASAT on vibroacoustic trials.

to co-ordinate military uses of space including Space Shuttle missions and anti-satellite (ASAT) weapon to be launched from F-15 Eagle aircraft. Based at NORAD Cheyenne Mountain underground complex near Colorado Springs.

September 4 Contact with India's combined communications/weather satellite, Insat 1A, is lost, probably because of premature depletion of fuel for attitude control.

September 9 Chinese People's Republic launches 12th artificial satellite into orbit of 107 x 244 miles (172 x 393km) inclined 62·98° to equator. Satellite experiment, including recovery technique. Capsule recovered after four days. LC Shuang-ch'eng-tzu. LV FB-1 (CSL-2).

September 9 First US private venture space rocket, Conestoga 1, launched from Matagorda Island, Texas, completed scheduled sub-orbital flight lasting 10·5 minutes. After reaching altitude of some 195 miles (314km) splashes down about 260 miles (418km) downrange in Gulf of Mexico. The 37·5ft (12·7m) rocket, based on 46,500lb (21,090kg) thrust government surplus Aerojet M56A-1 Minuteman 2nd stage motor, sponsored by Space Services Inc of America and cost about $2·5 million (£1·3 million). Company plans to develop satellite launchers.

September 10 Fifth ESA Ariane 1 rocket, carrying first revenue earning payload, fails to achieve orbit due to third stage turbopump failure. After 560 seconds of flight, nearly halfway into third stage burn, turbopump speed fell off followed by drop in chamber pressure. Lost was the Inmarsat Marecs B, Europe's second maritime communications satellite, and Sirio 2, a meteorological data distribution satellite. Marecs B insured for about $20 million, less than half its value. ESA investigating team concluded that most likely cause of turbopump failure was build-up of manufacturing tolerances in turbine assembly. LC Kourou, French Guiana. LV Ariane L05. LT 0212 GMT.

September 18-October 17 Soviets launch Progress 15 cargo spacecraft which docks with Salyut 7 space station on aft airlock at 1012 MT 20 September. Final approach and docking controlled by resident cosmonauts Berezovoi and Lebedev. Vehicle brought air, water, food,

scientific equipment and propellant for Salyut's engines. After supplies are transferred, craft is separated to make a controlled re-entry over central Pacific. LC Baikonur. LV A-2. LT 0859 MT.

September 29 NASA announces agreement to have Canadians trained as Space Shuttle mission specialists.

October 30 USAF launches first Titan 34D from Kennedy Space Center, Florida, carrying two Defense Satellite Communications System spacecraft for transfer to geostationary orbit by Inertial Upper Stage (IUS). Satellites are last of DSCS 2 series and first of DSCS 3.

October 31-December 15 Soviets launch Progress 16 which docks with Salyut 7 space station next day. Initial orbit 120 x 163 miles (193 x 263km) x 51·6°. Aboard are various consumables and replacement equipment. Craft is used to adjust the orbit of space station and remained attached after long-stay cosmonauts Berezovoi and Lebedev have departed. It is finally separated by remote command on 13 December to make a controlled re-entry over the central Pacific. LC Baikonur. LV A-2. LT 1420 MT.

November 11-16 Space Shuttle Columbia (STS-5) makes fifth flight into orbit marking first operational use. Astronauts: Vance D. Brand (commander), Col Robert F. Overmyer (pilot) and Dr Joseph P. Allen and Dr William B. Lenoir (mission specialists). Target lift-off weight is 4,494,556lb (2,038, 730kg); operational orbit is 160 nautical miles (296km) circular. First

A relaxed moment for the STS-5 crew.

revenue earning payload: two communications satellites for transfer to geostationary orbit, Satellite Business Systems SBS-3 and Telesat Canada's Anik C-3. SBS-3 is separated from cargo bay over Pacific 11 November; apogee motor PAM-D fires as planned by preset timer some 45 minutes after separation, when satellite is 20 miles (32km) behind Columbia and 16 miles (26km) above it. Anik C-3, separated above Atlantic the next day, is equally successful. Spacewalks by Lenoir and Allen to practise use of tools in cargo bay, delayed 24 hours from 14 November because of Lenoir's space sickness, are subsequently cancelled because of spacesuit problems. Lenoir's suit failed to fully pressurize because two plastic locking devices, each the size of a grain of rice, were omitted from pressure regulator during assembly. Oxygen circulation fan in Allen's suit failed because of a faulty magnetic sensor. Mission elapsed time is 5 days 2 hours 14 minutes. LC KSC. LV STS-5. LT 0719 EST. R 0633 PST, Runway 22, Edwards AFB.

December 22 NASA announces agreement to have Australians trained as Space Shuttle mission specialists. In 1985 an Australian will assist the launch from the Shuttle Orbiter's cargo bay of one of two communications satellites being developed for Aussat Pty Ltd., operator of Australia's national satellite system.

December 28 Soviet nuclear-powered satellite, Cosmos 1402, fails to eject section containing reactor into parking orbit at 600 miles (965km) altitude. Separates into three parts which re-enter Earth's atmosphere: rocket stage 30 December; reactor section (over Indian Ocean) 23 January 1983, and fuel core (over S. Atlantic) 7 February. One of a regular series of spacecraft designed to monitor Western shipping using radar. Launched 1 September 1982 into orbit of 156 x 164 miles (251 x 264km) x 65° sustained by low-thrust on-board rocket engines. Tass stated "... the satellite, equipped with a safety system in accordance with international recommendations, completed its programme of work and ceased active existence... extraction of the fuel core with radioactive products of fission from the reactor guaranteed its complete incineration." LC Baikonur. LV F-1-m. LT 1005 GMT.

1983

January 10 NASA postpones maiden flight of Space Shuttle *Challenger* scheduled for 24 January because of suspected hydrogen leak in engine compartment following 20 second on-the-pad engine test firing at KSC. At first decision is made to replace one main engine but replacement is found to be defective. Eventually, all three main engines are removed following discovery of hairline cracks in fuel coolant lines, which leads to further delay.

January 25 NASA launches 2,365lb (1,073kg) Infrared Astronomical Satellite (IRAS) by Delta 3910 from Vandenberg AFB, California into near-polar circular orbit of 560 miles

(900km). Designed to seek IR sources in surrounding Universe, it includes a sensitive liquid helium cooled telescope. The cryogenic liquid cools the IR detectors to 2 degrees above absolute zero which allows them to register the faintest impulses of IR from objects in space. First images reveal sources in Large Magellanic Cloud invisible to optical telescopes on Earth. Satellite is joint venture between NASA, the Netherlands and Britain which operates IRAS ground station at Rutherford Appleton Laboratory, Chilton.

March 2 Soviets launch Cosmos 1443 which docks automatically with Salyut 7 space station eight days later for "testing in various modes of flight a number of on-board systems, equipment and structural elements". Initial orbit of Cosmos 1443 123 x 167 miles (199 x 269km) x 51·6° Enlargement of space station permits wider range of experiments by cosmonauts. Said to resemble Cosmos 1267 which docked with Salyut 6 for engineering experiments 19 June 1981. LC Baikonur. LV D-1. LT 0932 GMT.

March 9 NASA announces programme SP-100 to assess and advance the technology required for nuclear reactor power systems for civil and military space applications. Cooperating are Department of Energy's Office of Nuclear Energy, NASA's Office of Aeronautics and Space Technology, and the Defense Advanced Research Projects Agency (DARPA).

March 15 Soviets repeat test of 2,205lb (1,000kg) class spaceplane research model. Flown under guise of Cosmos 1445, delta winged vehicle is recovered by parachute some 200 miles (322km) south-west of Cocos Islands, Indian Ocean after 1¼ orbits. Orbit 98 x 129 miles (158 x 208km) inclined at 50·7° to equator. Seven-ship task force in recovery area comprises Kara class GM cruiser, Kashin class GM destroyer, three space vehicle recovery ships, support ship and missile range instrumentation ship. Similar flight test made 3 June 1982. LC Kapustin Yar. LV SL-8. LT 2235 GMT (est).

The recovery of the Cosmos 1445 spaceplane from the Indian Ocean.

March US Defense Department publishes 2nd edition of *Soviet Military Power* which confirms that USSR "has under development a heavy-lift launch system, comparable to US Saturn V, and a re-usable space plane." Anticipated that expendable heavy-lift booster will place 330,688lb (150,000kg) into close Earth orbit; smaller vehicle will lift 28,660lb (13,000kg). A re-usable launch vehicle could be in regular use within a decade. Large manned space station expected by about 1990. Even larger station, possibly weighing more

than 100 tonnes, possible by end of century.

March 23 President Reagan tells nationwide TV audience that United States should move away from nuclear deterrence in favour of a new kind of anti-ballistic missile (ABM) system—the beam weapon. "Until now we have increasingly based our strategy of deterrence upon the threat of retaliation. But what if free people could live secure in the knowledge that their security did not rest upon the threat of instant retaliation to deter a Soviet attack: that we could intercept and destroy strategic missiles before they reached our own soil or that of our allies?"

March 23 Soviets launch observatory satellite, Astron, for UV and X-ray observation of Universe. Orbit 1,243 x 124,300 miles (2,000 x 200,000km) inclined at 51·5° to equator; period approximately 98 hours. Telescope, over 16ft (4·87m) long by 31·5in (80cm) diameter, weighs more than 3·5 tons and incorporates 31·5in (800mm) primary mirror; also X-ray spectrometers. Developed by Crimea Astrophysical Observatory; some equipment supplied by French specialists. Remotely controlled from Earth, Astron is designed to provide new information on the chemistry, temperature and density of stars and how matter is "leaked" from their surfaces. Also will investigate electromagnetic field associated with stars. First objects of study are star clusters and Crab Nebula in Taurus. LC Baikonur. LV D-1-e. LT 1250 GMT.

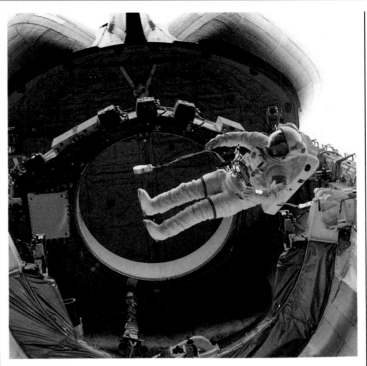

Story Musgrave during a tethered EVA in Challenger's payload bay.

April 4-9 NASA launches Space Shuttle *Challenger* on maiden flight from Cape Canaveral with commander Paul Weitz, a former Skylab astronaut; pilot is Air Force Colonel Karol Bobko, and mission specialists Dr Story Musgrave and Donald H. Peterson. *Challenger* is about 2,490lb (1,130kg) lighter than *Columbia;* its main engines are power rated at 104 per cent (compared with 100 per cent). Prime object is to launch first of four Tracking and Data Relay Satellites (TDRS) nearly 10 hours after lift-off. Satellite, to be transferred from 175 miles (281km) high orbit of Shuttle Orbiter into geostationary orbit by attached Inertial Upper Stage, is mis-directed into elliptical orbit of 12,000 x 19,000 miles (19,300 x 30,580km) due to fault in second stage. Subsequently, NASA nudged the satellite higher by firing small on-board thrusters. STS-6 mission features: First Shuttle EVAs into the payload bay (by Dr Story Musgrave and Donald Peterson) on 8 April, EVA duration: 3hr 45 min. First use of two-stage Inertial Upper Stage (IUS) to boost TDRS from Orbiter's cargo bay. Use of thermal-insulation blankets instead of certain white silica-foam tiles on upper surface of Orbiter. (A blanket was lost and two others bent on starboard side; three small pieces missing on port side). Removal of ejection seats for commander and pilot; four fixed seats fitted. First use of headup displays. First use of lightweight External Tank, approximately 10,000lb

(4,536kg) lighter than previous tanks. First use of lighter Solid Rocket Boosters, approximately 4,000lb (1,815kg) lighter than previous boosters. Small payloads include "Getaway Specials", an electrophoresis experiment by McDonnell Douglas Astronautics and a Monodisperse Latex Reactor. LC KSC. LV STS-6. LT 1330 EST. R 1053 PST, Runway 22, Edwards AFB, California.

April 9 Soviet spaceplane resembling NASA Space Shuttle is spotted at Ramenskoye airfield, SE of Moscow, mounted on back of My-4 Bison bomber. Airfield is associated with Central Institute of Aero-hydrodynamics (TsAGI). Soviet shuttle orbiter has double-delta configuration but omits main engines. Large shuttle booster is being developed as part of a family of modular boosters for application in both expendable and re-usable launch systems employing liquid propellants.

April 11 NASA announces that President Reagan has requested the Senior Interagency Group for Space to conduct a study to establish basis for an Administration decision on whether to proceed with NASA development of a permanently-based, manned space station. Issues addressed by study to include how such a station would contribute to the maintenance of US leadership and how a station would best fulfill national and international requirements versus other possible methods of satisfying them; also to be considered are foreign policy and national security implications and overall economic and social impacts.

April 17 India launches 91·5lb (41·5kg) satellite Rohini D2 by SLV-3 rocket from Sriharikota into orbit of 230·5 x 535 miles (371 x 861km) x 46·6°. Embodies two cameras with "smart" sensors, plus an L-band beacon for improved tracking.

April 20-22 Soviets launch Soyuz T-8 with cosmonauts Lt-Col Vladimir Titov (commander), Gennady Strekalov (flight engineer) and Alexander Serebrov (cosmonaut researcher). Fails to dock with Salyut 7/Cosmos 1443 complex on 21 April because of malfunction in rendezvous phase. Mission was intended to carry out "technical, medical and biological research." Strekalov—who flew in Soyuz T-3 in 1980—belongs to the spacecraft design bureau. Serebrov—who flew in Soyuz T-7 in 1982—is from the same bureau. LC Baikonur. LV A-2. LT 1711 MT. R 1729 MT, "several kilometres" SE of Arkalyk.

May Revealed that Vought anti-satellite (ASAT) will not be tested from F-15 Eagle with an active IR homing manoeuvring head until "early 1984". Two 6·5ft (2·0m) balloons to be launched by Vought Scout from Wallops Flight Center as orbiting targets; they can change thermal signature by louvres and assess ASAT miss distance by radar if head

does not impact. Technique involves (following separation from Altair stage) spinning up manoeuvring head to 20 revs/sec for stability, utilising laser gyro and liquid helium-cooled IR sensor to fire small rocket correction motors to track and align with ASAT target.

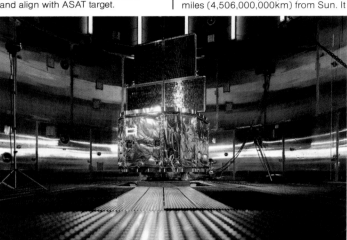

Exosat undergoing ground testing.

May 26 Exosat, the European Space Agency's first X-ray observatory satellite, is launched by Delta 3914 from Vandenberg Air Force Base, California. Orbit ranges between 186 x 124,278 miles (300 x 200,000 km) inclined at 72·5° to equator. Exosat will explore cosmic X-ray sources in the energy range 0·04keV to 80keV, parts of the spectrum which are cut off from ground observation by the Earth's atmosphere. Was originally to have been launched by ESA Ariane but mishap to the 5th launch vehicle intervened and it was decided to switch to an American rocket. Exosat weighs approximately 1,124lb (510kg) including 278lb (126kg) of payload and is 10ft (3·3m) high including solar array. Built by Cosmos member companies led by Messerschmitt-Bölkow-Blohm (W. Germany) with Aérospatiale (France); CASA (Spain); ETCA (Belgium); MSDS (UK); Selenia (Italy). Exosat ground station developed by MBB in co-operation with Krupp (W. Germany). Experiments involve nine institutes or universities from four countries involved in project.

June 2 Soviets launch Venera 15 for study of Venus from orbit. Unlike previous spacecraft of the series they do not have landing capsules but are designed to map the planet and investigate the atmosphere by radar. LC Baikonur. LV D-1-e. LT 0240 GMT.

June 7 Soviets launch Venera 16 for study of Venus from orbit. Objectives similar to those of Venera 15. LC Baikonur. LV D-1-e. LT 0240 GMT.

June 13 Pioneer 10, which departed Earth in March 1972, crosses orbit of Neptune at 30,552 miles/h (49,168km/h) on its way out of the Solar System. Designed to operate for 21 months, still relays data on solar wind more than 2,800,000,000 miles (4,506,000,000km) from Sun. It

may pass a nearby star after 10,500 years.

June 16 ESA launches first European Communications Satellite (ECS-1) by sixth Ariane rocket. Satellite, weighing 2,300lb (1,043kg) at launch and spanning more than 40ft (12·2m) with solar panels deployed, is subsequently positioned into geostationary orbit at 10° E longitude, above Gabon, Africa. Secondary payload is German-built satellite Oscar 10 for amateur radio enthusiasts. ECS-1, the first of five, is part of the Eutelsat network, providing telephone and telegraph services, TV distribution and (from ECS-2) specialised business services, covering Europe, the Middle East and Northern Africa; eg high speed data, audio and tele-conferencing, facsimile, remote printing of newspapers, computer-to-computer links, etc. LC Kourou, French Guiana. LV Ariane L06. LT 1159 GMT.

June 18-24 NASA launches Space Shuttle *Challenger* for second time on flight STS-7 from Kennedy Space Center, Florida, with Capt Robert L. Crippen (commander), Cdr Frederick H. Hauck (pilot) and mission specialists Lt-Col John M. Fabian, Sally K. Ride (first American woman in space) and Dr Norman E. Thagard. Deploys Telesat Canada Anik C2 and Indonesia Palapa B-1 satellites for subsequent positioning in geostationary orbit. First flight of German SPAS pallet satellite (commercially developed by MBB) deployed and recaptured by Canadian-built remote manipulator arm, in rehearsal for retrieval of failed Solar Maximum Mission (SMM) satellite during shuttle flight STS-13. First pictures of space shuttle in orbit by still, movie and TV cameras mounted on deployed SPAS pallet. Various experiments embodied in STS-7 were provided by the USA, Canada, Germany, Japan, Italy and Switzerland. One of several materials processing experiments was OSTA-2 provided by the USA and West Germany. Payload included Continuous Flow Electrophoresis System (CFES) and Monodisperse Latex Reactor (MLR), two mid-deck mounted experiments flown on previous shuttle missions for developing materials with potential pharmaceutical and medical uses. In experiment devised by students of two US high schools, Camden and New Jersey, colony of 150 carpenter ants, including queen "Norma", were found to be dead after the flight although plexiglas container, microprocessor and power equipment appeared to have operated normally. Many may have died during seven-week period aboard Challenger before lift-off. Objective of landing a Shuttle for first time at Kennedy Space Center was frustrated by bad weather conditions in Florida; flight diverted to Edwards Air Force Base, California, making six extra revolutions of Earth. Brake assembly of main landing gear damaged on landing which was otherwise normal. Some 25 thermal-tiles damaged. At time of STS-7 mission

America's first lady in space: Sally Ride communicates with ground controllers in Houston, Texas.

total space shuttle costs—development and production—amounted to some $20,000 million including allowances for inflation. LC KSC. LV STS-7. LT 0733 EDT. R 0957 EDT, Runway 15, Edwards AFB, California.

June 27-November 23 Soviets launch Soyuz T-9 with pilot-cosmonaut Col Vladimir Lyakhov and flight engineer Alexander Alexandrov. Docks with Salyut 7/Cosmos 1443 complex 28 June at 1046 GMT; combined mass of these vehicles about 103,000lb (46,720kg); orbit 203 x 213 miles (328 x 343km) x 51·6°. Objectives include technical and scientific experiments and bio-medical research. Lyakhov, 42, took part in 175-day space flight in 1979. Alexandrov, 40, making his first space flight, is from a spacecraft design bureau, specialising in control systems. Cosmonauts conducted more than 300 geological, astrophysical, technological and other research experiments during the 150 day flight. Visual observation alone of Earth and oceans took up about 50 hours. More than 100 medical and biological experiments conducted, and many experiments connected with space technology (including the processing of sample materials) were made for the first time. Electrical power of Salyut 7 was increased by the attachment of two additional solar panels on mountings installed during manufacture by resident crew during two spacewalks, "considerably widening the possibilities for research and experiments with the space station". The solar panels had previously been delivered to the station by Cosmos 1443. The first EVA began on 1 November at 0747 MT when the cosmonauts retrieved from the airlock a container in which the solar panels were

Cosmonauts Lyakhov and Alexandrov on their way to the Soyuz T-9 launcher.

folded. The men spent 2 hours 50 minutes in space installing and deploying the panels using special tools and welding equipment. On 3 November a second spacewalk lasting 2hr 55min began at 0647 MT to instal second, additional, solar panel. Soviets pointed out that Salyut 7 already had three large directional solar panels totaling some 538ft² (50m²) providing about 5kW of energy. Two extra panels, each of about 53·8ft² (5m²), would provide the extra power for the larger furnaces to be used for making semi-conductor materials— also to compensate for the slow degradation of solar panels under micrometeoroid bombardment in space. Pre-flight training included identical experiment in water tank at Gagarin Cosmonauts' Training Centre, during which an exact time table was worked out. Work is preparatory to bringing Salyut 7 into commission "as a pilot plant for the manufacture of semi-conductor components for use in high technology projects." Results of the Soyuz T-9 mission" laid the basis for a quantitatively new step in outer space exploration—a transition from the present space stations periodically visited by crews, replacing each other, to a multi-sectional, permanently inhabited orbital complex. This future complex was described as "a single system of structures of large size, placed in orbits at an altitude of 124 miles (200km) to 24,855 miles (40,000km), LC Baikonur. LV A-2. LT 1312MT. R 2258 MT, about 100 miles (160km) east of Dzhezkazgan, Kazakhstan.

July 1 Tracking & Data Relay Satellite (TDRS-A), launched by *Challenger* STS-6 but misdirected into lower-than-planned transfer orbit by Inertial Upper Stage (IUS), completes transfer to geostationary orbit under propulsion from small

The 16ft (4·9m) deployable antenna installed on TDRS satellites.

thrusters used for manoeuvre and control. Retains sufficient fuel for 10 year life on station. After being initially located at 67° W longitude (where radio interference is best for testing communications), satellite is manoeuvred to final location just off NE coast of Brazil (41° W) between 23 September and 17 October 1983.

July 1 NASA names Charles D. Walker, 35, as payload specialist for shuttle's flight STS-41D. An engineer with McDonnell Douglas Astronautics, Walker will run equipment developed by his company as part of its Electrophoresis Operation in Space Project (EOS) which has the object of separating large quantities of biological materials in space for ultimate use in new pharmaceuticals. Aim to provide enough materials for clinical testing.

August 6 Japan launches Sakura 2B communications satellite by Japanese-built NII rocket from Tanegashima for positioning in geostationary orbit at 135° E longitude. Satellite is cylindrical, enclosed in a drum-shaped solar panel with de-spun antenna. Launch weight 1,477lb (670kg), including 782·6lb (355kg) fuel and tank pressurant. Objective: provide telephone, TV and data links for Japanese mainland and smaller islands. Satellite built jointly by Ford Aerospace and Mitsubishi Electric for Japan's National Space Development .Agency. (Sakura 2A launched 4 February 1983).

August 10 Soviets launch three Glonass navigation satellites, Cosmos 1490-1492, by Proton D-1-e rocket from Baikonur cosmodrome. Second scheduled mission to form global positioning system similar to US

Navstar. Three other satellites launched 12 October 1982.

August 14 Cosmos 1443 separates from Salyut 7/Soyuz T-9 at 1804 under control of on-board cosmonauts Lyakhov and Alexandrov. Spends nine days in free flight before releasing re-entry capsule on 28 August which lands on target 65 miles (105km) SE of Arkalyk, Kazakhstan. Contains some 700lb (317·5kg) of exposed film, materials processing samples and expended hardware. Soviets describe Cosmos 1443 as "combined space tug and electric power module"—also a vehicle for transporting heavy cargo to and from large space facilities. Capable of returning 1,102lb (500kg) of cargo for water recovery. Module has about 430·5ft² (40m²) of solar panels providing some 3kW of electrical power. Propulsion system allows fuel and

A Soviet artist's impression of the Salyut 7/Cosmos 1443 complex.

oxidant to be passed in either direction between tug module and Salyut. Cosmos 1443 had docked with Salyut 7 on 10 March 1983. "On-board systems, power systems and structural elements of prospective spacecraft were tested and methods of controlling large-dimension complexes were practised during the joint flight. Flight path of manned complex was repeatedly adjusted by propulsion unit of Cosmos 1443. Brought to orbit about three tonnes of various cargoes necessary for functioning of Salyut 7 and conduct of scientific research and experiments.

August 15 Disclosed that Soyuz T-8 docking with Salyut 7 was unsuccessful in April because Soyuz rendezvous radar failed to deploy from its launch position. Commander, Titov, attempted visual approach in conjunction with data from ground control but abandoned the effort when he decided risk was too great.

August 17-September 18 Soviets launch unmanned Progress 17 cargo craft which docks with Salyut 7 on 19 August. On-board cosmonauts had previously separated Cosmos 1443 and transferred their Soyuz ferry to Salyut's forward docking port to clear aft port for cargo ship. Orbit after docking: 198 x 210·6 miles (319 x 339km) x 51·6°. After transferring propellant and other consumables, Progress 17 was undocked September 17 and made to re-enter the atmosphere over the Pacific Ocean. LC Baikonur. LV A2. LT 1208 GMT (est).

August 18 Soviet President Yuri Andropov, during Moscow meeting with nine US senators, proposes treaty banning anti-satellite weapons in space. Indicates that USSR would not conduct further anti-satellite tests if US refrained from doing so, pending negotiation of a treaty (according to Sen Clairborne Pell).

August 19 China launches thirteenth satellite as part of development programme. Orbit 106 x 248 miles (170 x 400km) x 63·59°. Ejects capsule for recovery on 24 August. Objectives: possibly largely photo-reconnaissance with other more general applications. On 4 August *People's Daily* reported that photographs obtained by Chinese satellites have been used for exploration of raw materials and analyses of river and coastal geographical and tidal influences, earthquakes and archaeology. LC Shuang-ch'eng-tsu. LV CSL-2. LT 0603 GMT (est).

August 30-September 6 NASA launches *Challenger* STS-8 with Capt Richard H. Truly (commander), Cdr Daniel C. Brandenstein (pilot) and three mission specialists, Lt Cdr Dale A. Gardner, Lt Col Guion S. Bluford, Jr, and Dr William E. Thornton. Bluford has a doctorate in aerospace engineering; he is the first US black astronaut. On second day of mission deploys Indian National Satellite (Insat 1B). Later

STS-8 touches down at Edwards: the first night landing for the Shuttle.

discovered that satellite was struck by unidentified object as it left cargo bay; a solar array had deployment problems, later rectified. Flight days three and four devoted to operations with Payload Deployment and Retrieval System test article using Canadian-built remote manipulator arm. Another major object was in-orbit test of Tracking and Data Relay Satellite System (TDRSS), mission being extended from five to six days for this purpose. (Proper operation of TDRSS was essential for STS-9 Spacelab mission launched 28 November 1983). Making its fourth flight was the Continuous Flow Electrophoresis System (CFES), the object of which is to develop techniques for the manufacture of pharmaceuticals under micro-gravity conditions. Live cell samples were used for the first time rather than simple protein samples used previously. Equipment, located on *Challenger's* mid-deck, weighed about 760lb (345kg) at lift-off. Six laboratory rats were carried in a special Animal Enclosure Module; the cage is to be used again in a subsequent student experiment. First night launch and landing. Post-flight analysis revealed that nozzle liner of Solid Rocket Booster almost burned through. LC KSC. LV STS-8. LT 0632 GMT. R 0440 GMT, Runway 22, Edwards Air Force Base, California.

September 27 Fire breaks out on Baikonur launch pad during final stage of countdown of Soyuz-T and two cosmonauts Lt-Col Vladimir Titov and Gennady Strekalov are forced to use emergency rocket escape system, which pulls their spacecraft clear of stricken A-2 launcher. Incident occurred shortly before 0140 local time. Their re-entry module lands within confines of cosmodrome after releasing recovery parachutes. Mission of Soyuz T-9 cosmonauts aboard Salyut 7 was

extended by this incident, who had to fit two exterior solar panels by EVA without the help of the men whose launch was aborted.

September Laser fired from NKC-135 Airborne Laser Laboratory puts BQM-34A drone out of control over Pacific Ocean, some 20 miles (32km) from US Navy Pacific Test Center, Pt Mugu, California. Carbon dioxide gas dynamics laser in aircraft operated at wavelength of 10·6 micrometres in IR band. Experiment—last of series—was part of joint programme by US Air Force Weapons Laboratory and Naval Weapons Evaluation Facility.

The BQM-34A drone flies out of control after being hit by a laser fired from the NKC-135 Airborne Laser Laboratory.

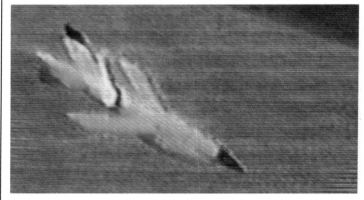

September 28 In bid to make first inspection of a comet, NASA deflects path (10 June 1982) of existing ISEE 3 satellite in a series of planned gravity-assist swings round the Moon. Third pass of the Moon occurs today, fourth 21 October and fifth 22 December taking the craft within 120 miles (194km) of lunar surface, accelerating it away towards a rendezvous with comet Giacobini-Zinner 5 September 1985.

Launched August 12 1978, the International Sun-Earth Explorer (ISEE-3) was the first spacecraft to orbit a point in space, i.e. Sun-Earth Libration Point—the first continuously to monitor solar wind conditions upstream from Earth; to explore distant geomagnetic tail between 317,000 and 990,000 miles (510,000 and 1,600,000km); to use multiple swingbys of Moon for orbital control and to use lunar gravity-assist manoeuvre to escape from Earth-Moon system.

October 10 Soviet space probe Venera 15 swings into orbit round Venus to begin joint radar mapping excursion with Venera 16 which arrives on 14 October. Images show objects little more than 0·5 mile (0·8km) across, including major fractures in crust, hills, mountain ridges and large impact craters. Plainly visible are traces of volcanic activity including hardened streams of lava. Continuous radar mapping covers an area 5,592 miles (9,000km) long by 93 miles (150km) wide. Analysis allows determination of heights of mountain ranges and individual mountains. Four maps prepared from this survey cover the northern geological structure of Venus; temperature distribution on the surface and composition of atmosphere and ionosphere.

October 13 Major expansion of Sentinel Project seeking evidence of intelligence elsewhere in Universe announced by Prof Carl Sagan. Organised by the Planetary Society, project will allow sky to be scanned on 8·4million radio channels simultaneously using radio receiver of advanced design. Already, the 84ft (27·5m) antenna of Harvard University Oak Ridge Radio Telescope is searching 131,000 channels. Prof Paul Horowitz (who built the new receiver) comments: "We shall have the biggest analyser on Earth. It will enable us to detect an extra-terrestrial civilisation that is not beaming a signal specifically at us."

October 17 TDRS-1 data relay satellite, launched by STS-6 in April, reaches final orbital position above Atlantic Ocean ready to link STS-9 Spacelab 1 mission with ground control.

October 18 ESA launches seventh Ariane rocket from Kourou, French Guiana with Intelsat V (F7) communications satellite for positioning in geostationary orbit.

October 20-November 16 Soviets launch unmanned Progress 18 cargo craft which docks with Salyut 7 on aft airlock on 22 October to transfer propellant and other expendables. Two of three oxidant tanks of Salyut are replenished following incident on 9 September which dumped fluids overboard and rendered inactive 16 of 32 control thrusters on the station. Progress 18 separates on 13 November and is made to re-enter the atmosphere over the Pacific three days later.

The Hubble Space Telescope during manufacture at Lockheed's plant.

October 24 NASA renames Space Telescope, to be launched by Shuttle, as the Edwin P. Hubble Space Telescope, in honour of one of America's foremost astronomers.

November Revealed that USSR plans 1986 mission to explore Martian moon Phobos at close range by placing robot spacecraft into coincident orbit. Hopes to fly within "few hundred metres" of moon for high-resolution photography and chemical analysis. Other Soviet plans include 1987-1990 missions to explore Moon from polar orbit, possibly in co-operation with France.

November 22 Infra-Red Astronomical Satellite (IRAS), launched 25 January 1983, runs out of helium refrigerant used to cool the telescope. During 300 days of observations, IRAS conducted first complete survey of the IR sky. Discoveries included detection of a ring of solid material around star Vega, seven comets, and

bands of dust around the Sun between orbits of Mars and Jupiter. Telescope provided a "new look" at Milky Way galaxy and detected many new mysterious objects; observations included more than 95 per cent of the sky, pinpointing the locations and intensities of more than 200,000 infra-red objects.

November 28 Following conclusion of 150-day mission by Soyuz T-9 cosmonauts aboard Salyut 7, *Pravda* describes future "multi-sectional, permanently inhabited orbital complex" as a single system linked to the Earth by transport cargo-passenger spaceships. The complex will include "specialised research laboratories, comfortable living modules, powerful energy systems, a refuelling station, repair workshops and even construction platforms for the manufacture and assembly of standard structural elements." Early objectives: round-the-clock observation of atmospheric conditions and agricultural crops, forest fires and "considerably increased effectiveness of prospecting for, and estimation of, mineral deposits." Subsequently, full-time monitoring of ships and aircraft, steady reception of TV programmes, batch production of electronic, optical and bio-medical materials and preparations having characteristics unattainable in usual terrestrial conditions. Looking further ahead, "it is possible to contemplate such vast projects as illuminating the long polar nights with reflected sunlight."

November 28-December 8 NASA launches Space Shuttle *Columbia* (STS-9) with astronauts Cdr John W. Young (USN retired), commander, Chief of Astronaut Office; Major Brewster H. Shaw, Jr (pilot); Dr Owen K. Garriott; Robert Allan Ridly Parker (mission specialists); Dr Byron

Left to right: Merbold, Lichtenberg and Parker attending to experiments during Spacelab's maiden flight.

K. Lichtenberg and Dr Ulf Merbold (payload specialists). Marks maiden flight of European Spacelab which remains fixed in Orbiter's cargo bay; also first mission to include a European crew member (Merbold). Configuration Spacelab 1: long module plus pallet; total mass 34,612lb (15,700kg) including 6,173lb (2,800kg) experiments. Orbit: circular at 155 miles (248km) x 57°. Objectives: verify Spacelab engineering performance by flying a variety of experiments in five broad scientific and technological disciplines (71 principal investigators, 13 NASA and 58 ESA). Experiment objectives: examine Earth's atmosphere and the space environment; biology and medicine; astronomy and solar physics; Earth observations, and space technology. Spacelab represents a European investment of almost $1,000 million. Nine ESA members contributed in the following percentage proportions: West Germany 54·94; Italy 15·57, France 10·29; UK 6·51; Belgium 4·32, Spain 2·88, Denmark 1·54 and Switzerland 1·0. Austria, which has associate member status, contributed 0·79 per cent of the endeavour. During off-duty periods Garriott uses a small radio to contact radio hams around the world (including King Husain of Jordan) in the 2 metre band, in the range 145·51 to 45·770 MHz FM. Mission, originally planned to last nine days, is extended a day to complete experiment programme; then re-entry is delayed by five orbits when two of five IBM general purpose computers fail (about 3hr 49min before planned re-entry burn) coincident with firing of small nose thrusters used for attitude control. Subsequently revealed that small fire broke out unnoticed in SSME compartment, damaging two of three auxiliary power units (APUs), after Orbiter re-entered atmosphere. (Fuelled by catalytic decomposition of hydrazine, APUs produce hot gas which operates a turbine in each unit to drive an

hydraulic pump. Hydraulic power is used to gimbal the SSMEs and orbiter control surfaces; hydraulic power also lowers the undercarriage. APUs operate independently, at least one being essential for flight.) Launch of STS-9 was postponed one month by discovery that nozzle of one of two Solid Rocket Boosters used on sister craft *Challenger* nearly burned through on 30 August lift-off, risking a disaster. *Columbia* was returned from launch pad to VAB for replacement of SRBs which had "new technology" nozzle liners. LC KSC. LV STS-9. LT 1100 EST. R 0347 PST, Runway 17, Edwards Air Force Base, California.

December Canada selects six Canadian scientists and engineers to train as payload specialists from more than 4,300 applicants. Planned that two of the six will eventually fly aboard the Space Shuttle to conduct two different Canadian experiments in life sciences and robotics in 1985-86.

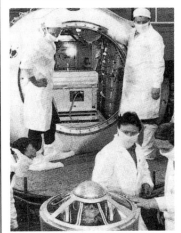

One of the Cosmos 1514 monkeys about to be retrieved after 5 days in orbit.

December 14-20 Soviets launch bio-satellite Cosmos 1514 containing small laboratory animals, fish, rats and (for the first time in .Soviet experiments) two monkeys "Abrek" and "Bion". Orbit: 140 x 179 miles (226 x 288km) x 82·3°. After recovery, animals are taken to Institute on Bio-Medical Problems of Ministry of Health. Objectives: development of manned space flight, study mechanisms of adaptation of living organisms to conditions of space flight, primarily weightlessness, in the first hours and days of flight.

December 20 Britain confirms decision to have two Skynet 4 military communications satellites launched by NASA Space Shuttles, late 1985 and 1986. Total cost about £60 million (See also 26 January 1984).

December 27 Soviets conduct third orbital flight test of sub-scale Kosmolyot (spaceplane) called

Cosmos 1517. At end of mission model makes "controlled descent in the atmosphere and splashes down in pre-set area of the Black Sea," indicating growing confidence in guidance and control. Previous test models were recovered in the Indian Ocean. LC Kapustin Yar. LV C-1.

1984

January 21 US Air Force announces successful first launch test of anti-satellite (ASAT) missile from F-15 interceptor over the Pacific. The 17ft (5·2m) missile, which omitted IR guided warhead, was aimed at a point in space rather than an actual target. It then dropped into the ocean, as planned.

January 23 Japan launches BS-2a direct-broadcast TV satellite by N-II rocket from Tanegashima Island for subsequent positioning in geo-stationary orbit at 110°E longitude. Owned by Japanese National Space Development Agency, the two direct-broadcast channels are leased to Japan Broadcasting Corporation for beaming TV programmes to remote parts of Japan, including outlying islands. Satellite has mass of 771lb (350kg) in final orbit. Prime contractor, General Electric with participation by Toshiba. Second satellite BS-2b to be co-located with BS-2a at 110°E in 1985.

January 25 President Reagan, in State of the Union address to joint session of Congress, says America must rebuild on its pioneer spirit "and develop our next frontier — space". He directs National Aeronautics and Space Administration to develop "within a decade" a permanent manned space station. NASA had previously published details of a 6-8 person space station which could be in permanent orbit by 1992. Assembled 310 miles (500km) above the Earth from prefabricated sections carried up by Space Shuttles, it would become a repair depot for satellites and a departure point for spacecraft making journeys into deep space; also an orbiting industrial centre where international companies could learn to exploit near-weightless conditions to produce ultra-pure semi-conductor materials, pharmaceuticals and new industrial alloys. Laboratories are planned that will be more advanced than Spacelab developed by the European Space Agency. Governments of Europe, Canada and Japan are invited to join project. Overall estimated cost about $8,000 million; a larger modular arrangement housing 12 to 18 astronauts about $17,000-20,000 million.

January 26 Revealed that Commander Peter Longhurst, 40, an electronics specialist serving in the Directorate of Naval Operational Requirements, MoD, has been nominated by RN as British astronaut. Further nominations are anticipated from Royal Air Force and British

Army. Selected astronaut candidates are expected to fly aboard Space Shuttles to monitor launch of British Skynet 4A and 4B military communications satellites in late 1985 and 1986.

January 26 Mr Larry Speakes, White House spokesman, confirms that President Reagan has "authorised a prudent research programme to determine if technology can be developed in the area of defence against ballistic missiles." The President's

defence budget request includes $5·6 billion for this purpose (see also entry for 23 March 1983).

January 29 China launches 14th Earth satellite. New China news agency says "important results" were achieved but gives no further information. NORAD confirms that after entering a low parking orbit of 191 x 279 miles (307 x 449km) x 31·04°, satellite was injected into eccentric orbit of 223 x 4,025 miles (359 x 6,479 km) x 36·03°. Possibly first orbital test from new launch site of three-stage launcher CSL-X3, developed from FB-1, having LO₂/LH₂ third stage.

February 3-11 NASA launches Space Shuttle *Challenger* mission 41-B with astronauts Vance D. Brand (C) (commander); Cdr Robert L. Gibson (pilot); Ronald E. McNair; Capt

Bruce McCandless, II, and Lt-Col Robert Stewart (mission specialists). Astronauts deploy first of two communications satellites, Westar 6 for Western Union, 3 February but Payload Assist Module (PAM), intended to achieve geostationary transfer orbit, underburns leaving satellite in 218 x 872 miles (352 x 1,403km) orbit, too low for adjustment by on-board propulsion. Deployment of second satellite, Palapa B-2 for Indonesia, is delayed 48 hours while mishap to Westar is investigated but Palapa also goes off course ending in 172 x 748 miles (278 x 1,204km) orbit. (Cause may have been defective batch of nozzle material, which resulted in break-up of rocket nozzle). Total insurance loss of two satellites about $180 million (£128 million). On 5 February, a 6·5ft (2·0m) Mylar balloon, released from cargo bay, bursts during inflation; was intended as rendezvous target for Orbiter prior to forthcoming shuttle mission to retrieve and repair Solar Maximum Mission satellite (SMM). Mission also features first shuttle flight of Manned Maneuvering Unit, a self-contained, propulsive backpack that enables astronauts McCandless and Stewart to move around freely in space without being

The world's first human satellite: Bruce McCandless flies his MMU up to 320ft (97·5m) away from Challenger.

tethered. On 7 February, McCandless becomes first human satellite orbiting alongside *Challenger* for more than one hour at 17,400mph (28,000km/h) up to 320ft (97·5m) away. Quotes: "That may have been one small step for Neil, but it was a heck of a big leap for me." "My impressions were of the immensity of the entire universe . . . what a beautiful Earth, what a beautiful flying machine!" Second EVA on 9 February, by Stewart, had to be modified because of jammed wrist action of remote manipulator arm. Both men were to practise docking with a shuttle pallet satellite (SPAS-01A) and perform work in preparation for the retrieval, at a later date, of the SMM, now tumbling in space. This involved simulating the spin rate of the SMM using a mockup but the experiment had to be abandoned. Instead, Stewart and McCandless conduct more free-flight trials with MMUs. At the end of the mission *Challenger* achieved first Shuttle landing at Kennedy Space Centre, Florida. LC KSC. LV STS 41-B. LT 0800 EST. R 0716 EST, KSC.

February 7 M. Mitterrand, the French President, in speech before Dutch Parliament in the Hague, proposes creation of a "Common Market in Space". He asks Western Europe to co-operate in setting up a defence early warning space system. "If Europe was capable of launching into space a manned satellite which would permit it to observe, transmit, and thus counter any eventual threat, it would take a great step forward in its own defence."

February 8 Soviets launch Soyuz T-10 with cosmonauts Col Leonid Kizim (commander); Vladimir Solovyov (flight engineer) and cosmonaut-researcher Oleg Atkov. After docking with Salyut 7 space station at 1743 MT 9 February, crew perform essential maintenance operations. Mission objectives: study of Earth's surface and atmosphere; astrophysical, technological and technical experiments; medical and biological research in conjunction with qualified doctor (Atkov). Particular attention is given to function of the human organism considered most important for ensuring man's prolonged stay in space, e.g. study of cardio-vascular system and water and salt exchange. LC Baikonur. LV A-2. LT 1507 MT.

February 8-October 2 Soviets launch Soyuz T-10 with cosmonauts Col Leonid Kizim (commander); Vladimir Solovyov (flight engineer) and cosmonaut-researcher Oleg Atkov. After docking with Salyut 7 space station at 1743 MT 9 February, crew perform essential maintenance operations. Mission objectives: study of Earth's surface and atmosphere; astrophysical, technological and technical experiments; medical and biological research in conjunction with qualified doctor (Atkov). Particular attention is given to function of the human organism considered most important for ensuring man's prolonged stay in space, e.g. study of cardio-vascular system and water and salt exchange. Kizim, Solovyov and Atkov returned in Soyuz T-11 capsule after record-breaking flight of 236 days 22hr 50min. During their time in space, cosmonauts were visited twice by different space crews and five times by Progress freighters which docked automatically. Six EVAs were made lasting a total of 22hr 50min. LC Baikonur. LV A-2. LT 1507 MT. R 1357 MT, some 99 miles (160km) E of Dzhezkazgan.

February 21-April 1 Soviets launch Progress 19 unmanned freighter which docks at rear port Salyut 7 at 0821 GMT 22 February to replenish propellant, water, food and other expendables; also provides new items of scientific equipment. Separates at 0940 GMT 31 March and re-enters atmosphere over Pacific Ocean. LC Baikonur. LV A-2. LT 0646 GMT.

April 3-11 Soviets launch Soyuz T-11 with cosmonauts Yuri Malyshev, Gennady Strekalov and Major Rakesh Sharma (India). Docks at 1831 MT 4 April with Salyut 7/Soyuz T-10 complex which contains cosmonauts Leonid Kizim, Vladimir Solovyov and Oleg Atkov. Objectives within Terra programme: study of natural resources of Indian sub-continent (oil, gas, minerals), agricultural crops, forests, coastal erosion, ocean conditions, etc. Also medical studies (Vector, Ballisto 3, Yoga, Optokinesis, Questionnaire and Poll) and, within Isparitel programme, microgravity processing of three alloys investigating borderline dividing liquids and solids. Cosmonauts returned in Soyuz T-10. LC Baikonur. LV A-2. LT 1709 MT. R 1450 MT, 29 miles (46km) E of Arkalyk, Kazakhstan.

April 6-13 NASA launches Space Shuttle *Challenger* (41-C) with Capt Robert L. Crippen (commander), Major Francis R. Scobee (pilot), George D. Nelson, James D. van Hoften and Terry J. Hart (mission specialists). Orbit approximately circular at 280 miles (450km) x 28·5° is achieved by direct insertion; subsequently Orbiter achieved record altitude of 309 miles (497km). On day two of mission, astronauts deploy Long-Duration Exposure Facility (LDEF) containing 57 experiments for US, Canada, Denmark, W Germany, France, Ireland, Netherlands, Switzerland and UK. Launch mass 21,400lb (9,707kg), length 29·8ft (9·1m), width 14·1ft (4·3m). LDEF, which lacks electrical power, attitude control and space-to-ground communications, is largest craft yet to be deployed from Shuttle by remote manipulator arm. Purpose is to expose various materials to cosmic rays, UV radiation, temperature extremes, micrometeorites and vacuum, and then to recover LDEF for post-flight analysis in February 1985, possibly during mission 51-D. On day three of 41-C mission, EVA astronauts, van Hoften and Nelson, attempt to retrieve and repair Solar Maximum Mission Satellite (SMMS) orbiting in same plane as *Challenger* at some 304 miles (490km) altitude. After Orbiter is brought within 200-300ft (61-91m) of Solar Max, George Nelson, wearing MMU, performs untethered EVA to reach satellite and stabilize it so that it can be grappled by Orbiter's remote manipulator arm and berthed in cargo bay. However, Nelson's

docking tool fails to engage satellite's docking fixture, and despite his valiant attempts to reduce satellite's rotation by manoeuvring out to grasp one of Solar Max's solar panels and using gas jets, he is forced to return to *Challenger* when gas runs low. This action leaves satellite with slight "wobble". After scientists at Goddard Space Flight Center unexpectedly re-established communications with Solar Max, satellite is brought under control and on 10 April Crippen and Scobee edge *Challenger* to within 33ft (10m) of the slowly revolving satellite. Hart, using the RMS, secures Solar Max which is then lowered into prepared berth in cargo bay. On 11 April Hart and van Hoften make 6hr EVA to repair satellite, replacing attitude control unit and electronic control box of coronograph/polarimeter. On 12 April Solar Max is released to continue study of solar flares and other activity on the Sun; also to study Halley's Comet in 1986. Heavy cloud over KSC prevents *Challenger's* return to Florida and flight is diverted to Edwards AFB, California. LC KSC. LV STS 41-C. LT 0859 EST. R 0538 PST, Runway 17, Edwards AFB, California.

April 8 Chinese People's Republic launches China 15, first experimental communications satellite for positioning (16 April) in geostationary orbit above 125°E longitude. Launch vehicle

Lift-off of Long March 3 from Xi Chang with the China 15 payload.

resembles Ariane 1 with "podded" nose fairing. Two liquid-propellant stages are derived from CSL-2/FB-1 launcher with LO₂/LH₂ third stage of smaller diameter. Base stage has four steerable fins. LC Xi Chang. LV Long March 3 (CSL-3). LT 1100 GMT approx.

April 15-May 7 Soviets launch Progress 20 unmanned freighter which docks with Salyut 7/Soyuz T-11 complex on rear port at 1322 MT 17 April. Orbit of space station complex is corrected by engine firing of Progress 20. Separates at 2146 MT 6 May and next day is de-orbited over Pacific Ocean. LC Baikonur. LV A-2. LT 1213 MT.

Leonid Kizim performing an EVA to attempt repairs to Salyut 7.

April 23 Cosmonauts Leonid Kizim and Vladimir Solovyov perform tethered EVA from Salyut 7 lasting 4hr 15min to begin repair of station's engine system. On 26 April the cosmonauts emerge again; using appropriate tools they open a protective cover on the engine bay and fit a new fuel valve in the pipe circuit. They re-enter station after some 5hr. Repairs are completed during two further EVAs, on 30 April and 4 May, each lasting about 2hr 45min. On the last occasion, the cosmonauts fitted a second pipe circuit and secured a thermal cover.

May 8 Soviets launch Progress 21 unmanned freighter which docks with Salyut 7/Soyuz T-11 complex on rear port at 0410 MT 10 May. Mission followed four record-breaking EVAs between 23 April and 4 May lasting a total of 14hr 45min by cosmonauts Kizim and Solovyov to repair station's engine. Progress 21 separated

26 May and was made to re-enter atmosphere over Pacific Ocean. LC Baikonur. LV A-2. LT 0247 MT.

May 18 NASA transfers ownership of Viking 1 Lander, which arrived on Mars in 1976, to National Air and Space Museum, Washington, DC. Transfer also includes loan of official Viking Lander plaque; this renames the Lander the "Thomas A. Mutch", after the Viking Lander Imaging Team Leader and NASA Associate Administrator for Space Science, who died in a climbing accident in the Himalayas, 1980. Plaque is scheduled to be placed on Lander by US astronauts when they travel to Mars at some indefinite time in the future.

May 18 Cosmonauts Leonid Kizim and Vladimir Solovyov make their fifth EVA from Salyut 7, this time to install additional solar arrays on solar panel no 2. They remain in open space for 3hr 5min. In total they have now spent a record 17hr 50min on EVA activity.

May 28-July 16 Soviets launch Progress 22 unmanned freighter which docks with Salyut 7/Soyuz T-11 on aft port at 1947 MT 30 May. On-board cosmonauts transfer propellant for repaired Salyut 7 propulsion unit, air, equipment, instruments, materials for scientific research including cassettes for MKF-6M multi-spectral camera and mail. On 11 July engine of Progress 22 is used to move station complex to new orbit of 198 x 222 miles (318 x 358km) x 51·6°. Separates at 1736 MT 15 July and is made to re-enter atmosphere over Pacific. LC Baikonur. LV A-2. LT 1813 MT.

June 9 Maiden flight of "stretched" Atlas Centaur (41-D) ends disastrously when upper stage goes out of control leaving geostationary communications satellite Intelsat 5 (F9) tumbling in lower-than-planned orbit. Valued at £21,500,000, satellite was meant to provide 12,000 voice channels and two colour TV programmes. Orbit achieved ranged between 93 and 759 miles (150 and 1,221km). Probable cause of failure was leak in LO₂ system of the upper stage; first stage performance was "nominal".

The June 10 intercept/kill vehicle.

June 10 Non-nuclear missile launched from Mech Island, Kwajalein Atoll, intercepts dummy warhead of Minuteman ICBM launched from Vandenberg AFB more than 100 miles (161km) out in space when travelling at 15,000mph (24,140km/h). Interceptor erected steel "umbrella" 15ft (24.1m) wide studded with weights, and locked onto its target by IR sensor which could theoretically detect heat emitted by a human body up to 1,000 miles (1,609km) away in space. Closing velocity 20,000ft/sec (6,096m/sec).

June 13 US Senate votes 61-28 to allow United States testing of anti-satellite weapon providing the President can convince Congress he is trying to negotiate with USSR on controlling such systems.

June 29 Soviet Union proposes talks on banning space weapons to begin in Vienna, September 1984; President Reagan agrees but states US intention to raise overall question of nuclear arms control. Soviets say this is unacceptable. In July US and USSR release joint statement affirming readiness to negotiate a ban on space weapons. Soviets want a moratorium on testing in space from the moment talks begin, but US Administration insists "no preconditions".

July 17-29 Soviets launch Soyuz T-12 with cosmonauts Col Vladimir Dzhanibekov (cdr), pilot cosmonaut Svetlana Savitskaya and researcher Igor Volk (world's 100th human space flight). Docks with Salyut 7/Soyuz T-11 complex on rear port at 2317 MT 18 July; Dzhanibekov making his fourth space

flight, Savitskaya her second. She now participates in tests of space vehicles and is attached to a design bureau. Volk, a newcomer to space, is a leading test pilot. Dzhanibekov and Savitskaya open the outer hatch at 1855 MT 25 July. Savitskaya, using a bulky 66lb (30kg) welder, then carries out three successive operations: 1) metal plate samples are cut and then welded together; 2) the plates are soldered; 3) a silver coating is sprayed onto an aluminium plate. The cosmonauts change places and the cycle of operations is repeated with other samples. Results look towards "an era of extensive space construction" when large antennae of radio telescopes and solar arrays will be set up for supporting orbital factories and other objects employing large amounts of electricity. Other experiments are concerned with the effects of exposure of materials in outer space, the production of vaccines, electrophoresis, molecular physics, the effects of spaceflight on human eyesight and the cardio-vascular system, and the use of filters for the purification of the cabin atmosphere. A Resonance experiment determined dynamic characteristics of orbital complex Soyuz T-11/Salyut 7/Soyuz T-12. Investigation also made of structure of Earth's atmosphere and distribution of interplanetary matter in outer space. Cosmonauts returned in Soyuz T-12. LC Baikonur. LV A-2. LT 2141 MT. R 1655 MT, some 87 miles (140km) SE of Dzhezkazgan.

The first launch of an Ariane 3.

August 4 Arianespace launches Ariane 3 (V-10) on maiden flight from Kourou, French Guiana; carries two geostationary communications satellites mounted in tandem, ECS-2 for Eutelsat and Telecom 1A for French national telephone/TV network. ECS-2 geostationary above 7°E; Telecom 1A 8°W. Launching of Ariane 3, made without prior test flight, is described as "a

calculated technological risk" at saving of nearly £40 million. LC Kourou, French Guiana. LV Ariane 3 (V-10). LT 1333 GMT.

August 8 Cosmonauts spacewalk from Salyut 7 to make additional repair to propulsion system using a new tool; also remove small section of solar cell so that photovoltaic wafers can be returned to Earth for examination. EVA lasts 3hr 35min.

August 14-28 Soviets launch Progress 23 unmanned freighter which docks with Salyut 7/Soyuz T-11 complex on rear port at 0811 GMT 16 August. It is fifth re-supply operation in support of long-stay cosmonauts. Separates at 1613 GMT 26 August and re-enters atmosphere over Pacific Ocean. LC Baikonur. LV A-2. LT 0628 GMT.

August 16 NASA launches Active Magnetosphere Particle Tracer Explorers (AMPTE) by Delta 3924 rocket from Cape Canaveral, Florida; triple payload studies interaction between solar wind and Earth's magnetic field. Three satellites mounted in tandem are: Charge Composition Explorer AMPTE 2 (US); Sub-satellite AMPTE 3 (UK) and Ion-Release Module AMPTE 1 (W Germany). LC Cape Canaveral. LV Delta 3924. LT 1448 GMT.

August 24 British Aerospace confirms existence of design study for pilotless spaceplane as satellite launcher which breathes air for burning in rocket engines. Code-named HOTOL (meaning

horizontal take-off and landing), the delta-winged craft would propel itself into orbit without dropping off boosters and return under its own power. Assisting the study are Rolls-Royce and Royal Aircraft Establishment.

August 30-September 5 NASA launches Space Shuttle *Discovery* (41-D) on maiden flight with Henry Hartsfield, Jr (Cdr), Cdr Michael Coats (pilot), Lt-Col Richard M. Mullane, Dr Judith Resnik, Dr Steven A. Hawley (mission specialists) and Charles D. Walker (payload specialist). Orbit: 184 miles (296km) x 195 miles (314km) x 28·47°. On 30 August communications satellite Leasat 1 (Syncom 4-2) is released for transfer to geostationary orbit. Mission did not fly Anik communications satellite as originally planned because of unresolved problem with PAM stage (see 3-11 February 1984). Resnik, an electrical engineer, helped test extension and retraction of 103ft (31·4m) solar panel which is part of Office of Aeronautics and Space Technology Pallet (OAST-1). Walker, an employee of McDonnell Douglas Astronautics, monitored apparatus designed to separate biological material for use in new drugs for clinical analysis. On 5 September crew successfully dislodge lumps of ice which had formed on the waste outlet of the Orbiter's toilet using remote manipulator arm. There had been concern that ice might dislodge during re-entry and damage the spacecraft.

The OAST-1 solar array experiment.

Mission was much delayed, first by need to replace one of three main engines with engine taken from sister craft *Challenger*, following static testing early June. This caused postponement from 22-25 June. Launch that day was abandoned within 30 minutes of lift-off because of transistor fault in a back-up computer. This computer was exchanged for one from *Challenger*. Second launch attempt 26 June was aborted four seconds before lift-off when No 3 main engine failed to ignite, causing other two to shut down automatically. Small fire at base of Shuttle was quickly doused by water jets. Problem was faulty valve on the computer signal system that activates the valve. Launch finally delayed for 24 hours on 29 August because of computer indication that separation mechanism of external tank and SRBs might be suspect and then for seven minutes because two private aircraft had strayed into KSC airspace. Satellite payload was revised to avoid delay in launching communications satellites for fare-paying customers: Leasat (on original rosta) plus Telstar 3-C and SBS-D dropped from mission; both employed PAM motors which gave trouble in February 1984. LC KSC. LV STS 41-D. LT 1242 GMT. R 1338 GMT, Runway 17, Edwards AFB, California.

September 12-17 People's Republic of China launches China 16 (SKW-12) into orbit of 106 x 241 miles (171 x 388km) inclined at 67·94° to equator. Descent module recovered five days later. Service module re-enters after 17 days. LC Jiuquan. LV FB-1. LT 0543 GMT.

September 30 Total number of satellites/spacecraft in space, according to NASA Goddard Spaceflight Center, is 1,462. There are 3,942 items of trackable "space junk" including spent rocket stages and payload shrouds. Decayed satellites since October 1957 number 9,944.

October 5-13 NASA launches Space Shuttle *Challenger* (41-G) with Capt Robert L. Crippen (cdr), Cdr John A. McBride (pilot), Dr Sally K. Ride, Dr Kathryn D. Sullivan, Lt Cdr David C. Leestma, Paul D. Scully-Power (mission specialists) and Dr Marc D. Garneau of Canada (payload specialist). Earth Radiation Budget Satellite (ERBS) deployed 5 October. Another primary payload was Shuttle Radar Laboratory (OSTA-3) named after the Office of Space Science and Terrestrial Applications. Designed to obtain radar images of Earth for map-making and interpretation of geological features, it comprised the Shuttle Imaging Radar (SIR-B), Large Format Camera, Measurement of Air Pollution from Satellites (MAPS) and Feature Identification and Location Experiment (FILE) which classifies areas according to water, vegetation, bare ground, snow and clouds. Tests also made of Orbital Reservicing System (ORS) which includes techniques for refuelling Landsat 4 in orbit. Scully-Power was added to crew at late stage to take advantage of 57° orbit which provided opportunity for a trained scientist to observe over three-quarters of Earth's surface. Opportunity was taken, with Large Format Camera, to photograph site of suspected Soviet nuclear accident in winter of 1957-58

located 56°N, 61°E. Several technical problems affecting communications were encountered which delayed planned EVA by Leestma and Sullivan for two days. An antenna did not fold back into place, delaying planned orbit-lowering manoeuvre. Ride used robot arm to fold antenna. On 11 October, Sullivan and Leestma spacewalked in Orbiter's cargo bay for more than three hours to test refuelling technique for restoring spent satellites to useful life. LC KSC. LV STS 41-G. LT 0703 EDT. R 1226 EDT, KSC.

November 8-16 NASA launches Space Shuttle *Discovery* (51-A) on second flight with Capt Frederick H. Hauck (cdr), Cdr David M. Walker (pilot) and Dr Anna L. Fisher, Lt-Cdr Dale A. Gardner and Joseph Allen (mission specialists). Launched geostationary communications satellites Canadian Telsat-H (Anik D2) 9 November and Hughes Syncom 4-3 (Leasat 2) 10 November and retrieved from orbit Palapa B-2 12 November and Westar 6 14 November. Recovery involved ground stations manoeuvring satellites from some 650 miles (1,046km) down to Shuttle orbit of about 225 miles (362km) by firing on-board thrusters. First retrieval entailed bringing *Discovery* within some 35ft (10·7m) of Palapa, enabling Allen wearing manoeuvring backpack (the MMU, manned maneuvering unit) to cross to it. He then inserted a 4ft (1·22m) "stinger" capture device into satellite's apogee rocket nozzle which expanded inside locking him to it. Thrusters in astronaut's backpack then stopped satellite's rotation and nudged man and satellite towards *Discovery*. After experiencing difficulty in attaching Orbiter's remote manipulator arm, method of securing satellite by means of a cradle device was abandoned and Allen and Gardner manhandled 1,200lb (544kg) Palapa into *Discovery's* cargo bay. Second recovery involved similar

Dale Gardner flying back to Discovery having retrieved Westar 6.

procedure, with Gardner flying out to retrieve Westar with Allen assisting. The highly successful 51-A mission also included Radiation Monitor Experiment and Aggregation of Red Blood Cells experiment installed in the mid-deck. LC KSC. LV STS 51-A. LT 0715 EST. R 0700 EST, Runway 15, KSC.

November 10 Arianespace launches second Ariane 3 carrying two geostationary satellites mounted in tandem, GTE Spacenet 2 and ESA's maritime communications satellite Marecs B-2. LC Kourou, French Guiana. LV Ariane 3 (V-11). LT 0114 GMT.

November 13 US Air Force conducts second live firing of anti-satellite (ASAT) missile from F-15 Eagle aircraft over Pacific Ocean. Target is simulated by fixing IR guidance system on a star.

December 3 USAF launches KH-11 manoeuvrable reconnaissance satellite by Titan D from Vandenberg AFB, California. Orbit 155 miles (250km) x 323 miles (520km) x 97°. Returns digital imagery to ground terminals at Ft Belvoir, Virginia, and elsewhere. Planned lifetime 3-4 years. LC Vandenberg AFB. LV Titan D. LT 1830 GMT approx.

December 15 Soviets launch Vega 1 interplanetary spacecraft on dual mission to investigate Venus and Halley's Comet. Equipped by scientists from Bulgaria, Hungary, E Germany, Poland, USSR, Czechoslovakia and W Germany, it will drop off capsule on Venus June 1985, then intercept the comet March 1986. Descent module to investigate atmosphere, cloud layer and surface of Venus; during descent 11·4ft (3·47m) balloon sonde released to study atmospheric circulation and meteorological phenomena. LC Baikonur. LV D-1-e. LT 0916 GMT.

December 19 Soviets launch sub-scale model of Kosmolyot (spaceplane) of blended wing/body design (Cosmos 1614). After completing single orbit, it makes controlled descent to planned recovery area in Black Sea. LC Kapustin Yar. LV C-1. LT 0400 GMT approx.

December 21 Soviets launch Vega 2 interplanetary spacecraft on dual mission to investigate Venus and Halley's Comet (see also 15 December). LC Baikonur. LV D-1-e. LT 0914 GMT.

1985

January 7 Japan launches 300lb (136kg) probe Sakigake (Pioneer) to study conditions in deep space during approach of Halley's Comet. Closest approach of 4·35 million miles (7 million km) achieved 11-13 March 1986. Measured solar wind plasma and interplanetary magnetic fields. LC Tanegashima. LV Mu-3S. LT 1915 GMT.

January 24-27 NASA launches Space Shuttle *Discovery* (51-C) into circular orbit of approximately 186 miles (300km)

A KSC landing for STS-51C Discovery.

x 28.5°; is first dedicated military mission with DoD astronaut Major Gary E. Payton and four NASA astronauts Capt Thomas K. Mattingly, II; Lt-Col Loren J. Shriver; Major Ellison S. Onizuka, and Lt-Col James F. Buchli. Payton (mission specialist) assists deployment of "national security satellite" with Boeing Inertial Upper Stage (IUS). Among details originally withheld are launch time and mission objectives. In fact, satellite was 30,000lb (13,608kg) new-generation Sigint 5 (Aquacade) designed to monitor military and diplomatic communications in USSR and large parts of Europe and Asia, including missile telemetry, radio, radar, telephone and satellite re-transmission. Deployment occurred some 16 hours into mission. First stage IUS burned for 145sec injecting satellite into elliptical transfer orbit; second stage propelled it into geosynchronous orbit, probably about 90°E downlinked to ground station in Western Australia. On 26 January it was announced that *Discovery* had completed its mission and would be landing at KSC the next day. NASA later reported that 13 protective tiles were damaged sufficient to need replacing. Launch was delayed 24 hours because of severe cold at the Cape, which raised concern that ice might form on External Tank. (At least four smaller Sigint satellites had been launched previously by USAF expendable rockets). LC KSC. LV STS 51-C. LT 1450 EST. R 1623 EST, Runway 15, KSC.

January 30-31 Ministers of eleven member-countries of European Space Agency (ESA) attend conference in Rome, and agree to co-operate in the development of the US Space Station project scheduled to become operational 1992, the 500th anniversary of Christopher Columbus's discovery of America. Possible ESA support includes Columbus space module (W Germany/Italy), polar platform (UK), Hermes spaceplane (France), Ariane 5 launcher (France/W Germany). Columbus is based on work already achieved with ESA Spacelab. Polar platform, defined by British Aerospace, would be assembled in space to operate in close proximity to space station or remotely from it for up to two years before being recalled for servicing. Typical applications: Earth observation, space factory in low-gravity, high-vacuum, environment.

February 8 Arianespace launches Arabsat 1 and Brazilsat 1 communications satellites by Ariane 3 from Kourou, French Guiana; both are subsequently positioned in geostationary orbit, Arabsat 1 at 19°E, Brazilsat at 65°W. LC Kourou, French Guiana. LV Ariane 3 (V-12). LT 2322 GMT.

March 1 NASA announces cancellation of Space Shuttle *Challenger* mission 51-E because of problem with TDRS satellite installed in cargo bay. Proposed to merge mission with that of *Discovery* (51-D), eventually flown on 12-19 April. Crew of 51-E were to be Col Karol J. Bobko (commander), Capt Donald E. Williams (pilot), S. David Griggs (flight engineer) Dr Margaret Rhea Seddon and Jeffrey A. Hoffman (mission specialists), Lt-Col Patrick Baudry (France) and US Senator E. J. "Jake" Garn (R-Utah)

(payload specialists). Garn, 52, an experienced jet-fighter pilot, is chairman of Senate appropriations sub-committee which oversees NASA's budget. Principal payloads: second Tracking and Data Relay Satellite and Anik C1 for Telesat of Canada. Baudry was to have monitored French echography experiment. Mission 51-E had already been delayed some weeks because of necessity to replace about 4,200 thermal insulation protective tiles following mission 41-G in October 1984.

April 12-19 NASA launches Space Shuttle *Discovery* (51-D) with Col Karol J. Bobko (cdr); Capt Donald E. Williams (pilot), S. David Griggs (flight engineer), Dr Rhea Seddon and Jeffrey A. Hoffman, mission specialists, Charles W. Walker, McDonnell Douglas payload specialist and Senator E. J. "Jake" Garn. Orbit: 196 x 285 miles (315 x 452km) x 28·52°. Mission lasted six days 23hrs 55min 23sec, following a one orbit delay caused by rain clouds over KSC. Successfully deployed are (12 April) Canada's Telesat-1 (Anik C-1) and (13 April) Hughes Syncom 4-3 (Leasat-3) leased to US Navy. Apogee motor of latter fails to ignite after 45min as planned. Mission is extended two days in unsuccessful attempt to fix inoperable satellite. Hughes engineers concluded that power switch had failed. Leasat is deployed by low-energy "frisbee" action which imparts both stabilizing spin and separation velocity. Centripetal force generated is supposed to pull out a pin which activates satellite's systems and starts

The unsuccessful attempt to activate Leasat's apogee motor.

sequence of events leading to ignition of apogee motor. Pin did not pull out leaving satellite inert. Leasat was not fitted with grapple that would have allowed it to be recaptured and returned to cargo bay. Unplanned EVA repair mission began 16 April. Astronauts improvised "flyswatter" tool from a few centsworth of plastic and tubing. Handle was made of 4ft (1.2m) extendable rod used to reach inaccessible switches in Shuttle cabin. This was sheathed in a hose from a portable vacuum cleaner and a plastic flap (with rectangular holes cut into it) was attached to one end. Astronauts Hoffman and Griggs space-

walked on 16 April to attach makeshift tool to end of manipulator arm but despite several attempts on 17 April to snag the Leasat switch their efforts were in vain (however, Syncom was successfully repaired during mission 51-I in August/September 1985). LC KSC. LV STS 51-D. LT 0859 EST. R 0855 EST, Runway 33, KSC.

April 29-May 6 NASA launches Space Shuttle *Challenger* (51-B) with Spacelab 3 and crew of seven: Col Robert F. Overmyer, (cdr) Lt-Col Frederick D. Gregory (pilot), Dr William E. Thornton, Dr Norman E. Thagard (mission special-

The Finger Lakes area of New York forms a backdrop to Spacelab 3.

ists) and Don L. Lind (physicist); Dr Taylor G. Wang (JPL fluid-mechanics specialist), and Dr Lodewijk van den Berg (EG&G specialist in materials processing) payload specialists. Considered first operational launch of Spacelab after Spacelab 1 check-out mission, 1983. Entered circular orbit of approximately 219 miles (352km) x 57°. Deployed "getaway special" sub-satellite NUSAT, 114lb (52kg), for air traffic control calibration, but GLOMR for DoD failed to leave its canister. LC KSC. STS 51-B. LT 1102 EDT. R 0912 PDT, Runway 17, Edwards AFB, California.

June 6-September 26 Soviets launch Soyuz T-13 with cosmonauts Col Vladimir Dzhanibekov and flight engineer Viktor Savinykh. Docks manually with Salyut 7 on forward port at 1250 MT 8 June using new range-finding device instead of ground-controlled automatic system. Objective: to repair space station which had been unmanned since October 1984 and was no longer responding to signals from mission control. Station was "lifeless" due to battery failure, with water and gas lines frozen. Cosmonauts began by examining antennas, solar batteries and other on-board systems and equipment. Over period of days they restored battery power and gradually restored the station to life. After repairs, cosmonauts participated with seven

Savinykh (left) and Dzhanibekov.

Intercosmos member-countries in major experiment, "Kursk-85", which tested new methods of forecasting crop yield. LC Baikonur. LV A-2. LT 1040 MT. R 1352 MT, 124 miles (200km) NE of Dzhezkazgan.

June 11 Soviet Vega-1 spacecraft en-route to rendezvous with Halley's Comet in March 1986 passes Venus after separating landing module two days earlier. After entering Venerian atmosphere releases 11·8ft (3·6m) diameter helium weather balloon which circulates around planet at some 33·5 miles (54km) altitude. Radio signals from balloon are received at JPL, California, who are co-operating in international venture. Soft-landing of descent capsule confirmed at 7° 11'N lattitude, 177° 48' longitude. Capsule made an hour-long descent measuring temperature, pressure and water content of clouds; also studied absorption and diffusion of light and gas composition of atmosphere. TV cameras not embodied because landing was made on night side of planet. Network of Soviet and international radio-telescopes in Europe, Asia, Australia, Africa and North and South America received balloon's signals (time interval in reception from probes nearly six minutes). Findings included: clouds around Venus were moving at 197-230ft/sec; balloon was blown 984ft (300m) up and down in atmosphere. Surface temperature 452°C (846°F); pressure 86 atmospheres. Experiment repeated 22 June with Vega-2. Both balloons drifted for approximately 46hr at average of 34mph (55km/hr) travelling some 7,450 miles (12,000km).

June 17-24 NASA launches Space Shuttle *Discovery* (51-G) with Cdr Daniel C. Brandenstein (cdr), Cdr John O. Creighton (pilot) and mission specialists Dr Shannon W. Lucid, Lt-Col Steven R. Nagel and Col John M. Fabian, and payload specialists Lt-Col Patrick Baudry (France) and Prince Sultan Salman Abdelazize Al-Saud (Saudi Arabia). Orbit is 219 miles (352km) x 28·5°. Successfully deployed 17 June are Mexican satellite Morelos-1A, geostationary above 113·5°W; 18 June Saudi-Arabian Arabsat-1A, geostationary above 26°E and 19 June AT&T Telstar 3-D, geostationary above 62°W. Also deployed and recovered by remote manipulator arm, day 4 and day 6 respectively, Spartan which uses X-ray sensors to search for hot gas clouds in galaxy clusters and carry out a survey of X-ray sources in local galaxy (examine possible Black Hole in galactic centre). Maximum separation distance from *Discovery* 99 miles (160km). On 21 June experiment was made to bounce ground-based low-energy laser beam from 8in (20·3cm), retro-reflector mounted in window of Orbiter's mid-deck side hatch. Beam was projected from USAF base 9,000ft (2,953m) up on Mt. Haleakala on the Hawaiian island of Maui to discover if ground computers could adjust beam to counteract distorting effect of Earth's atmosphere; also to test ability of Laser Beam Director accurately to track an object in low Earth orbit. Beam, originally pencil thin, was estimated to be about 30ft (9·14m) wide when it hit the Orbiter which was moving at 17,400mph (28,000km/h) some 220 miles (354km) overhead. LC KSC. LV STS 51-G. LT 0733 EDT. R 0612 PDT, Runway 23, Edwards AFB, California.

June 21-July 15 Soviets launch Progress 24 freighter which docks with Salyut 7 on rear port at 0234 GMT on 23 June. Re-supply mission followed repair and servicing of space station by on-board cosmonauts Dzanibekov and Savinykh, rendezvous and docking being controlled by Flight Control Centre and the cosmonauts themselves. The freighter brought propellants, food, air, water and research materials and mail. This enabled crew of Salyut 7 to restore vital systems, including replacement of three storage batteries. Progress 24 undocked at 1228 GMT on 15 July and was made to re-enter atmosphere over Pacific. LC Baikonur. LV A-2. LT 0040 GMT.

July 2 ESA launches Giotto space probe at 1123 GMT by Ariane 1 (V-14) from Kourou, French Guiana to intercept Halley's Comet on 13-14 March 1986. Launch mass 2,116lb (960kg) reducing to 1,129lb (512kg) after propellant depletion.

July 19 NASA selects first private citizen to go into space aboard Space Shuttle: Mrs Christa McAuliffe, teacher, of Concord, New Hampshire, mother of two children. Scheduled to fly on a six-day mission (see January 28 1986).

July 16-August 30 Soviets launch Cosmos 1669 freighter in test flight of new Soyuz/Progress type vehicle with solar arrays. Docks automatically with Salyut 7/Soyuz T-13 complex at 1905 MT 18 July. Undocked 29 August and re-entered atmosphere next day. LC Baikonur. LV A-2. LT 1705 MT.

July 29-August 6 NASA launches Space Shuttle *Challenger* (51-F) with Spacelab 2 two-pallet train plus single pallet and "Igloo". Astronauts are Col Charles Gordon Fullerton (cdr); Lt-Col Roy D. Bridges, Jr (pilot); Dr Story Musgrave (payload specialist; also 3rd pilot); Dr Karl G. Henize (astronomer), Dr Anthony W. England (geophysicist), Dr Loren W. Acton (payload specialist, Lockheed Palo Alto Research Lab), and Dr John-David Bartoe (payload specialist, NRL). Launch resulted in first major in-flight Shuttle emergency when sensor action shut down one of Orbiter's main engines some six minutes into launch sequence, causing an "abort to orbit" situation. Craft achieved orbit of 196 miles (315km) x 49·48° – some 41·5 miles (67km) lower than planned. Necessitated jettisoning about 4,400lb (1,996kg) of OMS propellants and use of additional OCS propellant. The fail-safe procedure was entirely successful and, in fact, mission was extended one day to allow increased observation time. A sub-satellite, Plasma Diagnostic Package (PDP), was deployed alongside *Challenger* on 1 August to detect effects on movement through natural plasma; also to measure electron emissions from Spacelab experiments. Was successfully recovered by manipulator arm 2 August; further experiments were performed with PDP still attached to arm. Mission validated pallet-only configuration of Spacelab which embodied 13 experiments in seven scientific disciplines: solar, atmospheric, plasma physics, IR astronomy, technology research, life sciences. After overcoming early problems in working pallet-mounted ESA/Dornier instrument pointing system (IPS), good data was obtained by associated instruments. "Igloo", pressurized automatic supply module, housed computers, data-handling equipment, etc. Previous launch attempt on 12 July was aborted because hydrogen chamber coolant valve on main engine no. 2 failed to close. LC KSC. LV STS 51-F. LT 1700 EDT. R 1245 PDT, Runway 23, Edwards AFB, California.

The Spacelab 2 experiments including the Dornier IPS (centre).

August 2 Cosmonauts Vladimir Dzhanibekov and Viktor Savinykh emerge from Salyut 7 airlock at 1115 MT to attach additional solar panels, delivered by Progress 24, to third solar array; now all three solar arrays have additional panels. EVA lasts total of 5hr.

August 16 Japan launches space probe Suisei (Planet A) by Mu-3S from Kagoshima for fly-by of Halley's comet. Spin-stabilized at 5rpm, 311lb (141kg) probe has low-thrust gas jets for minor course corrections; passed within 124,270 miles (200,000km) of the comet 8 March 1986. LC Kagoshima. LV Mu-3S. LT 2330 GMT approx.

August 27-September 3 NASA launches Space Shuttle *Discovery* (51-I) with astronauts Col Joe H. Engle (cdr), Lt-Col Richard O. Covey (pilot), Dr James D. A. van Hoften, John M. Lounge and Dr William F. Fisher (mission specialists). Deploys three communications satellites: Australia's Aussat 1, American Satellite Company's ASC-1 and Hughes Communications Services Leasat 4 (Syncom 4-4). Then, astronauts rendezvous with failed Leasat 3 and achieve capture by remote manipulator arm. Repair is effected during EVA by Hoften and Fisher and satellite is redeployed. When originally deployed during 51-D mission, 13 April 1985, satellite's automatic sequencer failed to initiate antenna deployment, spin-up and ignition of perigee kick motor. Orbits: 218 x 236 miles (351 x 380km) x 28·55° for satellite deployments; then manoeuvred to 195 x 279 miles (314 x 449km) x 28·53° for Leasat 3 retrieval. Leasat 3 geostationary above 175°W following boost motor firing 27 October. Conducted in *Discovery's* mid-deck was Physical Vapour Transport of Organic Solids (PVTOS) experiment for 3M Corporation. Mission duration: 170hr 18min 29sec. Mission was originally scheduled for 24 August but was postponed because of thunderheads over Cape Canaveral, and again on 25 August when back-up computer was "out of sync" with four primary computers. LV KSC. LV STS 51-I. LT 0658 EDT. R 0615 PDT, Runway 23, Edwards AFB, California.

August 28 Titan 34 carrying Lockheed KH-11 military reconnaissance satellite goes off course and is destroyed by range safety officer. Turbo-pump failure and "massive oxidiser leak" in Titan core resulted in premature shutdown after solid-propellant boosters had burned out. Estimated cost of satellite $150 m. KH-11 satellites are designed to return digital imagery to antennas at Ft Belvoir, Virginia and elsewhere.

September United States SDI test succeeds in directing ground-based low-power (4W) visible laser at missile target. Test is conducted from Air Force Maui Optical Site, Mt Heeakala, Hawaii, tracking a two-stage Terrier-Malemute launched from Pacific Missile Test Range, Kauai. Claimed to be first time that a laser beam, adjusted for atmospheric distortion, has been projected from the ground.

The ground-based laser (right) used to track a Terrier-Malemute target.

The lethal effect of the MIRACL laser on a Titan 1 second stage.

September 6 At White Sands, NM, Titan 1 second stage test vehicle, pressurized and loaded to simulate flight conditions of operational Soviet ICBM, explodes into fragments when hit "for several seconds" by US Navy mid-IR advanced chemical laser (MIRACL).

September 11 International Cometary Explorer (ICE) flies safely through tail of comet Giacobini-Zinner about 6,214 miles (10,000km) behind nucleus. Observed clear signatures of the interaction of comet with the solar wind within 18·6 million miles (30 million km) on sunward side of comet at end of March 1986. Before being re-directed, ICE was International Sun-Earth Explorer (ISEE-3)

launched from Cape Canaveral in August 1974 to study solar wind from "halo orbit" about libration point one million miles (1·6m km) sunward from Earth where gravitational fields of Sun, Earth and Moon are in balance.

September 12 Ariane rocket is destroyed by range safety officer within 10 minutes of launch, resulting in loss of two communications satellites, GTE's Spacenet 3 and Europe's ECS-3 valued at about $150M. Cryogenic third stage ignited late, due either to faulty ignition system or propellant supply failure (a leak in the LO_2 hydrogen injector valve?). Engine shut down automatically when proper ignition conditions were not met.

September 13 USAF launches ASAT from F-15 interceptor at 35,000-40,000ft

An ASAT test vehicle streaks skyward after launch from an F-15.

(10,668-12,192m) over Vandenberg AFB, California. Target is DARPA test program satellite P78-1 orbiting some 345 miles (556km) out in space. Hit confirmed at 1632 EDT by telemetry from target satellite and Spacetrack network (P78-1, which was still returning scientific data at time of attack, contained gamma-ray spectrometer).

September 17-November 21 Soviets launch Soyuz T-14 with cosmonauts Lt-Col Vladimir Vasyutin (cdr), Georgi Grechko (flight engineer) and Aleksandr Volkov (researcher). Docks with aft port of Salyut 7 space station complex at 1414 GMT 18 September; orbit 210 x 219 miles (338 x 353km) x 51·63°. Grechko returned with Vladimir Dzhanibekov on 26 September 1985. LC Baikonur. LV A-2. LT 1239 GMT. R 1031 GMT, 111 miles (180km) SE of Dzhezkazgan.

September 27 Soviets launch Cosmos 1686 Star Module which docks with Salyut 7/Soyuz T-14 space station complex on forward port at 1016 GMT on 2 October. Was further test for assembling "orbital complexes of large size and mass". Cosmos 1686 also delivered miscellaneous freight items. Similar to Cosmos 1267 and 1443. LC Baikonur. LV D-1-e. LT 0841 GMT.

October JPL scientists reviewing findings of Mariner and Viking spacecraft conclude that early history of Mars was shaped by ice, snow, flowing rivers and vast lakes. Today, however, surface water is frozen because thin Martian atmosphere (95 per cent carbon dioxide) cannot effectively trap solar heat. Thin mantle of dry ice covers polar regions with underlying layers of water ice. Some evidence of water ice in places above 30 deg latitude, with evidence of "terrain softening" in regions of impact craters, indicating possibility of liquid water perhaps 0·6 miles (1km) down, subject to thermal heating.

The ELA 2 launch pad at Kourou.

October Second launch pad, ELA 2, is completed at Kourou Space Centre, French Guiana. Consecutive use of two pads allows Ariane 3/4 launch rate to rise to 10 per year. Construction has already started on third launch pad for Ariane 5.

October 3-7 NASA launches Space Shuttle *Atlantis* (51-J) on maiden flight with astronauts Col Karol J. Bobko (cdr); Lt-Col Ronald J. Grabe (pilot), Major David C. Hilmers and Col Robert L. Stewart (mission specialists) and Major William D. Pailes (payload specialist). Was dedicated DoD mision achieving orbit of 296 x 320 miles (476 x 515km), a new Shuttle altitude record. Launched by single IUS booster two geosynchronous satellites DSCS Phase 3. Mid-deck experiment studied damage to biological materials from high energy cosmic rays. LC KSC. LV STS 51-J. LT 1115 EDT. R 1000 PDT, Runway 23, Edwards AFB, California.

October 21-26 Chinese People's Republic launches China 17 (SKW-13) for Earth observation into orbit of 106 x 244 miles (171 x 393km) x 62·98°. Ejects capsule for recovery after five days. Satellite body re-enters after 17 days. LC Jiuquan. LV CZ-2 (Long March 2). LT 0504 GMT approx.

October 24 Austria and Norway are accepted by council of ESA into full membership; brings membership to 13.

October 25 Soviets launch Cosmos 1700 (Lutch) tracking and data relay satellite as part of triple satellite system in support of Mir space station. However, satellite drifts out of position over Indian Ocean. Was to be geosynchronous above 95°E. LC Baikonur. LV D-1-e. LT 1545 GMT approx.

October 30-November 6 NASA launches Spacelab D-1 aboard Space Shuttle *Challenger* on mission 61-A. Astronauts are Col Henry W. Hartsfield, Jr (cdr), Lt-Col Steven R. Nagel (pilot), Col James F. Buchli, Dr Bonnie J. Dunbar, Col Guion S. Bluford, Jr, Dr Reinhard Furrer (W Germany); Dr Ernst Messerschmid (W Germany) and Dr Wubbo Ockels (Netherlands). Spacelab experiments – primarily materials, life sciences, communications and navigation – are managed by W Germany and controlled from German Operations Control Centre, Oberpfaffenhofen, near Munich. Biorack experiments provided striking evidence of effects of microgravity on bacteria, unicellular organisms, white blood cells and insect development. Vestibular sled comprised a seat for a test subject that could be moved backward and forward with precisely adjusted accelerations along rails fixed to floor of Spacelab's aisle. Mission also launched 150lb (68kg) GLOMR message relay satellite which failed to deploy during Spacelab 3 mission (see April 29-May 6 1985). Was 22nd Shuttle mission; carried largest Shuttle crew; mission duration 168hr 44min 51sec. Orbit: 200 x 207 miles (322 x 333km) x 57°. LC KSC. LV STS 61-A. LT 1200 EST. R 0944 PST. Runway 17, Edwards AFB, California.

Sherwood Spring checks the assembly of the ACCESS tower from his perch on the end of the RMS arm.

November 26-December 3 NASA launches Space Shuttle *Atlantis* (STS 61-B) with astronauts Lt-Col Brewster H. Shaw, Jr (cdr), Lt-Col Bryan D. O'Connor (pilot), Mary L. Cleave (mission specialist), Lt-Col Sherwood C. Spring, Major Jerry L. Ross, Rudolfo Neri Vela (Mexico) and Charles D. Walker (McDonnell-Douglas payload specialist making his third space flight). Orbit is 219 miles (352km) x 28·46°. Successfully deployed are: 26 November, Mexican satellite

Morelos 2; 27 November, Australian satellite Aussat 2 and 28 November RCA Satcom K-2 with PAM D2 perigee boost stage. On-board experiments include: McDonnell-Douglas biological processing of erythropoietin (a red blood cell stimulant); 3M Corp commercial materials processing (development of materials for advanced light-powered communications and data handling); Alabama/Birmingham protein crystal growth. Spring and Ross, during two EVAs lasting more than 11hr, erected and dismantled 44·3ft (13·5m) tower (ACCESS) and 11·8ft (3·6m) pyramid (EASE). Mary Cleave, from *Atlantis'* mid-deck, controlled manipulator arm on which astronauts worked. LC KSC. LV STS 61-B. LT 1929 EST. R 1333 PST, Runway 22, Edwards AFB, California.

December Soviet Union establishes civilian space agency, Glavkosmos, to manage space science, space applications and co-operative international space programmes.

December 13 USAF launches two 6·5ft (1·98m) instrumented inflatable balloon satellites in cylindrical container (USA 13/USA 14) as future targets for ASAT missiles launched from F-15 interceptor. Balloons have louvres which can be adjusted to vary IR images; they also carry instruments to measure test results. Orbits range between 194 x 481 miles (313 x 774km) x 37·07°. LC Wallops Island, Virginia. LV Scout AF-16. LT 0055 GMT approx.

December 28 Pioneer 12 Venus Orbiter begins observations of Halley's Comet. Passes within 25 million miles (40 million km) of comet on 4 February 1986 (five days before comet's closest approach to the Sun). Pioneer's UV spectrometer observed comet's gas composition and water vaporisation rate. Particle field sensors observed solar wind.

1986

January 12-18 NASA launches Space Shuttle *Columbia* (61-C) with astronauts Cdr Robert L. Gibson (cdr), Col Charles F. Bolden, Jr (pilot), George D. Nelson (mission specialist), Steven A. Hawley, Franklin R. Chang-Diaz, Robert Cenker (RCA payload specialist) and Bill Nelson (Congressional flight observer). Communications satellite RCA Satcom K1 is deployed with PAM-D2; subsequently positioned in geostationary orbit above 85°W longitude. Astronauts conducted materials science experiments, tested SDI-related surveillance equipment and its ability to obtain atmospheric signature of USAF aircraft. Bill Nelson assisted protein crystal growth experiment sponsored by Alabama-Birmingham; obtained photographic documentation of crystal growth. Three days of bad weather at KSC resulted in mission terminating at Edwards AFB. LC KSC. LV STS 61-C. LT 0655 EST. R 0559 PST, Runway 22, Edwards AFB, California.

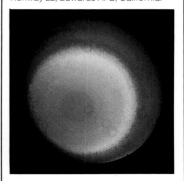

A Voyager 2 false colour image of the polar regions of Uranus.

January 24 Voyager 2 passes within 66,500 miles (107,00km) of Uranus. The fly-by also features encounters with moons Miranda, Umbriel, Ariel, Titania, Oberon and the planet's ring system. Discovered 14 new moons by mid-January, including one of about 50 miles (80km) diameter midway between Miranda and outer rim of Uranus' ring system which orbits planet every 18hr 17min 9sec. Following thrust manoeuvre on 14 February, spacecraft is re-directed towards Neptune for 24 August 1989 encounter.

January 28 Space Shuttle *Challenger* (51-L) is destroyed in mid-air explosion 73 seconds after lifting off from KSC with total loss of crew, Francis R. Scobee (cdr), Cdr Michael Smith (pilot), Dr Judith Resnik, Lt-Col Ellison Onizuka and Dr Ronald McNair (mission specialists), Gregory Jarvis (Hughes payload specialist) and Christa McAuliffe (teacher observer). Primary objective had been to deploy TDRS-B in geostationary orbit for high capacity communications and data links between Earth, Shuttle and other spacecraft and launch vehicles in conjunction with previously-launched TDRS-1. TDRS-B was scheduled for Pacific station above 171°W longitude.

A telltale puff of smoke escapes from Challenger's defective right-hand SRB just seconds after launch.

Was first Space Shuttle launch from newly-activated Pad 39B, and 25th Shuttle mission, *Challenger's* tenth. Launch photographs revealed plume of flame coming from right hand SRB impinging on attachment structure. Jerrol W. Littles, assistant director of engineering Marshall SFC (7 March) gave the probable cause: 1) Damage to primary and secondary O-rings caused by out-of-round segment when boosters were stacked. 2) Blowby or leakage of primary O-ring 3) Putty sealant (asbestos-filled zinc chromate) that keeps pressure off primary O-ring. The question remained if sub-zero temperature at the Cape before 28 January had affected RH booster O-ring used to seal the aft booster segment. Recovered section of SRB had a 1·96ft (0·6m) x 0·98ft (0·3m) hole where hot exhaust gases had burned through destroying the base attachment of the SRB and allowing it to

pivot into the External Tank. (A subsequent report suggested that the aft attachment might have failed because of a combination of abnormal side gust loads). Crew compartment, with astronaut remains, was recovered from a depth of some 85ft (26m) 16·8 miles (27km) NE of KSC. It had fallen practically intact from 72,200ft (22,000m) and broke up on impact with the water. Launch, originally scheduled 20 January, was delayed because of hydrogen leak during flight readiness firing 18 December 1985. LC KSC. LV STS 51-L. LT 1138 EDT.

February 1 People's Republic of China launches China 18 (STW-2) for domestic communications for positioning in geostationary orbit above 103°E longitude. STW-1, launched 8 April 1984, located 125°E. LC Xi Chang. LV Long March 3. LT 1240 GMT approx.

February 12 Soviet scientists reported to be finalizing "Atlas of Venus" from radar and optical probing carried out by

orbiting stations Venera 15 and Venera 16 between October 1983 and July 1984. Surface of Venus resembles that of Earth with mountain ranges and valleys, volcanic peaks and craters; there are signs of tectonic activity. Highest mountain stands 7·1 miles (11·5km).

February 19 Soviets launch core of permanent space station Mir (Peace) into staging orbit of 107 x 187 miles (172 x 301km) x 51·62°; subsequently raised by on-board propulsion to 201 x 211 miles (324 x 340km). Developed from Salyut, the overall length is about 42·6ft (13m); maximum diameter 13·6ft (4·15m); mass about 21 tonnes. At forward end a spherical docking unit will accept four laboratory modules on laterally disposed docking ports; fifth and sixth ports are located on the axis front and rear. The rear port is surrounded by the ODU engine compartment. A "lab" module to be attached radially will first dock on the forward axial port, then be transferred by manipulator arm to its final position. Inside the station much of the scientific equipment found in Salyut has been removed to the "lab" modules which arrive separately. Cosmonauts now have their own compartments with table, chair and intercom. Life-support and air-conditioning systems are improved and water is reclaimed from the atmosphere. After orbital adjustments, on 16 March, orbit is 206 x 220 miles (332 x 354km) x 51·6°; period 91·2min. Mir is officially described (*Pravda*) as "a test site for practising in-flight assembly and maintenance of large structures of different shapes... utilising new structural materials and fundamentally new approaches to durability estimates and design methods, and the use of multi-functional space robots". New training programmes have been prepared for future orbital stations – "continually growing and developing multi-functional complexes". It may be supposed, says Vladimir Shatalov, that crews will later be increased to six and even 12. LC Baikonur. LV D-1. LT 2119 GMT.

February 22 Ariane launches dual payload: French SPOT-1 Earth resources satellite and Swedish Viking scientific satellite. SPOT achieves Sun-synchronous orbit of 512 x 515 miles (824 x 829km) x 98·74°. Mass including propellant is 4,035lb (1,830kg). Obtains Earth resources multispectral images of high quality including many showing features of military interest, e.g. Sary Shagan test site for Soviet ABM, ASAT and strategic laser weapons. Viking is designed for electrical, magnetic and UV studies of auroral regions. Satellite operations carried out in real time from Esrange, Kiruna, northern Sweden. LC Kourou, French Guiana. LV Ariane 1 (V-16). LT 0145 GMT.

March National Commission on Space, tasked by President Reagan to formulate space policy for next 50 years, recommends establishment of permanent base on Moon by 2017 and base on Mars by 2027. Total estimated cost $7,000,000 million.

March 6 Soviet comet probe Vega 1 flies within 5,520 miles (8,889km) of Halley's Comet.

March 9 Soviet comet probe Vega 2 flies within 4,990 miles (8,030km) of Halley's Comet. Observations from Vega 1/2 suggest to Professor Yuri Makogon that heads of comets are made of gas hydrates in which methane and water are combined in a ratio of 200 to 1. Measurements made during comet fly-by suggest nucleus comprises a hydrate of carbon dioxide and water in the ratio of 300 to 1 by volume mixed with mineral dust and metals.

March 13/14 ESA's Giotto comet probe flies within 335 miles (540km) of nucleus of Halley's Comet. Discovers that nucleus is potato shaped about 9 miles (14·5km) long by 5 miles (8·05km) wide. Surface is uneven with valleys, hills and what appear to be impact craters. Maximum brightness is observed to be closest to the Sun; two bright dust jets spring from sunward side which pour tons of dust particles per second deep into space. Most of the activity of nucleus seems to come from only a few sources; the remainder of the surface appears to be sealed beneath a black crust. From launch 2 July 1985, Giotto travelled some 435 million miles (700 million km) to intercept the comet at a distance from Earth of 93 million miles (149·6 million km). Will arrive back in Earth's vicinity 1990, when it may be given another scientific task.

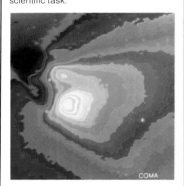

Giotto's multicolour camera reveals the dynamic nature of Halley's comet as it approaches its rendezvous.

March 13-July 16 Soviets launch Soyuz T-15 with cosmonauts Col Leonid Kizim and Vladimir Solovyov; docks with Mir core module on forward port 1638 MT 15 March. On 5 May, cosmonauts undocked and transferred to unmanned Salyut 7/Cosmos 1686 complex entering that station on 6 May. On 12 May Kizim and Solovyov checked the orientation system and replaced an instrument in the engine control loop. On 13 May they carried out a full check of electrical circuits. After performing other essential maintenance tasks, they were able to resume visual observations of Earth's surface seven days later. On 28 May, the cosmonauts spacewalked from the Salyut 7/Cosmos 1686/Soyuz T-15 complex, taking out segments of a 49·2ft (15m) truss from a cylinder and joining sections together by "automatic devices". The whole structure was then secured to a platform. On 31 May Kizim and Solovyov make their eighth spacewalk opening the hatch at 0857 MT. As before they unfolded a lattice and pin frame and with its help built a 36·5ft (12m) tower resembling an oil derrick; mounted on a platform atop the structure were the "Fon" wide-band instrument to measure atmospheric density and a seismic unit to monitor vibrations in the framework. The data obtained helped to forecast the behaviour of large structures and estimate their strength. For the first time an optical communications system, employing a low-power laser, relayed data to a ground station from the outside. Next the cosmonauts employed a portable beam-welder to weld lattice and pin frames. Altogether, in eight EVAs, Kizim and Solovyov worked on the outside of the station for 31hr 40min. In total they spent 50 days aboard Salyut 7/Cosmos 1686, leaving at 1858 MT on 25 June, and re-docking with Mir at 2346 MT the following day. On 2 July Kizim broke human space endurance record, having accumulated 362 days during three missions. LC Baikonur. LV A-2. LT 1533 MT. R 1634 MT, NE of Arkalyk.

Leonid Kizim chases an elusive film canister during his Soyuz T-15 visit to the Mir space station.

March 19-April 21 Soviets launch Progress 25 freighter which docks with Mir/Soyuz T-15 space station complex on aft port at 1416 MT 21 March with propellants, air, food, water and other expendables. On 25 March Progress 25 engine is fired to adjust orbit of station complex; other thrust corrections follow. Separates at 2324 MT 20 April and is made to re-enter atmosphere. LC Baikonur. LV A-2. LT 1308 MT.

March 28 Ariane 3 launches dual communications satellite payload, G-Star 2 and Brazilsat S2. US satellite G-Star 2 is subsequently positioned in geostationary orbit above 105°N longitude. Brazilsat S2 is positioned in geostationary orbit above 70°N longitude.

The payload fairing about to be closed around G-Star 2 and Brazilsat.

LC Kourou, French Guiana (first use of ELA-2 pad). LV Ariane 3 (V-17). LT 2330 GMT.

April Japanese space agency NASDA, in 1986-87 budget, includes funds for study of unmanned spaceplane Himes. The highly manoeuvrable vehicle 42·6ft (13m) long, weighs about 14 tonnes; propellants are LO_2/LH_2. Objective: to carry sounding-rocket size payloads on sub-orbital trajectories but for periods longer than a conventional sounding-rocket. Also receiving financial support are plans to build two free-flying platforms, one for use in conjunction with NASA Space Shuttle and the other with US International Space Station.

April 7 NASA initiates Shuttle Crew Egress and Escape Review to be completed December 1986. Considers emergency escape possibilities for pad abort, bale out, ejection systems, water landings and powered flight separation.

April 12 On 25th anniversary of world's first manned venture into Earth orbit (Yuri Gagarin, Vostok 1), *Izvestia* reveals identity of eight previously unknown cosmonauts in group of 20 chosen in 1960. Includes Valentin Bondarenko, killed in a spacecraft fire during a ground test 23 March 1961 only 20 days before Gagarin's epic space flight.

April 18 Titan 34-D rocket carrying Lockheed Big Bird photo-reconnaissance satellite explodes some 800ft (244m) above Vandenberg AFB launch pad after 9sec of flight. Fault in a solid propellant booster activated vehicle's self-destruct system. Believed that flaw in insulation and its bonding to rocket motor casing resulted in "burn-through".

April 23-June 23 Soviets launch Progress 26 freighter which docks with Mir-Soyuz T-15 complex on rear port at 0126 MT 27 April. Delivers propellant, water, food and "assorted cargo". Undocks 2225 MT 22 June and is made to re-enter atmosphere next day. LC Baikonur. LV A-2. LT 2340 MT.

April 25 Fourth anniversary of launch of astrophysics station Astron into high elliptical orbit, with joint experiments by USSR, E Germany, France and Italy. Using UV and X-ray telescopes, Astron found an unusually high content of superheavy elements in the atmospheres of certain stars; also, a new type of star flare and peculiarities of UV radiation of certain galaxies.

May 3 Delta 178 rocket carrying Geostationary Environmental Satellite (GOES-G) is destroyed by range safety officer after 91sec of flight. Main stage engine suffered abrupt shutdown at about 71sec, causing vehicle to tumble uncontrollably. Believed that wire insulation in electrical system of Delta's main engine damaged by in-flight vibra-

tions, causing two electrical surges when led to engine shutdown. Satellite value: $57·5 million. LC Cape Canaveral Air Force Station, complex 17-A. LV Delta 178.

May 21-30 Soviets launch Soyuz TM spacecraft, unmanned, into preliminary orbit of 124 x 149 miles (200 x 240km) x 51·6°. Docks with unmanned Mir/Progress 26 complex on forward port at 1412 MT 23 May. Developed from Soyuz T, craft has new systems: approach and docking; radio communications; emergency rescue; new combined propulsion unit and a new lighter and stronger recovery parachute. Mutual search, rendezvous and docking were carried out with aid of onboard automatic systems of both space vehicles. Instead of the previous "Igla" (Needle) system, it involves new system "Kurs" (Course) in which only TM ship manoeuvres for docking and Mir expends zero propellant. New communications system allows communications with Earth via the Luch geostationary relay satellite. Before separating at 1323 MT 29 May, Soyuz TM used its combined propulsion unit to adjust orbit of Mir complex. LC Baikonur. LV A-2. LT 1222 MT. R 1049 MT, "designated area of Soviet territory".

May 31 Ariane launches Intelsat 5A (F14) but rocket's third stage HM-7 LO_2/LH_2 engine suffers ignition failure; rocket and satellite are destroyed by range safety officer. Rectification involved detailed study of ignition conditions, redefinition and qualification of more powerful third stage igniter. Testing of cryogenic engine with modified igniter began 4 August 1986. LC Kourou, French Guiana (ELA-1 pad). LV Ariane (V18). LT 0053 GMT.

June 19 Dr James C. Fletcher, NASA Administrator, cancels Shuttle-Centaur programme for reasons of safety.

July France confirms existence of Helios military reconnaissance satellite programme based on Spot technology (which supersedes Samro project shelved in 1982). Objective: to launch four satellites for operation in 497 x 559 miles (800 x 900km) Sun-synchronous orbit. Payload includes optical and IR sensors; electronic intelligence, radar and advanced communications systems. Optical ground resolution less than 3·28ft (1·0m). Estimated cost of satellites, ground terminals and rapid-processing facilities $550-700 million. First launch scheduled 1992.

July ESA responds to Arianespace request to up-rate design of Ariane 5 launcher to include capability of putting 5·2 tonnes into geostationary transfer orbit. New design also conforms to a CNES requirement to build extra safety provisions into Hermes spaceplane, increasing launch mass from 17 to 20 tonnes. Modifications to Hermes include: provision of second orbit manoeuvring engine; launch escape system of four solid propellant rockets mounted externally between second stage and spaceplane and, possibly, a crew compartment escape pod.

July W Germany considers design of two-stage re-usable spaceplane, Sänger 2, as competitor to BAe-Rolls-Rolls

HOTOL project. Stage 1 is conceived as winged ramjet carrying a rocket-plane which separates at Mach 6 velocity 18 miles (30km) above the Earth. Like HOTOL it takes off horizontally and payloads are placed in low-Earth orbit for about one-fifth cost of NASA Space Shuttle. Spaceplane, designed by MBB, is named after German rocket pioneer Dr Eugen Sänger who designed rocket-powered "antipodal bomber" 1938-42.

July 30 Cosmos 1767 launched by "new type of rocket" (according to DoD) fails to achieve useful orbit; decays from orbit 15 August 1986. Orbit actually achieved: 123 x 140 miles (198 x 226km) x 64·9°. LC Baikonur. LV MLLV. LT 0830 GMT approx.

July 31 French national space agency, CNES, picks Jean-Loup Chrétien to make a joint flight with Soviet colleagues to the Soviet Mir space station in 1988. Lt-Col Michel Tognini is appointed back-up cosmonaut. "We are planning to conduct medical experiments... The

Jean-Loup Chrétien (left) and Michel Tognini, the French prime and back-up candidates for a flight to Mir.

research is essential for further work in France under the Hermes programme to develop a re-usable spaceplane", said Chrétien.

August Prime Minister Jacques Chirac confirms go-ahead for French TDF 4-channel direct-broadcasting satellite programme. Total programme cost FFr 3,500 million. First of two satellites, TDF-1, to be launched by Ariane 1988; TDF-2 1989.

August Cockpit voice recording released by NASA reveals that *Challenger* astronauts were unaware of impending disaster until pilot Michael Smith's last words, "uh oh!" at the moment of the explosion at about 47,900ft (14,600m) altitude 73sec after launch. After crew compartment was torn away from Orbiter by aerodynamic forces, subjecting occupants to 12-20g for brief periods, it

depressurised and crew members were probably conscious for between 6-12sec. Severed crew compartment, travelling at almost 2,953ft/sec (900m/sec), climbed on to altitude of 63,320ft (19,300m) before falling back towards Atlantic Ocean. It impacted the water at some 207mph (334km/h).

August USAF launches fourth ASAT from F-15 interceptor using a hypothetical target by fixing IR guidance system on a star. Earlier the US Senate had adopted an amendment to the defense budget, banning ASAT tests against actual targets although two such targets were already in orbit.

August President Reagan announces that a Space Shuttle replacing *Challenger* will be built at a cost of some $3,000 million. Will enable NASA to establish International Space Station in 1994 but will involve paring down other NASA projects.

August 12 Japan launches Ajisai (EGS) for geodetic studies into orbit of 919 x 930 miles (1,479 x 1497km) x 50·01°. Satellite is 7ft (2·15m) sphere covered with mirrors and retro-reflectors, mass 1,510lb (685kg). Secondary payload is Fuji (JAS-1), an amateur radio relay satellite placed in a similar orbit. Was first successful Western launch since *Challenger* disaster. Launcher was H-I with only first two stages live in test of Japan's new LE-5 cryogenic second

The Ajisai satellite which is used to improve geodetic surveys.

stage engine which tested operation in orbit of flywheel with a magnetic bearing. LC Tanegashima. LV H-I (two stage version). LT 0845 GMT approx.

August 22 Salyut 7/Cosmos 1686 orbital complex is boosted into a higher orbit using propulsion systems of both vehicles. Modified orbit is 294 x 306 miles (474 x 492km) x 51·6°; period of revolution 94min.

September 1 *Novosti* reveals that Soviet design team head investigating orbital

mirror systems is Nikolai Lidorenko, a corresponding member of USSR Academy of Sciences. Object is to place mirrors in geostationary orbit so that they remain stationary above that part of Earth they illuminate. As a further development light energy will be converted into electricity for transmission to Earth at laser or microwave frequencies.

September 1 Rolls-Royce announces start of rig testing at Ansty, near Coventry, of critical components of combined airbreathing rocket engine, the RB545, being investigated as propulsion system for HOTOL spaceplane. The RB545,

The key to the HOTOL concept is a revolutionary hybrid power plant, known as the RB545, which is under study by Rolls-Royce.

classified "secret", uses atmospheric oxygen with liquid hydrogen fuel until about nine minutes after launch, then switches to on-board liquid oxygen to achieve orbit. Two year study is funded jointly by Department of Trade and Industry and Rolls-Royce. Engine designer is Alan Bond, former employee of Rolls-Royce.

September 5 Delta rocket launched from Cape Canaveral Air Force Station releases two experimental satellites into different orbits as part of SDI programme. Object was to track a missile launch to the point where it released a "warhead" and an "interceptor". The latter was then to manoeuvre in a game of "space pursuit" and destroy the "warhead". Launch was first to be made successfully from the Cape since Shuttle disaster on 28 January.

September 8 Japanese government elects to co-operate with United States in research for Strategic Defense Initiative. Major factor is concern that Japan might fall behind in "high tech" race related to computing, automation and lasers.

September 8 Reported by *Pravda* that Salyut 7/Cosmos 1686 complex has been manoeuvred into higher orbit averaging 298 miles (480km) from Earth, extending lifetime by eight years. Although station is in "suspended animation", an expedition may be sent to it "in several years time" to examine conditions on board and to recover parts for analysis.

September 19 Italy becomes fourth country to join Strategic Defense Initiative; others are UK, W Germany and Japan.

September 26 Soviets confirm that two Phobos spacecraft will be launched in summer of 1988 to study Mars and its moons. International project involves specialists from Socialist countries, as well as Austria, W Germany, France, Sweden and ESA.

September 27 NASA reveals "single-keel" space station re-design which allows assembly to be accomplished by eight Shuttle flights per year. More emphasis is placed on accommodating equipment *within* space station, reducing number of EVA's by astronauts.

September 30 USAF F-15 interceptor successfully launches ASAT missile with guidance system locked on a star; was fifth test of series.

October 1 Protocol is signed in Moscow between representatives of Soviet Institute for Space Research and British National Space Centre opening possibilities for joint research, including astrophysics, space medicine and biology, studies of space materials and radio astronomy. First joint project involves launch of space probe Roentgen which has X-ray telescope designed with the help of scientists from Birmingham University.

October 6-11 Chinese People's Republic launches China 19 Earth observation satellite into orbit of 107 x 239 miles (173 x 385km) x 65·96°. Descent capsule is recovered 11 October in Gansu province. Satellite body re-enters after 17 days. LC Jiuquan. LV Long March 2C. LT 0540 GMT approx.

November NASA/JPL scientists increase Voyager 2 miss-distance from Neptune in 1989 fly-by from 795 miles (1,280km) above cloud tops to 27,840 miles (44,800km) in case atmospheric drag causes significant diversion.

November 14 USAF launches 275lb (125kg) auroral satellite, Polar Bear, by Scout rocket from Vandenberg AFB, California. Satellite is refurbished Transit-type, with navigational beacons replaced by experiments. Orbit: 598 x 633 miles (962 x 1,019km) x 89·56°.

December NASA reveals details of Space Shuttle crew escape systems for emergency use in gliding flight. Favoured scheme involves "blowing" side hatch in crew compartment under deck, allowing astronauts to escape sequentially by attached tractor rockets. Alternative is telescoping pole down which astronauts slide for conventional parachute recovery. (The second technique was adopted).

December 5 NASA launches FltSatCom F 7 satellite by Atlas-Centaur from Cape Canaveral for subsequent positioning in geostationary orbit at 105°W longitude. Provides US Navy and other agencies with real-time global UHF communications. LC Cape Canaveral Air Force Station, (pad 39). LV Atlas-Centaur. LT 0235 GMT approx.

December 26 Soviets launch Cosmos 1801, bringing total of year's satellite launchings by USSR to 91. Compares with twelve launched by rest of world. (The USSR total in 1985 was 98). Many satellites launched in the Cosmos programme have unspecified military objectives.

December 31 Total number of satellites and spacecraft in space, mainly in Earth orbit, is 1,655 plus 4,582 trackable items of debris including discarded rocket stages, payload shrouds, etc. There are also thousands of unrecorded fragments resulting mainly from deliberate or accidental explosions.

1987

January British Aerospace redefines HOTOL spaceplane concept following windtunnel model testing. Wing shape revised for improved aerodynamic performance, canard foreplanes deleted. Primary structure: titanium/Rene 41 sandwich, with carbon-carbon nose cone and wing leading edges withstanding up to 950°C (1,742°F). Launch weight 230-240 tons from laser-guided trolley at 334mph (537km/h). Landing weight 40-42 tons. Payload to 186 miles (300km) orbit 7-8 tons. Aims to reduce launch cost to $5 million.

January Caspar Weinberger, US Defense Secretary, requests "budget supplemental" of $2.8 billion to start development of heavy lift vehicle (HLV) capable of launching "heavy space structures" into low Earth orbit, including SDI experiments, up to 145,500lb (66,000kg) mass.

January 5 Debris of Space Shuttle *Challenger* is buried in two disused Minuteman ICBM silos at Cape Canaveral Air Force Station, Florida.

January 16-February 25 Soviets launch Progress 27 freighter which docks with Mir space station on aft port 1027 MT on 18 January, delivering propellant and other consumables. Engine fired to raise orbit of Mir complex to 204 x 225 miles (328 x 363km) 18 January. Undocks 1429 MT on 23 February and is made to re-enter atmosphere. LC Baikonur. LV A-2. LT 0906 MT

February US Air Force anticipates that Space Shuttle *Atlantis* will launch KH-12 reconnaissance satellite from KSC in May 1988 into orbit inclined at 57° to equator. Launch was originally to have been into near-polar orbit from Vandenberg. KH-12, designed to be serviced in orbit, will be capable of resolving surface objects less than 4in (10·2cm) across; also carries thermal IR sensors for night-time imaging. KH-12 was cancelled in 1988.

February Alexander Arkhipov of Moscow's Radio Astronomy Institute reveals that nine sites in Universe have been identified as possible locations of intelligent life, based on a "new approach" to SETI investigations. Assumes that any developed civilization will have an industrial base giving off

radiation in a band of frequencies between 100 and 1,000MHz, similar to that of our own. Life is likely to be found, Arkhipov argues, where a radio source of this kind exists very close to a yellow dwarf star, like the Sun. A search near 4,500 stars of this type has discovered nine with an appropriate source nearby.

February 5 Japan launches 924lb (419kg) satellite Astro-C (Ginga) by Mu-3C at 0630 GMT from Tanegashima into 314 x 416 miles (505 x 670km) x 31.09° orbit. Object: detect X-ray emissions from neutron stars and black holes, believed to result from dust and gas being drawn into gravity wells. Largest satellite-borne X-ray detector yet flown weighs more than 220lb (100kg) and has a sensitive area of 5·38ft² (0·5m²).

February 6-July 30 Soviets launch Soyuz TM-2 with cosmonauts Col Yuri Victorovich Romanenko (commander) and Alexander Leveykin (flight engineer). Docks with Mir/Progress 27 space station complex at 0228 MT on 8 February using new "Kurs" automatic docking system. Spacecraft has improved computers, upgraded propulsion, lighter launch escape tower. Flight crew "manual" is held in Strela information retrieval system. First tasks were to re-activate Mir's radio and TV communications, etc. On 11 February propulsion system of Progress 27 was used to adjust orbit of

The night-time launch of Soyuz TM-2 cosmonauts Romanenko and Leveykin.

Soyuz TM-2/Mir/Progress 27 complex. Other improvements: engine assembly has new base unit of propellant tanks, feed system and sustainer engine with uncooled nozzle; power unit and altimeter for landing rockets. Inertial guidance system and computer diagnosis allows revision of flight programme. Main electrical system triplicated. Redundant hydraulic and pneumatic systems; back-up life support system provides oxygen during re-entry if main system fails. Weight reduced to 309lb (140kg). Weight and space saving allows capsule to carry 551lb (250kg) extra payload. LC Baikonur. LV A-2. LT 0038 MT. R 0504 MT.

February 11-12 Representatives of NASA, ESA, Japan and Canada concerned in US International Space Station programme meet at US State Department to discuss new draft intergovernmental agreement. Proposed accord gives NASA overall control of Station operations, bars ESA and Japan from using US laboratory module and allows only limited use of their own laboratory modules; US Defense Department retains option to use Station for "peaceful research purposes". New draft reflects fact that "foreign" participation in dual-keel Station is only about one-quarter of the original $8 billion estimate; latest estimates put total costs at $14·5-$20 billion.

February 12 USAF launches classified payload from Vandenberg AFB by Titan

3B-Agena D, possibly Satellite Data System (SDS) for relaying communications between US command centres and strategic forces in northern hemisphere; also reconnaissance images from KH-11 satellites to ground stations. Orbit 248 x 24,716 miles (400 x 39,775km) x 63°. LC Vandenberg AFB. LV Titan 3B-Agena D. LT 0630 GMT approx.

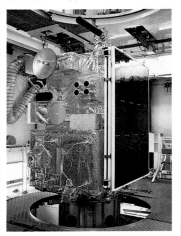

MOS-1 during qualification testing.

February 18 Japan launches Marine Observation Satellite MOS-1 (Peach Blossom) at 0120 GMT by last N-II rocket from Tanegashima Space Centre. Orbit is Sun-synchronous at 561 x 570 miles (903 x 917km) x 99·10°. Returns surface images of quality comparable with NASA Landsat. Has multi-spectral electronic self-scanning radiometer (MESSR); visible and thermal IR radiometer (VTIR); and microwave scanning radiometer (MSR).

February 26 NASA launches Geostationary Observation Environmental Satellite (GOES-7) by Delta 3920 at 2240 GMT from Cape Canaveral, Florida. Satellite is eighth of series for international Global Atmospheric Research Program (GARP). Geostationary above 83°W.

March Soviet plans for Mars exploration (yet to be approved in detail) according to Valery Barsukov, director USSR Academy of Geochemistry and Analytic Chemistry at 18th Lunar and Planetary Science conference, Houston, Texas: 1992 Large Mars orbiter carrying surface penetrators, balloon sonde, and possibly small roving vehicle. Landing module to contain two penetrators, double-walled "rise and fall" balloon to drift in thin Martian air up to 3·7 miles (6km) when heated by Sun, obtaining high-resolution images; where it lands at night soil type and composition are measured by on-board instruments. 1994 Large Mars Rover plus robot "mole" capable of tunnelling 66 to 98ft (20 to 30m) beneath soil to obtain samples for chemical and biological analysis. 1996/98 Sample return mission.

March Sixth edition of US Department of Defense publication *Soviet Military Power*

claims that USSR spends $1 billion a year on laser weapons research. Most research is concentrated at Sary Shagan where anti-ballistic missile tests are made. Estimates that ground-based high-energy air defense laser could be deployed early 1990s and aboard ships mid-1990s. Prototype space-based particle-beam weapon capable of disrupting electronics of satellites might be tested 1990s.

March 3 Attempt to re-establish contact with Pioneer 9 space probe fails despite use of NASA's ultra-sensitive Search for Extra-terrestrial Intelligence (SETI) receiver. Last signal received 18 May 1983.

March 3-28 Soviets launch unmanned Progress 28 freighter which docks with Mir space station complex on aft port 1443 MT 5 March. Delivers more than two tonnes of propellant, equipment, food, letters, newspapers and magazines for on-board crew. Payload includes Korund semi-industrial plant for growing industrial crystals under microgravity; KATE-140 topographic mapping camera. Engine used to raise orbit of station complex 26 March. Undocks at 0807 MT March 26 and is made to re-enter atmosphere. LC Baikonur. LV A-2. LT 1414 MT.

The first launch of India's ASLV which ended unsuccessfully.

March 24 India's first attempt to fly Augmented Satellite Launch Vehicle (ASLV-DL1) from Sriharikota ends disastrously when second stage fails one minute after lift-off; rocket and satellite descend into Bay of Bengal. Concluded that central core failed to ignite at T + 48·5sec, due either to electrical short-circuit or "random malfunction of safety arm device". Satellite was first of Stretched Rohini Series (SRS) with

gamma-ray detectors, monocular optical scanner, and ionospheric monitoring and X-ray astronomy instruments.

March 26 Attempt to launch satellite FltSatCom F-6 fails when Atlas-Centaur AC67 goes out of control shortly after lifting off from Cape Canaveral. Rocket yawed to right, broke up and was finally destroyed by range safety officer after 71 seconds of flight. Approx cost: Atlas-Centaur $78m; FltSatCom $83m.

March 31 Soviets launch astrophysics module Kvant (Quantum) into 110 x 199 miles (177 x 320km) orbit for subsequent docking with Mir space station central core. However, orientation problems cause temporary suspension of docking manoeuvres on 5 April when module is within 1,968ft (600m) of station. On-board cosmonauts Romanenko and Laveykin had previously taken up positions in the Soyuz TM-2 ferry on the nose of Mir at the time of the planned docking at the station's rear, ready for an emergency breakaway. Second docking attempt 9 April was only partially successful; although Kvant functioned normally through every stage of rendezvous and docking before it finally linked up with Mir, the docking was not positive. Romanenko and Laveykin began 3hr 40min spacewalk 11 April at 2341 MT. By extending the boom of Kvant's docking unit, the two craft were pulled as far apart as possible; the cosmonauts found that a "foreign object" (a plastic bag) was impeding hard docking. After this was removed, Kvant was successfully docked with Mir by ground control under the cosmonaut's visual supervision. At 0018 MT on 13 April the 10·6 tonne service module or "tug" was detached, leaving the 12·1 tonne Kvant module attached to Mir with its axial docking unit exposed ready to receive Progress freighters. Combined mass Soyuz TM-2/Mir/Kvant 51 tonnes; overall length 114·8ft (35m). LC Baikonur. LV D-1. LT 0406 MT.

April Chinese People's Republic declares interest in marketing facilities aboard recoverable space-stabilised satellites FSW-I and FSW-II which have "useful loads" of up to 661lb (300kg) and 1,102lb

The FSW-I recoverable payload during simulated landing tests.

(500kg) respectively. Re-entry capsules are 330lb (150kg) and 551lb (250kg) respectively.

April NASA's revised estimate for US space station baseline configuration is $10·9 billion (compared with original $8 billion), plus $1·3 billion for ground support. New plans put greater emphasis on growth in later years, reducing start-up costs. Deleted from initial construction are upper and lower trusses, solar dynamic power station, servicing facility and co-orbiting space platform. Central cross-member now supports US and international crew modules, four "resource nodes" and non-pressurized experiments. Retained are US and ESA polar-orbiting platforms, and first-phase of Canada's mobile servicing system. Future activity to be devoted to developing station for satellite servicing, materials processing, scientific payloads and enhanced power generation.

April Feasibility study by Government of Queensland backs proposal to establish international launch centre on Cape York peninsula. Launch azimuths are ES-E over water for geosynchronous orbits; SW over Gulf of Carpentaria and thinly populated central Australia for polar orbits.

April 8 Academician Vladimir Kotelnikov, chairman of Intercosmos Council, says Soviet specialists are exploring possibilities of establishing orbital power systems. Problems of placing in orbit "large-scale structures, solar cell arrays and batteries as well as mirrors with diameters up to 0·62 miles (1km) are being tackled".

April 21-May 11 Soviets launch Progress 29 freighter which docks with Mir/Kvant/Soyuz TM-2 space station complex on rear port at 2105 MT on 23 April. The complex – almost 115ft (35m) long – has a total mass of nearly 50 tonnes. Undocked 0710 MT 11 May and re-entered atmosphere. LC Baikonur. LV A-2. LT 1914 MT.

May NASA delays re-launch of Space Shuttle *(Discovery)* until June 1988 to allow more time for validation testing. Following qualification of modified SRBs about six weeks before launch, a "wet" countdown demonstration test is planned on the pad followed by a 20

second flight-readiness firing of the three main engines. Under revised programme, three Shuttle flights are scheduled in 1988, seven in 1989, building up to 14 per year by 1992.

May 15 Soviets launch new generation heavy-lift rocket Energiya 1 (SL-W) (Energy) at 2130 MT from Baikonur cosmodrome. Carried side-mounted "dummy satellite" with apogee "kick motor" for orbital injection but orientation fault caused motor to fire in wrong direction; it fell into Pacific Ocean. Chief designer G. Gubanov blamed malfunction of circuit in an on-board instrument. However, according to *Tass*: "All the aims and objectives of the launch were met and the high standard of Energiya's design and engines were confirmed".

The four strap-on version of Energiya before its maiden flight.

May 19-July 19 Soviets launch Progress 30 freighter which docks with Soyuz TM-2/Mir/Kvant space station complex on rear Kvant port at 0953 MT on 21 May with propellant, water, food, equipment, mail, etc. Undocks 19 July at 0420 MT and is made to re-enter atmosphere. LC Baikonur. LV A-2. LT 0802 MT.

June NASA sets up Office of Exploration with astronaut Sally Ride as acting associate administrator. Object to coordinate effort that could "expand the human presence beyond Earth", e.g. intensive use of Earth systems to protect the environment; robotic exploration of Moon and planets; permanent Moon base; manned expedition to Mars.

June International Council for Scientific Unions designates 1992 – 500th anniversary of Columbus' voyage to the New World – International Space Year, dedicated to a global understanding of the benefits of space to mankind.

June 12/June 16 Yuri Romanenko and Alexander Leveykin spacewalk from Mir/Kvant space station complex to erect third solar array on core module.

Additional solar array boosts Mir's power supply by 10kW, needed to run gyroscopes which keep station correctly orientated; also to furnish additional power for Kvant astrophysics module and microgravity processing equipment.

July Launch of final US Navy FltSatCom communications satellite, F8, on last NASA Atlas-Centaur (AC68), is delayed indefinitely because hydrogen tank of Centaur stage is punctured on launch pad by scaffolding. Was originally to have been launched 11 June 1987 but delayed until Fall by 27 March launch mishap to Atlas-Centaur (AC67) and loss of FltSatCom F6.

July Sally Ride, former US astronaut, submits to Congress NASA Committee report on long-term space goals. Recommends "evolution and natural progression" rather than one-shot spectaculars: 1. "Mission to planet Earth", systematically examining global cloud cover, rainfall, vegetation, chlorophyll, ozone and carbon dioxide. 2. Solar System exploration, including Mars sample return mission 1996. Others, asteroid flyby 1993; Cassini probe to Saturn 1998. 3. Construction of lunar outpost around turn of century as part of long-term strategy for human exploration of Solar System. 4. Manned mission to Mars. Favoured is two-stage mission in which cargo vehicle is followed by manned ship. Advocates series of three one-year missions culminating in manned landing 2010.

July 10 Twenty-fifth anniversary of launch of Telstar, world's first commercial communications satellite. To date communications satellites have relayed some 3·6 billion telephone calls and broadcast news bulletins to more than 2,000 million people in 100 countries.

July 22-30 Soviets launch Soyuz TM-3 with joint Soviet/Syrian crew: Alexander Viktorenko (cdr), Alexander Alexandrov (flight engineer) and Mohammed Faris (Syrian Arab Republic). Docks with Soyuz TM-2/Mir/Kvant complex on Kvant aft

Mir/Kvant/Soyuz TM-3 as seen by the departing Soyuz TM-2 spacecraft.

port 0731 MT 24 July. Objectives, in conjunction with resident cosmonauts: comprehensive mapping of Syrian republic, study of Euphrates basin, Syrian desert, Arabian-African fissure, etc; experiments related to raw materials, mineral and oil exploration, energy and ecology; ionospheric studies, medical experiments, materials technology. Laveykin, the resident Mir flight engineer, whose electrocardiogram had indicated irregularities in heart rhythm during physical exercises, returned with Viktorenko and Faris in Soyuz TM-2 which had been docked to Mir complex for 174 days. Alexandrov was left behind as his replacement. After investigation at national heart research centre, Laveykin's heart function was declared to be sound. After TM-2 had departed from forward berth, cosmonauts undocked TM-3 from Kvant module on 31 July at 0328 MT; commands from mission control caused space station complex to turn through 180° and at 0348 MT crew re-docked TM-3 on forward port thereby releasing Kvant docking port for Progress freighters. LC Baikonur. LV A-2. LT 0559 MT. R 0504 MT in TM-2 capsule, 87 miles (140km) NE of Arkalyk, Kazakhstan. Parachute-supported capsule, blown off course by strong winds, came down within 1·2 miles (2km) of a village.

July 23 UK Government rejects space plan proposed September 1986 by British National Space Centre (BNSC) which called for tripling British civilian space spending. Defending decision in the House of Commons, Mrs Thatcher commented: "We spend some £4·5 billion on research and development. We are not able to find any more resources without switching funds from one research and technology development to another . . . We shall continue our subscription to the European Space Agency but at present we are not able to find any more money." She hoped the private sector, if interested in the results of space research, would come forward with considerable resources.

July 25 Soviets launch Cosmos 1870, a 20 tonne remote-sensing platform into near polar orbit; possibly large enough to be man-tended following rendezvous and docking operation. After adjustment, orbit ranges between 147 x 154 miles (237

x 249km) x 71·9°. Carries large imaging radar and array of scientific instruments related to hydrology, cartography, geology, agriculture and the environment. LC Baikonur. LV D-1. LT 0855 GMT.

August Confirmed that French 2.5 tonne military reconnaissance satellite Helios will be launched in 1993 by Ariane 4 into Sun-synchronous orbit at 528 miles (850km) altitude. Will have powerful optical telescope with electronic-scanning sensors capable of resolution about 3·3ft (1m). Italy contributing 15 per cent of estimated FFr 7·6 billion funding, Spain 5 per cent.

August Manufacture of new Shuttle Orbiter, estimated to cost $2.12 billion, begins at Rockwell's Palmdale facility. Possible that Vandenberg Shuttle operations could begin 1993, with delivery of first of 82 sets of Block II SRBs. This would allow 31,966lb (14,500kg) payload to be placed in polar orbit. Vandenberg facility, now mothballed, cost $3·6 billion to build.

August 3-September 23 Soviets launch Progress 31 freighter which docks with Mir space station complex on Kvant's rear port at 2028 GMT 5 August to replenish propellant, air, water, food and other supplies. Undocked 2358 GMT 21 September and made to re-enter atmosphere. LC Baikonur. LV A-2. LT 2044 GMT.

August 4 Roy Gibson, director-general of British National Space Centre (BNSC), resigns because of failure of UK Government to provide adquate funding for UK and ESA civilian space ventures.

August 5-10 Chinese People's Republic launches China 20 (SKW-15) with microgravity materials processing experiments in recoverable capsule. Orbit 107 x 247 miles (173 x 400km) x 62·96°. Two experiments prepared by French Matra company, combined mass 33lb (15kg). LC Jiuquan. LV Long March 2 (CZ-2). R 0530 GMT Sichuan Province (capsule); remainder of spacecraft re-entered atmosphere 23 August.

August 25 Woomera rocket range in South Australia is re-opened for scientific research by sounding rockets under $A10 million up-grading programme. First launch campaign involves 11 NASA sounding rockets and at least one British Skylark.

The first H-I launcher lifts off.

August 27 Japan launches Engineering Test Satellite ETS-5 (Kiku 5), three-axis stabilized communications satellite, by first three-stage H-I rocket. Embodies C-band communications package and L-band transponders for use by aircraft in Pacific area and for navigation and search and rescue for ships. H-I launcher features Japanese LE5 cryogenic engine in second stage with Nissan solid propellant third stage. LC Tanegashima. LV H-I. LT 0920 GMT.

August 27 Criticism of SDI programme is voiced by Lawrence Livermore Laboratory specialists. Although it is conceivable that a "few thousand" kinetic projectiles could deal with an attack by presently operational Soviet SS-18s, defence will cease to be effective as Soviets deploy faster SS-24s and SS-25s in the 1990s.

September Japan reveals plans to replace Nissan Mu-3S2 launcher with new-generation M-booster in mid-1990s. Length 98·4ft (30m); diameter 8·2ft (2·5m). Will place 2 tonnes into low Earth orbit.

September British Aerospace completes two year £2 million HOTOL spaceplane "proof-of-concept study". Advocates HOTOL "enabling technology programme" starting 1994 with anticipation of first flight about the year 2000. Aim to bring recurring costs to about $5 million, based on five vehicles performing 28 missions/year with 120-mission design life, turnround between flights 48 working hours.

September 16 Arianespace launches satellites ECS-4 and Aussat K3 by Ariane 3 (V-19) from Kourou, French Guiana. Was first launch since V-18 which suffered third stage ignition failure 31 May 1986; for this launch a more powerful twin-jet engine igniter was substituted with delayed ignition start and faster LH_2 ignition valve opening. ESA spent £52 million to correct the fault. When positioned 10°E in geostationary orbit, ECS-4 on 1 November was re-designated Eutelsat I F-4. Complements ECS-1 and ECS-2 to extend communications services including telephone, business and TV distribution. Aussat K3, located 164°E, used to extend TV broadcasting for Australia's main networks. LC Kourou, French Guiana. LV Ariane 3 (V-19) LT 0045 GMT.

September 16 Soviets launch three Global Navigation System (GLONASS) satellites by Proton D-1-e from Baikonur. Orbital distribution 11,874 x 11,900 miles (19,108 x 19,151km) x 64·89°.

September 18 US Government declares intention of stepping up "Star Wars" anti-missile programme. Research "within constraints of 1972 Anti-Ballistic Missile Treaty" concentrates initially upon: space platforms capable of discharging rockets against incoming missiles; satellites capable of tracking missiles and discriminating real warheads from decoys; ground-based tracking system, including rockets that would be fired to the "edge of space"; computerised "battle management" system to coordinate various anti-missile defences.

September 23-November 18 Soviets launch Progress 32 freighter which docks with Mir-Kvant space station complex at 0108 GMT 26 September. After Mir cosmonauts have finished transferring supplies, freighter undocks 0409 GMT 10 November, retreats some 1·55 miles (2·5km) and is re-docked 90 minutes later after two Earth orbits to check new computer software in Mir and stability of station's modified solar arrays. Finally, undocks 1925 GMT 17 November and re-enters atmosphere. LC Baikonur. LV A-2. LT 2344 GMT.

September 29-October 12 Soviets launch Vostok-type biosatellite Cosmos 1887 carrying two Rhesus monkeys, Yerosha (Trouble-Maker) and Dryoma; 10 rats, fish, single-celled organisms and plants. Mission is organised jointly with United States and ESA, including more than 50 NASA-sponsored scientists from Ames Research Centre and US universities participating in 27 major joint experiments. Experiments investigated effects of space flight on major body systems. One of the monkeys, Yerosha, succeeded in freeing its left paw from harness on day five and pulled off its name tag. Return of capsule on 12 October was misdirected, the intention being to land in Kazakhstan. LC Baikonur. LV A-1. LT 0050 GMT approx. R 0403 GMT near Kakut city of Mirny district some 1,988 miles (3,200km) off target probably because of misalignment at time of retro-fire.

September 30 NASA's Goddard Space Centre reveals that 3,668 payloads have been launched into space since 4 October 1957. Including trackable debris, there are some 18,400 man-made objects in space.

October 1 Yuri Romanenko aboard Mir space station breaks human space endurance record of 236 days 22 hours 50 minutes set by Soyuz T-10/Salyut 7 cosmonauts in October 1984.

October 18 World's first telephone call via satellite from scheduled airliner is made between Boeing 747 of Japan Airlines and Tokyo HQ of Kokusai Denshin Denwa via Inmarsat Pacific Ocean satellite and Japanese Earth Station at Ibaraki.

October 29 Soviets achieve 2,000th satellite launch with Cosmos 1894.

November 20 Arianespace launches Ariane 2 (V20) at 2319 local time from Kourou, French Guiana, with Franco-German TV-Sat 1. Is Europe's first direct-broadcast satellite built by Aérospatiale and MBB under Eurosatellite label; has four TV channels and 16 digital radio links. Although successfully positioned in geostationary orbit 5°W, one of satellite's two solar panels fails to open. Subsequently, 14 January 1988, ground control reports failure to control satellite's momentum wheel. If backup fails attitude control thruster must be used, reducing operational life.

The TV-Sat direct broadcasting satellite during testing at MBB.

November 20-December 19 Soviets launch Progress 33 freighter which docks with Mir/Kvant complex 0139 GMT on rear port 23 November. Delivers propellant, food, water, equipment and mail including 1,000 envelopes with a stamp commemorating 30th anniversary of Sputnik 1. Cancellation of covers aboard space station is world's first such act performed for commercial purposes. Undocks 0816 GMT 19 December, and re-enters atmosphere. LC Baikonur. LV A-2. LT 2347 GMT.

November 29 US Air Force launches Defense Support Program early warning satellite into geostationary orbit by Titan 34D from Cape Canaveral. Joins five earlier satellites for early warning of ballistic missile attack (system requires three satellites operational at any one time). LC Cape Canaveral AFS. LV Titan 34D/IUS. LT 0327 approx.

December 1 NASA selects prime contractors to build NASA-International Space Station. Objectives: research and

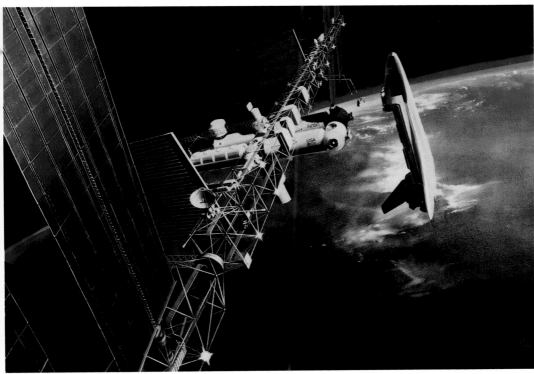

A Boeing artist's impression of the single keel Freedom space station being approached by a Shuttle.

development of new technologies/private sector R&D activites. Later, staging base for continued manned and unmanned exploration of Solar System. Capable of growth both in size and capability; intended to operate well into the 21st century. First construction phase consists of a "single keel" complex to house eight astronauts, serving as a base for scientific and technological research, for commercial space activities and as a "springboard" for missions beyond low Earth orbit. Construction period spans 1994-1997 (20 Shuttle missions); station to be man-tended from 1995. Four work packages in 10-year Phase 1 program to establish single-keel complex (Phase 2 extends configuration to two-keel).

1. Boeing Aerospace Company responds to Marshall Space Flight Center, Huntsville, Alabama. Associated are Lockheed, Teledyne, Grumman Aerospace, ILC Industries. Laboratory and habitation modules, logistics elements, resource node structures, airlock systems, environmental control and life support, thermal, audio and video systems, etc. Contract value: $750 million (Phase 2 adds $2·5 billion to make station "dual-keel").

2. McDonnell Douglas Astronautics Co., Huntington Beach, California, responds to Johnson Space Center. Associated are IBM, Lockheed, RCA, Honeywell and Astro Aerospace. Integration, management, integrated truss, airlocks,

propulsion and mobile servicing system, mobile transporter; also outfitting of resource nodes. Contract value $1·9 billion. Phase 2 adds $140 million.

3. General Electric, responding to Goddard Space Flight Center. Associated is TRW Incorporated. Free-flying, unmanned, polar-orbiting platform to carry scientific experiments in Sun-synchronous or other near-polar orbits plus two "attach points", including pointing system, for accommodating scientific instruments on the manned base; also integration of telerobotic service to the space station, software, planning NASA's role in satellite servicing, etc. Contract value $800 million. Phase 2 includes free-flying, unmanned, co-orbiting platform, three additional attach points, another pointing system and a satellite servicing facility. Phase 2 adds $570 million.

4. Rocketdyne, responding to Lewis Research Center. Associated are Ford Aerospace, Garrett, General Dynamics, Lockheed, Harris (solar dynamics mirrors). Electrical power system using photovoltaic arrays and batteries, with 75kW delivery. Also solar array, battery assemblies and common power management and distribution components for polar platform. Proof of concept for possible Brayton cycle solar dynamics power system. Contract value $1·6 billion. Phase 2 adds solar dynamics 50kW power system $740 million.

December 21-29 Soviets launch Soyuz TM-4 with cosmonauts Col Vladimir Titov (cdr), Musa Manarov (flight engineer) and Anatoli Levchenko (researcher/

pilot). Docks with Mir/Kvant complex on rear port at 1551 MT 23 December. Levchenko returned with resident Mir/Kvant crew Romanenko and Alexandrov in Soyuz TM-3, undocking at 0555 GMT 29 December. LC Baikonur. LV A-2. LT 1418 MT. R 1216 MT, 50 miles (80km) from Arkalyk.

December 29 Soyuz TM-3 undocks from Mir-Kvant space station complex at 0555 GMT returning to Earth cosmonauts Yuri Romanenko, Alexander Alexandrov and Anatoli Levchenko. Romanenko had spent record 326 days in space exceeding previous record by some 90 days. Alexandrov was aloft 160 days and

The return of Soyuz TM-3 brought (l to r) Alexandrov, Romanenko and Levchenko back to Earth from Mir.

Levchenko 8 days. Romanenko, 43, had grown taller by 0·39in (1cm) but lost 3·5lb (1·6kg) in weight; circumference of his calf muscles had shrunk by 15 per cent. Alexandrov had grown taller by 10·59in (1·5cm), gained about 5lb (2·27kg).

December 29 Soviets launch Cosmos 1907 photo-reconnaissance satellite, bringing year's total of USSR launchings to 94. Total all other nations, 13.

December 30 Vladimir Titov and Musa Manarov aboard Mir/Kvant complex undock their Soyuz TM-4 at 1210 MT from Kvant module and pull clear. The station complex, on command from mission control, then turns through 180° allowing crew to redock at 1229 MT on Mir forward axial port. This is now routine procedure with Soyuz TM.

1988

January President Reagan approves go-ahead for Advanced Launch System (ALS) to place payloads of 100,000-150,000lb (45,360-68,040kg) into low Earth orbit by late 1990s. Under DoD funding, ALS will launch SDI and other military payloads but NASA will have vehicle use under separate funding; will also manage studies into liquid propellant engine systems and associated technologies. ALS could feature in early 21st century Mars expedition.

January 20-March 4 Soviets launch Progress 34 freighter which docks with Mir/Kvant complex on Kvant aft port at 0009 GMT 23 January. As well as replacing expendables, craft brought new systems equipment to replace parts of station complex which had completed their service life. Undocks at 0340 GMT 4 March and is made to re-enter atmosphere. LC Baikonur. LV A-2. LT 2252 GMT.

February NASA reports that International Ultraviolet Explorer (IUE) still operates in geostationary orbit after 10 years; now investigating supernova 1987A. Discovered hot gas in "halo" of Milky Way.

February 8 As part of Phase 1 SDI layered defense technology programme, DoD launches 6,000lb (2,722kg) SDIO Delta 181 in $250 million bid to improve knowledge (1) of ballistic missile characteristics before individual warheads are separated, and (2) backgrounds against which space sensors will view missiles, warheads and decoys. In test lasting 12hr satellite ejected 14 mock-up targets, each representing a Soviet missile, warhead or decoy which were observed both from the satellite itself and hundreds of ground stations using radars, lasers, optical, IR and UV sensors. Satellite made up to 200 attitude changes to observe objects it deployed; also tracked other launchings carried out from the ground. LC Cape Canaveral AFS. LV Delta 3910. LT 2208 GMT.

February 11 President Reagan announces National Space Policy, confirming recommendations of Sally Ride committee (July 1987). Also supports development of Advanced Launch System (ALS) and commercialization of space, including Industrial Space Facility (ISF), a Shuttle-launched free-flying space factory. FY 1989 budget contains $100 million request to study "enabling technologies" within Pathfinder Project.

February 16 NASA launches first Black Brant IX sounding rocket from Woomera, Australia. Observes supernova 1987A.

February 17 *Tass* reveals that a Proton rocket launched from Baikonur failed to place three Glonass (Global Navigation Satellite System) satellites into desired circular orbit of 11,806 miles (19,000km) following fourth stage failure. Was third Proton failure in a year; two others stated to have been due to "malfunctions of experimental stages".

February 17 Air-launched anti-satellite missile programme is cancelled in US Defense Budget for FY 1989.

February 26 Mir/Kvant cosmonauts Vladimir Titov and Musa Manarov spacewalk to modify third solar array of Mir's core module; replaced one of two lower panels with new panel embodying samples of "photoelectric transducers of semi-conductors with improved energy properties". EVA lasts 4hr 25min.

March NASA confirms details of re-usable Orbital Maneuvering Vehicle (OMV), or "space tug", deployed from Space Shuttle to retrieve satellites from orbits higher than Shuttle can reach. OMV is disc-shaped, 4·66ft (1·42m) deep by 14·66ft (4·47m) diameter; mass 17,926lb (8,130kg).

March MBB confirms Sänger feasibility study for two-stage re-usable spaceplanes for the cost-effective transport of crews and freight into low Earth orbit. First stage is hypersonic aircraft powered by turbo-ramjets; can be used independently as passenger transport. Optional upper stages have rocket engines. Winged, re-usable, HOROS to have accommodation for two to six astronauts and payload of two to four

An MBB concept of the Sänger two-stage re-usable aerospace plane.

tonnes. CARGUS, an expendable payload carrier, will take up to 15 tonnes into low Earth orbit and up to 2·6 tonnes to geostationary orbit.

March Soviets reveal that Cosmos weather satellites have tested "a new form of radar" which simultaneously gives a picture of cloud cover and underlying surface. Combination of the two images "improves flood predictions, Arctic navigation and monitoring of grain ripening".

March 7 People's Republic of China launches China 22, STW domestic communications satellite, into geostationary orbit by Long March 3 from Xi Chang. Geostationary above 87·5°E. Was fourth launch of rocket type: STW-1 1984 (not entirely successful); STW-2 1984; STW-3 1986.

March 11 Arianespace launches Ariane 3 (V-21) with US Spacenet 3R for GTE Spacenet and piggy-back radio-determination satellite RO2; also French Telecom 1C. Spacenet 3R, geostationary above 87°W, incorporates satellite radio positioning system for Geostar Corporation. Telecom 1C geostationary above 5°E. LC Kourou Space Centre (ELA 1). LV Ariane 3 (V-21). LT 2328 GMT.

March 17 Soviets launch India's remote-sensing satellite IRS-1A by A-1 Vostok rocket at about 0643 GMT from Baikonur. Was first launched under commercial arrangements negotiated with Glavkosmos but price (7·5 million roubles) did not reflect actual cost. Orbit is Sun-synchronous 539 x 567 miles (867 x 913km) x 99·03°; mass 2,072lb (940kg).

March 23-May 5 Soviets launch Progress 35 freighter which docks with Mir/Kvant complex on Kvant rear port at 2222 GMT on 25 March. Replenished propellants, air, water, food and other expendables. Engine used to lift orbit of station complex 22 April. Undocked at 0136 GMT 5 May and is made to re-enter atmosphere same day. LC Baikonur. LV A-2. LT 2105 GMT.

March 18 ESA announces that agreement has been reached with NASA to join development of International Space Station; also involves Canada and

Japan. Britain is only major industrial nation abstaining. ESA's contribution comprises: attached lab module; manned free-flier; polar orbiting platform. (Later, see April 18, UK agreed contribution to polar orbiting platform).

April NASA submits to Congress plans for Advanced Solid Rocket Booster (ASRB) which retains segmented design features. Will boost Shuttle payload capability by 12,000lb (5,443kg). If rigorously pursued, could fly in 1994. Precludes necessity to throttle Shuttle's main engines during period of Max-q (maximum dynamic pressure).

April 18 Kenneth Clarke, UK Minister for Trade and Industry, announces that Britain will after all join ESA Columbus programme-concentrating on the Polar Orbiting Platform. Financial commitment is £250 million plus £5 million from British industry. Mr Clarke added that this would be the limit of UK contribution to ESA's Columbus optional programme.

April 20 United States becomes 21st nation to accept INMARSAT amendments to extend mobile satellite communications services to aircraft. Will include cockpit data and voice communications, as well as direct-dial global telephone

The Vandenberg Shuttle launch area.

April US Air Force elects to "mothball" Shuttle launch facility at Vandenberg AFB which currently costs some $50 million a year to maintain. Spending is limited to about $7 million p.a. to maintain Shuttle pad and main control centre.

April NASA approves use of telescopic pole for emergency escape from Shuttle Orbiter during gliding flight. Housed in the mid-deck, pole extends from open hatch (cover explosively released) to enable each astronaut, in turn, to slide out on a ring attachment sufficient to clear Orbiter's wings and tail for conventional parachute recovery. Pole-bale-out technique is effective during gliding flight following an "abort" between 24,000-11,000ft (7,315-3,353m) before water or ground impact. Astronauts wear Crew Altitude Protection System partial pressure suits, with emergency oxygen supply, parachute, flotation gear and survival equipment.

services for passengers. INMARSAT is the 54-member-nation cooperative organisation currently providing satellite communications services to almost 7,000 ships and other units around the world.

April 26 Soviets launch Cosmos 1970 by Proton rocket from Baikonur cosmodrome which subsequently enters geostationary orbit above 24oW. Is first geostationary satellite "for research into processes taking place in Earth's atmosphere and in the world's oceans".

May Japan reaches agreement with NASA to equip international space station with permanently attached Japanese experiment module (Jem) comprising: (1) pressurized module; (2) exposed experiment pallet; (3) experiment logistics module; (4) remote manipulator, and (5) science equipment airlock. Assembly requires two Shuttle flights with Japanese astronaut participation. Supplementary projects may include small re-entry capsule to return samples of processed materials and life-science experiments from space station directly to Japan. Communications to be relayed initially via Japanese ETS-VI satellite, later by planned data relay satellite.

May NASA reveals that three-stage commercial winged booster, Pegasus, being developed by Orbital Sciences Corporation and Hercules Aerospace, will be launched from B-52 No 0008, the same "mother" that air-launched X-15 research aircraft. Aims to place up to 900lb (408kg) payloads into low Earth orbit. Performance gains stem from use of new solid-propellant motors with lightweight cases of graphite composite construction. Lift generated by graphite composite delta wing of stage 1, combined with B-52 launch at 39,700ft (12,100m) at Mach 0·80, yields significant payload benefits.

A model of the Pegasus booster in front of its B-52 mothercraft.

May Lawrence Livermore National Laboratory studies nuclear fusion powered spaceship, Vista, for interplanetary flight. Funnel-shaped spaceship, 1,300ft (396m) diameter, mass 6,000 tons, would be assembled in Earth-orbit during 30 flights of heavy lift boosters. Powered by detonation of 30 marble-sized nuclear pellets per second, ship would carry six astronauts to Mars and back in 100 days, including 10-day excursion to Mars' surface in associated lander. Propulsion system is reminiscent of Project Daedalus studed by BIS for interstellar flight.

May 13-June 5 Soviets launch Progress 36 freighter which docks with Mir/Kvant space station complex on rear port at 0213 GMT 15 May to replenish propellant, water, food and other expendables. Engine used to raise orbit of station complex 3 June. Undocks 5 June at 1112 GMT and is made to re-enter atmosphere. LC Baikonur. LV A-2. LT 0030 GMT.

May 17 Arianespace launches Intelsat 5-F13 into geostationary transfer orbit by Ariane 3 at 1158 GMT from Kourou Space Centre for subsequent positioning at 53°W. Launch mass of satellite 4,438lb (2,013kg). Capacity is 15,000 telephone channels at C-band and L-band.

June Rockwell International reveals it has begun work on extended duration Orbiter kit designed to increase Shuttle time in space to 16-18 days. Includes cryogenic fuel kit inside cargo bay (complementing existing fuel cells), improvements to life-support system and astronaut equipment in general.

June 7-17 Soviets launch Soyuz TM-5 with Anatoli Solovyov (cdr), Viktor Savinykh (flight engineer) and Alexander Alexandrov (Bulgaria) which docks with Mir/Kvant complex on Kvant rear port at 1557 GMT on 9 June. Forty-two experiments conducted under Shipka programme involved space physics, space biology and medicine, remote sensing and materials processing. Cosmonauts returned in Soyuz TM-4 with samples of alloys and computer disks containing results of astrophysical experiments; undocked Mir front port 0618 GMT 17 June. On 18 June Mir/Kvant resident cosmonauts Vladimir Titov and Musa Manarov entered Soyuz TM-5 and transferred it to the forward axial port of Mir in readiness for another Progress docking. LC Baikonur. LV A-2. LT 1403 GMT. R 1013 GMT, 125 miles (202km) SE of Dzhezkazgan.

June 15 Ariane 4 on maiden flight, in 44LP configuration, launches three satellites: Meteosat P2, Amsat IIIC (OSCAR 13) and PanAmSat 1, combined mass 7,745 lb (3,513kg). Spelda dual launch structure of 13ft (3·97m) diameter in nose of launcher allows two satellites stacked one above the other to be launched independently; third satellite mounted above Spelda's roof employs

The first flight of Ariane 4; note two liquid and two solid boosters.

adaptor Apex (Ariane Passenger Experiment). LC Kourou Space Centre. LV Ariane 4 (V-22). LT 1119 GMT.

June 30 Soviet cosmonauts Vladimir Titov and Musa Manarov spacewalk from Mir space station for five hours in unsuccessful bid to repair X-ray telescope mounted on Kvant module built jointly by University of Birmingham and Netherlands Space Research Laboratory. However, a wrench broke in the hands of one of the cosmonauts who was using it to force off a clamp. The telescope was not designed for in-orbit repair.

July 4 Space Shuttle *Discovery* is rolled out to launch complex 39B at Kennedy Space Center in readiness for STS-26 mission to deploy NASA's Tracking and Data Relay Satellite, TDRS-D. Follows successful test-firing of modified Solid

Rocket Booster (SRB) at Morton Thiokol on 14 June.

July 5 Soviets launch new satellite, Okean 1, for sea and ice survey by microwave sounders and side-looking radar. Orbit ranges between 404 and 422 miles (661 x 680km) inclined at 82·5° to equator. LC Plesetsk. LV F-2. LT 0946 GMT approx.

July 7 Soviets launch Phobos 1 which is course-corrected 16 July with object of being inserted into orbit around Mars on 23 January 1989. Intended to make close inspection of inner moon Phobos but incorrect signal sent by Soviet mission control immobilizes spacecraft's systems (see September 2); probe is officially declared "lost" 3 November. LC Baikonur. LV D-1-e. LT 2138 MT.

July 12 Soviets launch Phobos 2 with objectives similar to Phobos 1 (see July 7). Primary objective is the inner Martian moon Phobos which has dimensions of

Technicians prepare one of the Phobos craft for its flight to Mars.

about 16·8 x 13·0 x 11·8 miles (27 x 21 x 19km). Flight into Mars orbit lasts about 200 days, spanning 118 million miles (190 million km). Mid-course corrections 21 July and one or two weeks before arrival 29 January 1989. Midcourse observations: X-ray, UV and visible of Sun's chromosphere and corona plus French experiments on plasma density, temperature, wave measurements. LC Baikonur. LV D-1-e. LT 2102 MT.

July 13 India's Augmented Satellite Launch Vehicle (ASLV), launched from Shriharikota, goes out of control following ignition of core stage after 48·5 seconds of flight. Propulsion continued but rocket was yawing and rolling; the top end, containing 330lb (150kg) SROSS-2 satellite, broke off and debris descended into Bay of Bengal.

July 18 President Reagan names US International Space Station "Freedom". Subsequently, he signs Bill fixing NASA's FY 1989 budget at $10·6 billion of which $900 million is allocated to space station.

July 19-August 12 Soviets launch Progress 37 freighter which docks with Mir/Kvant space station complex on rear port on 21 July to replenish propellant, water, food and other expendables. Also brings new tools for cosmonauts to use in second attempt to repair TTM telescope mounted in Kvant module. Undocks 12 August at 1232 MT and is made to re-enter atmosphere. LC Baikonur. LV A-2. LT 0113 MT.

July 21 Arianespace launches geostationary communications satellite ECS-5 and India's combined communications/meteorological satellite Insat 1C at 2312 GMT by Ariane 3 (V-24) from Kourou, French Guiana. ECS-5 enclosed within Spelda payload canister within launcher; satellite redesignated Eutelsat 1-F5 in orbit co-located with Eutelsat 1-F1 at 13°E (after TV and radio channels are transferred, older satellite is repositioned to 16°E). ECS-5 is last of series leased to Eutelsat. Insat 1C, built for India by Ford

Aerospace, is located 93·5°E but loss of one of two power "buses" as it was being moved onto station reduced TV services by 50 per cent; meteorological services normal.

July 25 British Government refuses further financial backing for Hotol spaceplane project. Mr. Kenneth Clarke, in one of his last acts as Industry Minister (he is newly appointed Secretary of State for Health) declares Hotol too expensive for Britain to develop alone. The Government, he said, would help British Aerospace and Rolls-Royce find "suitable collaborators" but would not provide further funds for "the foreseeable future".

July 26 Soviets launch operational meteorological satellite Meteor 3 by Tsyklon rocket from Plesetsk (prototype Meteor 3-1 launched October 1984). Supersedes Meteor 2 series which began 1975. Object to establish three operational satellites in circular orbit at 621 miles (1,000km) with orbital planes spaced 120° apart.

August Israel announces intention to develop two geostationary communications satellites, Amos 1 and Amos 2. Participants are: Israel Aircraft Industries, Dornier (W Germany), General Satellite Co (Euro-US consortium) and Bezek, Israeli Government Telecommunications Corporation. First launch by Ariane 1993.

August 5-13 People's Republic of China launches FSW satellite with recoverable capsule. Orbit 127 x 194 miles (204 x 312km) x 63°. Carried 104 experiments by 20 scientists including study of protein crystallisation to find new ways of making cancer drug Interferon. Crystal growth experiment sponsored jointly by MBB, the European Consortium Intospace, and West Germany's DFVLR. Capsule recovered after 8 days. LC Jiuquan. LV Long March 2C. LT 0730 GMT approx.

August 6 Cosmonaut Anatoly Levchenko, 47, dies in Moscow following surgery for removal of a brain tumour. Flew in Soyuz TM-4 to Mir space station and was training to fly Soviet space shuttle. Another cosmonaut training to fly the shuttle, Alexander Shchukin, was killed on 18 August in a Sukhoi Su-26M which crashed after aerobatic manoeuvres.

August 22 British National Space Centre announces decision to spend up to £76 million on the ESA programme to develop and launch two scientific spacecraft in the mid-1990s. Soho – the Solar and Heliospheric Observatory – will study tiny oscillations on the Sun's surface, which may provide clues to processes going on within the core, where temperatures reach 27 million degrees F. Cluster consists of four satellites to provide greater understanding of the way in which Earth's magnetic field traps particles of the solar wind.

August 29-September 7 Soviets launch Soyuz TM-6 with cosmonauts Col Vladimir Lyakhov (cdr), Dr Valeri Poliakov (physician) and Capt Abdol Ahad Mohmand (Afghan researcher). Docks with Mir/Kvant space station complex at 0941 MT on 31 August on Kvant rear port. Main task of Dr Poliakov is to check

health of resident cosmonauts Titov and Manarov attempting to break 326-day space endurance record set by Yuri Romanenko in 1987. Afghanistan is 20th nation to have a human being launched into space. Return is made in Soyuz TM-5 capsule. Mission went smoothly until cosmonauts started re-entry sequence when navigation computer received different readings from primary and back-up IR horizon sensors (possibly because of sunglare) which inhibited engine firing. Then computer accepts sensor readings indicating that spacecraft was oriented correctly, starting ignition sequence seven seconds late. After three seconds Lyakhov shuts down engine; it would have meant landing in Manchuria! Two orbits later Lyakhov tries retro-fire again using spacecraft's inertial measuring unit but engine cuts off again after six seconds (it should have burned for 230 seconds). Lyakhov re-starts manually and engine continues to burn for about 60 seconds when computer detects orientation error and stops engine again. Mission control advises waiting another day. After on-board back-up computer had been re-programmed, retro-fire at 0401 MT 7 September is successful and cosmonauts land in primary recovery zone. LC Baikonur. LV A-2. LT 0823 MT. R 0450 MT, about 100 miles (161km) SE of Dzhezkazgan.

September 2 Surveillance satellite Vortex is launched by Titan 34D from Cape Canaveral AFS at 0805 EDT, but Transtage, intended to deliver it into geosynchronous orbit, fails to refire to complete manoeuvre. Satellite, designed to erect a large antenna to monitor Soviet missile tests, radar, and external diplomatic communications, is stranded in elliptical orbit.

September 2 Phobos mission controller sends incorrect signal to Phobos 1 space probe en-route to Mars, causing its de-stabilization. Solar panels lose lock on the Sun and electronic systems are deprived of power. According to Dr Roald Sagdeev, on-board computer chips were "probably damaged beyond repair . . ." He saw no hope of restoring craft to working order. Craft officially declared "lost" 3 November.

September 5 Cluster of four US Navy surveillance satellites, White Cloud, launched by modified Titan II from Vandenberg AFB. Satellites track Soviet shipping by monitoring radio/radar transmissions. Was first use of 13 Titan II ICBMs made available for conversion to space boosters; 20 more Titan IIs are in storage.

September 7 People's Republic of China launches metereological satellite Feng Yun (Wind and Cloud) which embodies both optical and infra-red sensors. Achieves Sun-synchronous orbit at 547 x 562 miles (881 x 904km) x 99·12°. This is first launch of Long March 4, from new launch site at Taiyuan, south of Beijing. Mass approximately 1,653lb (750kg); downlink frequency 137·78 MHz. LC Taiyuan. LV Long March 4. LT 2030 GMT.

September 8 Arianespace launches two US communications satellites by Ariane 3 (V-25), using Spelda payload canister, at

1100 GMT from Kourou, French Guiana. SBS-5, located 122°W. G-Star, to be located 124°W, was initially stranded in an orbit some 12,000 miles (19,312km) too low because of problem with apogee kick stage fired 15 September.

September 10 Soviets launch Progress 38 freighter which docks at 0522 MT 12 September with Soyuz TM-6/Mir/Kvant complex on Kvant rear port. Replenished basic services and carried new X-ray detector and tools needed for repair of Anglo-Dutch X-ray telescope (see October 20). LC Baikonur. LV A-2. LT 0334 MT.

September 19 Israel becomes eighth nation to launch an artificial satellite by independent effort. Spin-stabilized 344lb (156kg) test satellite Offeq (Horizon) 1 ascends from site in Negev desert south of Tel Aviv, taking a north-westerly course over the Mediterranean (against the direction of Earth's rotation). Retrograde orbit ranges between 155 x 717 miles (250 x 1,154km) inclined at 142·86° to the equator. Shavit launcher is derived from Jericho II ballistic missile developed by Israel Military Industries. LC Palmachim, Negev desert, S. Tel Aviv. LV Shavit. LT 1132 local time.

The Israeli satellite Offeq which was launched by a Shavit rocket.

September 29 US Secretary of State George Shultz and government representatives of Japan, Canada and nine ESA member-states, in Washington, D.C., sign inter-governmental agreement (IGA) for $23 billion US International Space Station *Freedom*.

September 29-October 3, NASA launches Space Shuttle *Discovery* (STS-26) on first US manned spaceflight since *Challenger* disaster in January 1986. Aboard are Capt Frederick H. Hauck (cdr); Col Richard O. Covey (pilot) and John M. Lounge, Lt-Col David C. Hilmers and George D. Nelson (mission specialists). Primary payload is Tracking and Data Relay Satellite (TDRS-C) deployed with associated Inertial Upper Stage 6hr 13min into the mission; satellite is subsequently located in geostationary orbit at 171°W longitude. Operated from the mid-deck was environmental experiment Oasis to measure TDRS vibration, strain, acoustics and temperature during Orbiter ascent, using transducers affixed to the payload. In addition to TDRS and Oasis, 11 mid-deck experiments involved the study of electrical storms, microgravity research and materials processing. Orbit approximately circular at 184 miles (296km) x 28·45° allowed photography of storm damage in East Mexico due to Hurricane Gilbert; flooding in Khartoum, and monitoring of drought conditions in Senegal. Flew 1·7 million miles (2·7 million km), completed 64 orbits. *Discovery* incorporated many modifications following *Challenger* disaster, affecting several major sub-systems including main rocket engines and solid rocket boosters (SRBs). In particular, changes were made to SRB field joints, case-to-nozzle joint, nozzle, local propellant grain contour, ignition system and ground support equipment. Crew, for the first time, had telescopic pole for emergency escape in gliding flight and new partial pressure suits. Re-design and testing to restore Shuttle programme cost some $2·4 billion. Shuttle launch costs now averaging nearly $500 million, several times original estimates. LC Pad 39B, KSC. LV STS-26. LT 1137 EDT. R 0937 PDT, Runway 17, Edwards AFB, California.

The STS-26 crew pay lighthearted tribute to Hawaii's tracking station.

October Soviets confirm intention to launch two Mars orbiters by Proton D-1-e booster in October 1994, to arrive August 1995. Three components: Mothercraft orbiter, with 441lb (200kg) payload instruments. Landing module with 330lb (150kg) roving vehicle, range 62 miles (100km). Balloon with instrument gondola (released from landing module just before touchdown). Ascends during Martian day; descends to surface during Martian night. Employs Soviet/French technology. Embodies: cameras, radar altimeter, magnetometer, IR spectrometer, gamma spectrometer, meteorological instruments. (Roving vehicle later deferred until 1996 mission).

October 20 Mir cosmonauts Vladimir Titov and Musa Manarov repair Anglo-Dutch TTM X-ray telescope installed in attached Kvant module during EVA lasting 4hr 12min. The telescope, built by scientists at Birmingham University and the Space Research Laboratory at Utrecht, was not designed to be serviced in space and a defective X-ray detector had to be replaced using parts and tools flown up by Progress 38.

October 28 Arianespace launches French-built TDF-1 direct-broadcasting TV satellite by Ariane 2 at 0217 GMT from Kourou, French Guiana. Geostationary above 19°W.

October 29 First attempt to launch Soviet space shuttle *Buran* (Snowstorm), unmanned, by Energiya 2 from Baikonur is aborted 51 seconds before planned lift-off when service gantry arm fails to retract properly. Launch attempt had previously been delayed four hours from 0623 MT because of difficulty with "support systems".

November 11 Cosmonauts Vladimir Titov, 41, and Musa Manarov, 37, aboard Mir/Kvant space station complex break space flight endurance record of 326 days set by Yuri Romanenko. Cosmonauts report small changes in weight and muscle sizes; otherwise in good health.

November 15 Soviets launch re-usable space shuttle *Buran* (Snowstorm), unmanned, by Energiya. Lift-off is made entirely under control of on-board computers switched on at 0549 MT.

Human controllers no longer interfere with pre-launch preparations; "craft itself decides whether to go for launch or to abort". Within the last minute "escape" arm and external services disengage. Stages 1 and 2 of Energiya ignite together developing total thrust of some 3,500 tonnes. Unlike US Space Shuttle, *Buran* has no main engines and depends on Energiya to obtain high sub-orbital velocity. *Buran's* manoeuvre engines burn as third stage to inject craft into preliminary orbit at 99 miles (160km) x 51·6°; then re-fire to circularise at 155 miles (250km). Elapsed time 47 minutes. At 0820 MT on second orbit, under computer control, craft turns through

Buran, the Soviet shuttle, awaits first launch by Energiya booster.

180° and fires propulsion unit as braking engine. Re-enters atmosphere at 62 miles (100km) and at 24·8 miles (40km), with nose pitched up, begins re-entry glide using elevons and airbrakes. Return is made to Baikonur concrete runway 2·8 miles (4·5km) long x 275ft (84m) wide, located some 7·4 miles (12km) from launch pad. Completed two Earth orbits; flight duration 3hr 25min. LC Baikonur. LV Energiya. LT 0600 MT. R 0925 MT, Baikonur runway.

November 26-December 21, Soviets launch Soyuz TM-7 (Aragatz) with cosmonauts Col Alexander Volkov (cdr); Sergei Krikalev (flight engineer) and Brig-Gen Jean-Loup Chrétien (French researcher). Docks with Mir/Kvant complex on Kvant rear port at 2016 MT, 28 November. Experiments: technological, astrophysical and medical. First West European EVA, by Chrétien, with Volkov 9 December; hatch opened 1257 MT. Set up on outside of Mir experimental carbon-fibre pin-jointed erectable structure (made by Aerospatiale) stowed as bundle of rods which springs open, by remote control, into 12·5 x 11·8ft (3·8 x 3·6m) lattice. However, EVA lasted approximately 6hr instead of 4hr 20min largely because lattice initially failed to open. Objective: evaluate vibration modes of structures suitable for large antennae and space station unit assembly. After tests completed, lattice structure is rejected overboard automatically at 1·64ft/sec (0·5m/sec). During spacewalk Chrétien and Volkov erected panel of materials samples with different coatings, paints and films; also experimental solar panel, Armedeus, to test deployment mechanism. Other mission experiments related to monitoring blood flow/ hormonal response using French-supplied echocardiograph and radiobiological apparatus; also measurement of radiation field inside Mir/Kvant complex. Chrétien was making his second space flight, having flown to Salyut 7 in Soyuz T-6 in 1982. Chrétien returned in TM-6

with Vladimir Titov and Musa Manarov whose total flight lasted record 366 days 18 hours 7 minutes. Re-entry was delayed some three hours because on-board computer was overloaded and automatically stopped preparations for descent sequence. However, following the problems with Soyuz TM-5, orbital module was retained until after retro-fire (reverting to earlier practice) to safeguard crew in the event of prolonged delay in achieving safe return. LC Baikonur. LV A-2. LT 1850 MT. R 1257 MT, 110 miles (177km) SE of Dzhezkazgan.

December Soviets modify plans to explore Mars with unmanned spacecraft (see also March 1987): *1994* Orbiter and Lander with penetrators "to be anchored to its surface". Instrumented helium balloon about 82ft (25m) diameter; will rise 2·5 miles (4km) during day and descend to ground at night. Objectives: photography, chemical analysis and electromagnetic soundings of Martian soil; study of atmosphere. *1996* Mars Orbiter plus Lander with 1,102lb (500kg) roving vehicle with soil sampler/analyser. Total mass 1994/96 spacecraft 14,330lb (6,500kg) of which scientific instruments aboard orbiter account for 441lb (200kg). *1998/2000* Sample return mission to lift off from Mars with up to 6·6lb (3kg) soil samples, returning to Earth or space station.

December 2-6 NASA launches Space Shuttle *Atlantis* (STS-27) with all-military crew: Cdr Robert L. Gibson (cdr); Lt-Col Guy S. Gardner (pilot); Lt-Col Jerry L. Ross, Cdr William M. Shepherd and Col R. M. (Mike) Mullane (mission specialists). Classified DoD military payload is Lacrosse radar imaging reconnaissance satellite deployed in space by manipulator arm on fifth orbit. Orbit approximately circular at 242 miles (389km) x 57°, later manoeuvred to 415 x 437 miles (668 x 703km). Crew observations related to ground and ocean surveillance. Insulation debris falling from Shuttle's right hand Solid Propellant Booster caused impact damage to some 170 thermal protection tiles about 85 seconds into the flight;

one tile was lost beneath the crew compartment – also an insulation panel from the RH orbital manoeuvring system pod LC Pad 39B, KSC. LV STS-27. LT 1430 GMT. R 2336 GMT, Runway 17, Edwards AFB, California.

December 11 Ariane 4 launches double satellite payload using Spelda: Skynet 4B military communications satellite built for MoD by BAe with Marconi communications package, located 1°W; Astra 1A 16-channel TV direct-broadcasting satellite sponsored by SES Luxembourg, located 19·2°E. LC Kourou. LV Ariane 4 (V-27) LT 0038 GMT.

December 15 ESA confirms Cassini mission to Saturn as joint venture with NASA/JPL; aims to study Saturn from orbit and land an instrumented probe, Huygens, on the large moon Titan. Orbiter is NASA-supplied Mariner Mk II Interplanetary Platform; descent probe, released 12 days after arrival is ESA supplied. Huygens' total mass 424lb (192·3kg); seven experiments 88lb (39·9kg). Launch vehicle: Titan 4/Centaur G. Departs April 1996; fly-by asteroid 66 Maja 1999; fly-by Jupiter late 1999; enter orbit Saturn October 2002.

December 22 People's Republic of China launches communications satellite for subsequent positioning (30 December) in geostationary orbit at 110·5°E. LC Xi Chang. LV Long March 3. LT 2040 Peking time.

December 25 Soviets launch Progress 39 freighter which docks with Mir/Kvant space station complex on Kvant rear port at 0835 MT on 27 December. Brings propellants, water, food and other expendables; also equipment, mail and New Year gifts for resident cosmonauts. Undocks at 0946 MT on 7 February and is made to re-enter atmosphere over Pacific Ocean later that day. LC Baikonur. LV A-2. LT 0712 MT.

December 31 Total number of satellites (including Space Shuttles) launched in 1988: USSR 90; others 26, including USA 11, Arianespace 7, China 4; Japan 2; Italy/NASA 1 and Israel 1.

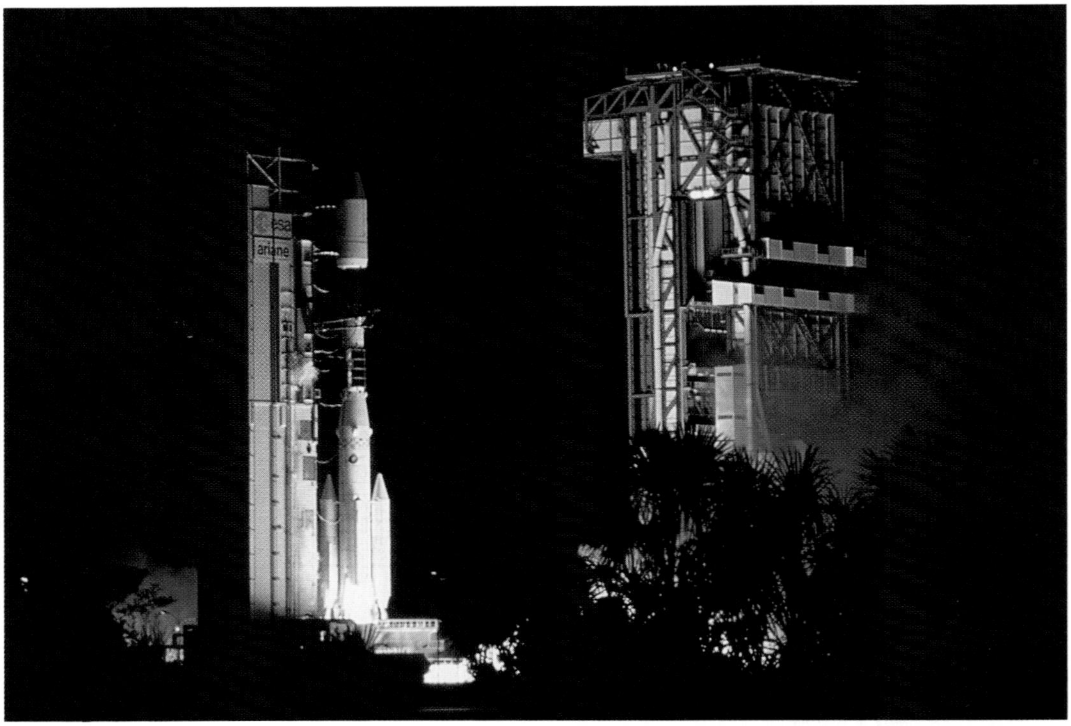

The moment of ignition for the Ariane 4 V27 mission carrying Skynet 4B and Astra 1A to orbit.

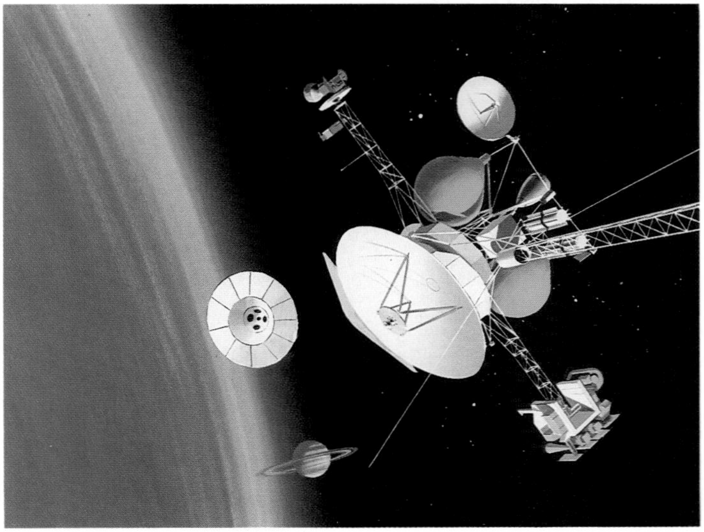

The Cassini spacecraft releases its probe towards the moon Titan (right) after arrival at Saturn in 2002. Cassini will spend four years studying Saturn's system of rings and moons.

1989

January Oleg Borisov, Academy of Soviet Sciences, reveals Soviet plan for landing cosmonauts on Mars from two nuclear-electric powered spaceships between 2005 and 2010. Assembled in Earth-orbit after eight Energiya launchings, ships are propelled by 80-tonne nuclear-electric engines located 328ft (100m) behind 10-tonne crew compartments. Two men descend from Mars orbit in 60 tonne landing craft with roving vehicle, returning to Mars orbit in ascent stage for return flight.

January 10 Soviets launch triple satellite payload: two Glonass navigation satellites (Cosmos 1987 and 1988) and Etallon (Cosmos 1989) – all orbits roughly circular at 11,860 miles (19,083km) x 65°. Etallon 1, mass exceeding 3,000lb (1,361kg), is geodetic target embodying retro-reflectors for ground-based lasers.

January 11 Novosti confirms names of first pilots who will fly Soviet Space Shuttles: I. Volk; R. Stankevicius; U. Sultanov and M. Tolboyev.

January 12 Novosti confirms Soviet plan to put unmanned spacecraft into polar orbit round the Moon in 1992. Will photograph large areas of lunar surface, including polar regions, with a resolution down to a few metres. Also aboard will be gamma and x-ray spectrometers to analyse soil composition; infra-red spectrometer to study mineral composition, and magnetometer to measure magnetic fields, and other instruments. Spacecraft is based on Phobos spacecraft sent to Mars.

January 24 Arianespace confirms order for 50 Ariane 4 launch vehicles for delivery between 1991-1999. Contract, worth approximately FFr18 billion ($3 billion), brings total number of rockets on order to 71.

January 26 Arianespace launches Intelsat V (F15) communications satellite

Payload integration for Intelsat V.

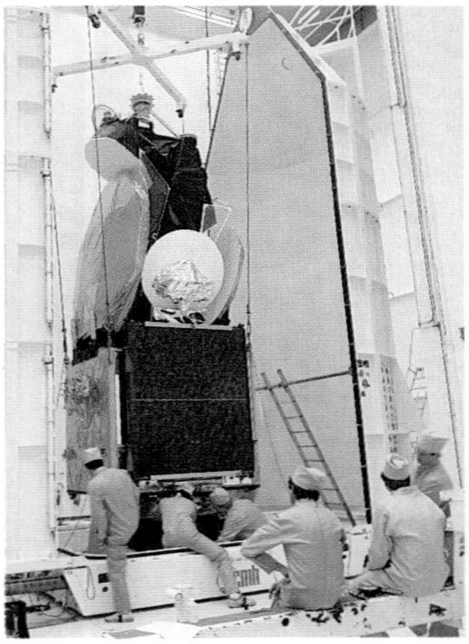

by Ariane 2 for positioning in geostationary orbit. LC Kourou. LV Ariane 2 (V28). LT 2221 local time.

January 29 Phobos 2 swings into orbit round Mars having travelled nearly half a billion kilometres in 200 days. Braking engines switched on at 1555 MT operated for about 200 seconds to put craft into orbit of 497 x 49,710 miles (800 to 80,000km) inclined at 1° to equator. First orbit correction 12 February changes this to 3,977 x 50,457 miles (6,400 x 81,200km) x 0.9°.

February 10-March 5 Soviet launch Progress 40 freighter which docks with Mir/Kvant complex on rear port at 1330 MT on 12 February to replenish expendables. New equipment and scientific apparatus are also on board. On 24 February orbit of station complex is raised by Progress engine to 222 x 240 miles (358 x 386km) x 51.6°. Separates 0446 MT 3 March when two large "multi-link" structures are automatically deployed from sides of craft, testing "form-remembering" materials. Sequence is filmed from space station. After braking manoeuvre initiated 0408 MT 5 March, craft re-enters atmosphere and is destroyed. LC Baikonur. LV A-2. LT 1154 MT.

February 10 Soviets launch 2,000th Cosmos satellite into near-polar orbit by SL-4 Soyuz booster from Plesetsk. Priroda natural resources/ecology satellite orbits at 119 x 171 miles (191 x 275km) x 82.3°. Secures oblique photographs of Earth's polar regions yielding data on ice cover, rock outcrops, formation of glaciers and icebergs, picture resolution to within 16.4ft (5m). Allows first precise mapping of central regions of Antarctica.

February 14 USAF launches Navstar 2-1 by Delta 2. First satellite of Global Positioning System Block 2 series. Full complement of 21 satellites (18 operational, 3 standby) to be launched at approx 60 day intervals. LC Pad 17, Cape Canaveral. LV Delta 2. LT 1329 EST.

February 18 Phobos 2 orbiting Mars is switched to new path having average radius of 6,009 miles (9,670km) inclined at 0.5° to equator. Main engine is discarded so that craft, using 28 small thrusters, can manoeuvre within 164ft (50m) of moon Phobos for close inspection and deployment of landers. First TV images of moon received 21 February from distances of 534-702 miles (860-1,130km).

February 21 Japan launches 660lb (200kg) auroral research satellite EXOS-D by Mu-3S-2 from Kagoshima. Orbit 168 x 6,520 miles (270 x 10,493km) x 75°.

March 6 Arianespace launches dual payload by Ariane 4 from Kourou: Japanese communications satellite JC-SATI and European Meteosat 4 (MOP-1) JC-SAT1 (Hughes HS-393 series), launch mass 5,026lb (2,280kg) located 150°E. Meteosat 1, prime contractor Aérospatiale, launch mass 1,501lb (681kg), located 3°W (later 0°). LC ELA-2, Kourou. LV Ariane 4. LT 2329 GMT.

March 13-18 NASA launches Space Shuttle *Discovery* (STS-29) with Capt Michael Coats (cdr); Col John Blaha; Col James Buchli; Col Robert Springer and James Bagian (physician). Launches data relay satellite TDRS-D by two-stage IUS for positioning 1°W. Secondary objectives: test within cargo bay of Space Station heat pipe advanced radiator element (SHARE), only partly succeeds

The External Tank tumbles towards Earth after separation from STS-29.

because of formation under micro-g of "bubbles" in ammonia fluid system preventing proper heat transfer. Also: Oasis payload bay environmental monitoring unit; protein crystal growth, chromosomes and plant cell division; IMAX camera, two student experiments. *Discovery* was rolled out 3 February. Mission was delayed because of requirement to replace liquid oxygen turbopumps of main engines following discovery of stress corrosion in pump bearing during STS-27 mission

December 1988. LC 39B, KSC. LV STS-29. LT 1457 GMT. R 1436 GMT, Runway 22, Edwards AFB, California.

March 16 Soviets launch Progress 41 freighter which docks at 2351 MT 18 March with Mir Kvant complex. LC Baikonur. LV A-2. LT 2154 MT.

March 24 US Air Force launches Delta Star satellite from Cape Canaveral by Delta 3920 (last of series) for Strategic Defense Initiative Organisation (SDIO). Comprises sensor module and attached McDonnell Douglas command/control module; total length 18ft (5.5m) x 7.6ft (2.3m) diameter; mass approximately 6,000lb (2,722kg). Sensor system, designed and integrated by Johns Hopkins Applied Physics Laboratory, includes laser radar and seven IR and UV imaging sensors – also Laser Illumination Detection System (LIDS). Object: by precise manoeuvring, to point sensors to observe "rocket plumes and other phenomena from space".

March 27 Tokyo Broadcasting System confirms that a Japanese television reporter will visit the Soviet Mir space station in 1991, under arrangements made with Glavkosmos costing £6.7 million ($11.4 million).

March 27 Soviet lose contact with Phobos 2 spacecraft orbiting Mars during final manoeuvres to approach moon Phobos within 164ft (50m). With rendezvous achieved, craft was set to drift slowly past the moon for some 20 minutes while TV, radar, laser and ion-gun equipment probed the surface. Two landers were to be released, one static with TV and soil sensors, the other capable of hopping up to 65.6ft (20m) to investigate soil chemistry at different points.

April 1 Power depletion aboard Mir space station and late delivery of two 20 tonne "building block" modules for attachment to Mir's multiple docking unit, lead to abandonment of plans to launch Soyuz TM-8 with Alexander Viktorenko (cdr) and Alexander Baladin on 19 April. Moscow anticipates that Mir will be left unmanned after the return of resident crew Alexander Volkov, Sergei Krikalev and Valery Polyakov on 27 April. Before leaving the station, cosmonauts monitored a number of engine firings which raised the orbiting altitude. Mir could remain "mothballed" for "several months".

April 2 Arianespace launches Swedish Tele-X communications satellite by final Ariane 2 for positioning in geostationary orbit. Provides television services to Sweden, Norway and Finland.

May 4-8 NASA launches Space Shuttle *Atlantis* (STS-30) with astronauts Capt David M. Walker (cdr); Col Ronald J. Grabe (pilot), Dr Mary L. Cleave, Norman E. Thagard and Major Mark C. Lee (mission specialists). Deploys Magellan probe and attached IUS two-stage booster from cargo bay; 7,604lb (3,449kg) spacecraft is injected into transfer orbit to Venus. Braked into orbit around Venus August 1990, it will map up to 90 per cent of the surface normally hidden by cloud by synthetic aperture radar.

SOVIET LAUNCH VEHICLES

Western authorities have applied various codes to identify Soviet launchers. The scheme followed throughout this volume is that devised by the late Dr Charles Sheldon II of the US Library of Congress. Sheldon's system assigns a capital letter, ranging from A to J (but omitting E, H, and I) to the basic first/second stages of the launch vehicle which are common throughout the family. Orbital stages are given the numbers 1 or 2, the latter indicating an orbital stage of second generation. (The 1 stage may vary between families of vehicles, however.) Additional stages are indicated by lower case letters: "e" (meaning escape stage), "r" (re-entry stage), or "m" (manoeuvre stage). "E" was not used to avoid confusion with the "e" stage of A-2-e and D-1-e. "H" was reserved by Sheldon because of an anticipated high-energy (LO$_2$/LH$_2$) upper stage for the "D" vehicle; D-1-h is now used to denote this. "I" was omitted to avoid confusion with figure 1.

Department of Defense designations reflect the input of USAF satellite reconnaissance information. In the case of Sheldon's "G" vehicle, the DoD initially assigned this the letter "J" signifying the ninth launch complex identified at the Baikonur cosmodrome. When the vehicle itself was photographed, it became the TT-5, the fifth launch vehicle type to be detected at the cosmodrome. In the next phase the vehicle is normally given an "SL" or Space Launcher designation, e.g. SL-15.

SHELDON	DoD	DERIVATION	TYPICAL PAYLOADS
A	SL-1	* SS-6 Sapwood ICBM (Soviet R-7)	Sputnik 1
A	SL-2	SL-1	Sputnik 2 & 3
A-1	SL-3	SL-2	Korabl-Sputnik, Vostok, 1st generation, Cosmos reconsats, biosats, Meteor, etc. Soviet name "Vostok".
A-2	SL-4	SL-3	Voskhod, Soyuz, 2nd gen. Cosmos reconsats, etc. Soviet name "Soyuz".
A-2-e	SL-5	SL-3	Obscure. Polyot 1 & 2.
A-2-e	SL-6	4 stage version SL-4	First gen. lunar/planetary probes; Molniya, etc. Soviet name "Molniya".
B-1	SL-7	* SS-4 Sandal	1st gen. Cosmos/Intercosmos (1962-1977)
C-1	SL-8	* SS-5 Skean	2nd gen. Cosmos/Intercosmos, navsats, ferret, etc. Soviet name "Cosmos".
D-1	SL-9	–	Proton 1, 2 & 3.
D-1-e	SL-12	SL-9	2nd gen. lunar/planetary probes including Zond circumlunar.
D-1/D-1-e	SL-13	SL-12	Proton 4, Salyut, Mir, Kvant, Raduga, Gorizont, Ekran, etc. Soviet name "Proton".
F-1	SL-11	*SS-9 Scarp	FOBS, ASAT, ocean survey, etc. Soviet name "Tsyklon".
F-2	SL-14	3 stage version SL-11	Meteor 2, Meteor 3, ocean survey, etc. Soviet name "Cyclone".
G	SL-15	–	1st gen. heavy-lift launcher abandoned after three test failures (1969-72).
G	SL-17	–	2nd gen. heavy-lift launcher. Large orbital modules; space shuttle; lunar/interplanetary spacecraft. Soviet name "Energiya".
J-1	SL-16	–	Medium-lift launch vehicle. Related to 1st stage strap-on SL-17
?	SL-10	SL-3	Obscure designation circa 1965. Vostok/Soyuz. Cosmos 102, 125 (?)

Notes: * NATO designation of ballistic missile.
FOBS = Fractional Orbit Bombardment System.
ASAT = Anti-Satellite. SL = Space Launcher.